Qualitative Methodologies and Data Collection Methods

Toward Increased Rigour in Management Research

New Teaching Resources for Management in a Globalised World

Print ISSN: 2661-4774
Online ISSN: 2661 4782

Series Editor: Professor Léo-Paul Dana

The classic economic view of internationalisation was based on the theory of competitive advantage, and over the years, internationalisation was seen in various lights, as an expansion option. With the reduction of trade barriers, however, many local small enterprises face major international competitors in formerly protected domestic markets. Today, competitiveness in the global marketplace is no longer an option; it has become a necessity as the acceleration towards globalisation offers unprecedented challenges and opportunities.

This book series will bring together textbooks, monographs, edited collections and handbooks useful to postgraduates and researchers in the age of globalisation. Relevant topics include, but are not limited to: research methods, culture, entrepreneurship, globalisation, immigration, migrants, public policy, self-employment, sustainability, technological advances, emerging markets, demographic shifts, and innovation.

Published:

Resources for
Management
and
Globalisation
Volume 1

Qualitative Methodologies and Data Collection Methods

Toward Increased Rigour in Management Research

Edward Groenland

Nyenrode University, The Netherlands

Léo-Paul Dana

Montpellier Business School, France

World Scientific

NEW JERSEY · LONDON · SINGAPORE · BEIJING · SHANGHAI · HONG KONG · TAIPEI · CHENNAI · TOKYO

Published by

World Scientific Publishing Co. Pte. Ltd.

5 Toh Tuck Link, Singapore 596224

USA office: 27 Warren Street, Suite 401-402, Hackensack, NJ 07601

UK office: 57 Shelton Street, Covent Garden, London WC2H 9HE

Library of Congress Cataloging-in-Publication Data

Names: Groenland, Edward, author. | Dana, Leo Paul, author.
Title: Qualitative methodologies and data collection methods : toward increased rigour in
    management research / Edward Groenland (Nyenrode University, The Netherlands),
    Léo-Paul Dana (Montpellier Business School, France)
Description: 1 Edition. | New Jersey : World Scientific, [2019] | Series: New teaching
    resources for management in a globalised world ; Volume 1 | Includes bibliographical
    references and index.
Identifiers: LCCN 2019020534 | ISBN 9789811206535
Subjects: LCSH: Management--Research. | Quantitative research. |
    Social sciences--Research--Methodology.
Classification: LCC HD30.4 .G764 2019 | DDC 658.0072/1--dc23
LC record available at https://lccn.loc.gov/2019020534

British Library Cataloguing-in-Publication Data
A catalogue record for this book is available from the British Library.

For any available supplementary material, please visit
https://www.worldscientific.com/worldscibooks/10.1142/11449#t=suppl

Desk Editor: Shreya Gopi

Typeset by Stallion Press
Email: enquiries@stallionpress.com

Contents

Foreword

This compelling work by Edward Groenland and Léo-Paul Dana, *Qualitative Methodologies and Data Collection Methods,* is an interesting and valuable contribution for the academic community. Without too many frills, it clearly explains in an analytic way a large array of research methodologies and methods in the domain of qualitative research. While many other illustrious authors have already studied these issues, my personal opinion is that this book is able to bring all these approaches and techniques together in a succinct and ready-to-use format, that I am sure many readers will appreciate. Indeed, in many cases, the real problem with qualitative research is not structuring and carrying out the study; rather scholars, especially young ones, may struggle with thinking of and designing the most appropriate methodology in relation to the phenomenon they are approaching and in relation to the data they want to collect. This is a real obstacle that is hard to correct once the actual collection of data started. For this reason, having an *ex-ante* clear picture and a deeper understanding of many qualitative methodologies and techniques is a prominent advantage. This book responds exactly to such a need in a comprehensive way.

The book specifically delves into eight research paradigms, i.e., case studies, critical incident methodology, ethnography, field simulation, grounded theory, content analysis, semiotics, and narrative inquiry; and six research techniques, i.e., the Delphi method, document analysis, focus groups, interviews, elicitation techniques, and observation and participant observation. The dedicated chapter for each of these methodologies and techniques offers: a brief overview of the topic, its uses and tips from best practices, and related advantages and disadvantages of its implementation. This structure contributes to the ready-to-use format of the book. In some cases, the specific chapters also present and analyse an example of a study that uses this approach, thus providing the reader with contextualised knowledge of successful research designs and data collections. In sum, the book is extremely useful for fully understanding a methodology and/or a technique, but it can also allow researchers to clearly picture their research design, weighing and comparing several solutions to their problem.

This book will be beneficial to a wide audience of academics and practitioners interested in qualitative methods. I am sure it will become a 'must-have' on every bookshelf of both amateur and expert qualitative researchers! Surely, on my shelf, this book already has a space reserved.

Massimiliano M. Pellegrini
Qualified Associate Professor of
Organisational Studies and Entrepreneurship
University of Rome 'Tor Vergata'
Past Chair of the Entrepreneurship SIG
at the European Academy of Management (EURAM)

About the Authors

Edward Groenland is Professor of Business Research Methodology at Nyenrode Business Universiteit, the Netherlands. He is also Academic Director BBA at the Nyenrode New Business School in Amsterdam. Finally, he teaches students from market research agencies and companies the skills for conducting in-depth interviews and focus groups. Past positions include Associate Professor of Economic Psychology at Tilburg University, Academic director of the Nyenrode PhD School, and Research Director at a market research agency in the Netherlands. His main topics of interest include research methodology, qualitative research methods, online qualitative research, qualitative research skills, multivariate analysis and consumer psychology.

Léo-Paul Dana, a graduate of McGill University and of HEC Montreal, is Professor at Montpellier Business School/Montpellier Research in Management, and a member of the Entre-preneurship & Innovation chair, which is part of LabEx Entrepreneurship (University of Montpellier, France). This "laboratory of excel-lence" is funded by the French government in recognition of high-level research initiatives in the human and natural sciences (LabEx Entreprendre, ANR-10-LabEx-11-01). He has published extensively in a variety of leading journals including *Entrepreneurship & Regional Development, Entrepreneurship: Theory & Practice, International Small Business Journal, Journal of Business Research, Journal of Small Business Management, Journal of World Business, Small Business Economics,* and *Technological Forecasting & Social Change.*

Chapter 1

Introduction

This chapter provides a basic introduction to science and research for scholars who wish to acquire an elementary orientation of the domain of the empirical social sciences. Based on this knowledge, a researcher is able to choose among the prime approaches of this domain with respect to the design of a research project. These major research approaches are presented in the subsequent chapters.

This chapter addresses the following aspects of science and research:

- Science;
- Research;
- Theories and models;
- Methods of research;
- Qualitative research versus quantitative research — essential contrasts.

Thus, the reader moves from notions about the philosophy of science to their consequences for the research approach, and theories and models to be tested and developed to the corresponding research methods. Finally, the essential differences between qualitative research approaches and quantitative research approaches are discussed.

1.1 Definitions

This book is about qualitative methodologies for management research, but what are methodologies and what is qualitative research?

Ontology is the study of what constitutes the reality in the world. *Epistemology* is the study of how to obtain valid knowledge. A *methodology* is a plan of action involving a structured set of strategic guidelines to assist researchers in scientific enquiry. Veryard (1985, p. 12) described methodologies as systems. Robson (1993) explained methodology as the background to social research and its implications for research practice and for the use of particular research methods. Adherence to a methodology results in structured and coherent procedures.

Qualitative methodologies are those that do not involve formalised and objectified measurement or statistics. Instead, they comply with the defining characteristics of qualitative research as described above. In recent years, the legitimacy of qualitative research has increased resulting in an increase in qualitative projects funded and articles published (Creswell, 2009). A *de facto* acceptance may be found by checking the number and level of scientific journals devoted to qualitative studies.

Qualitative research is a type of scientific research focused on holistic inquiry; it involves a vast and complex area of methodology that is used to describe phenomena from the participant's viewpoint, with rich, descriptive detail of the human context, and preferably it does so by observing subjects in their natural setting. The objective is not to count, but rather to understand a wide holistic picture. Qualitative research generally involves direct interaction, of some kind, between the researcher and the individual/household/company to be studied. In contrast to quantitative approaches, qualitative research aims at directly reaching the idiosyncratic inner world of individuals by this interaction and this is considered to be a unique advantage over quantitative approaches.

Geertz (1973) referred to thick description in qualitative research. Sieber (1973) emphasised that qualitative research is deep. Rist (1977) emphasised the adjective *holistic*. Schmid (1981) explained qualitative research as the investigation of the empirical world from the viewpoint of the subject(s) under study without statistical manipulation. It tends to be less generalisable than quantitative research, the latter being optimal to summarising large amounts of data and reaching generalisations based on statistical analysis. Nevertheless, qualitative outcomes may be generalised in an analytical manner, convincingly portraying the patterns found in research as they exist in the population under study.

As summarised by Sandelowski, "qualitative descriptive studies have as their goal a comprehensive summary of events in the everyday terms of those events. Researchers conducting qualitative descriptive studies stay close to their data and to the surface of words and events" (2000, p. 334). As Lincoln wrote, "The topic is complex not only because it involves taxonomizing, but because it is deeply implicated in considerations of validity, verification, the politics of knowledge, and what we consider not only 'evidence' itself, but also what we consider 'knowledge,' and what knowledge we consider worth having" (2002, p. 3). Qualitative research is conducted using qualitative methodology.

1.2 Science

1.2.1 *Objectives of science: Truth and reality*

In the broadest sense of the word, science and scientific endeavours are aimed at finding out whether phenomena and, by extension, the world as we humans experience it are really describing reality. That is, reality has to be established somehow, and there are two reasons for this: we wish to gain more control in our lives and it satisfies our curiosity.

This raises the question of how many "realities" may exist for various different individuals, each with their own educational background, learning history, and cultural influences. For instance, for many people, a chair may be a device to sit on, and that mostly has a back and chair legs. The same may not be true for an individual who has never come across such a device. Consequently, the reality of what most would call a chair is different for this person. The same is true for phenomena, such as safety, pet animals, and the experience of time.

Things become even more complicated when we contemplate phenomena such as falling in love or out of love. Are causes involved, which create effects? We enjoy books and movies, which describe or portray extended sequences of steps of these processes. The reason may be that, while our brains essentially have the same structure and build, each of us has learned in an idiosyncratic way how to process and interpret the events we come across. Consequently, we individuals may recognize or imagine a certain sequence of events without being part of it. "Why does not she love him anymore?" "Why did he have to kill her when she rejected his hand? Why did not he just make the rounds of the bars with his friends while sobbing his heart out about his loss?" At moments like this, we are trying to make sense of this process. We may be trying to find causes that create a certain (end) effect. We are trying to understand reality. Because the point is: not everybody will harm an ex-girlfriend once she has rejected him. Why, or under which circumstances or conditions will this happen, or fail to happen? What are the true forces that will bring about a certain outcome? What is the true nature of this phenomenon, what is the truth in that matter?

1.2.1.1 *Human language*

Humans only have their senses, their consciousness, and their mental processes to touch their inner world and the outside world. In order to make sense of the world, perceptions of events are compared and categorised, as what one has experienced, processed, and learned earlier. And, based on that, one attaches a certain meaning to the event. A prime tool available during this process is language (Chomsky, 1957). Some would speak of the "language dimension of reality." In this way, an individual develops basic interpretations of the world and eventually the experience of life or even worldly wisdom. However, we are now talking about interpretations, which are individual and subjective approaches to reality, or individual variations of the truth of the matter. Moreover, language and interpretations may change over a lifetime, and generations of people for that matter. One could speculate that language has come into existence and has been shaped by successive generations of humans while fighting for their existence and survival. As a consequence, they formed and invented concepts, and relations between concepts, that were functional aids for living their lives, for showing activities, for developing their thoughts and for living through their experiences, and for construing their self-image and the image of others, and finally, for communicating while choosing both content and the party to be addressed. One could say that language and culture thus remain heavily intertwined in a long-lasting process of continued change over time. Over time, language has adapted to these circumstances. Changes have occurred with respect to the meaning of words, their connotations, sentence structure, length of sentences used, the use of vowels and consonants, and pronunciation. And during this perpetual process of change, language is used to describe and experience ever-changing pictures of truth and reality.

1.2.1.2 *Mathematical language*

We may compare human language with the formal language of mathematics. When studying mathematic formulae and laws as expressed in mathematics (e.g., Einstein's theory of general relativity: $E = MC^2$), we can see both similarities and differences. Similarities pertain to the use of parameters in mathematics that resemble concepts in common language, and arithmetic operations resemble the causal relationships between concepts of the conceptual model. A major difference concerns the formal precision with which parameters in mathematics are connected. When compared with common language and the conceptual model the latter connections are fuzzier, less logical, and less formal. Humans seem to appreciate language, which allow them to be less consequential regarding their thoughts and their behaviours. Be that as it may, both types of language seem to have the capacity to capture truth and reality.

We continue with some notes on the notion of objective reality regarding Einstein's theory of relativity as quoted earlier. According to his theory, space and time are not unaltered or fixed. Instead, they change as a function of the position and movement of the observer. Moreover, his introduction of the "quantum" demonstrates that the world as we observe it is in a major way connected to the position of the observer. Therefore, the Newtonian view of the universe (the universe functions as a clock) has to be rewritten: these clocks depend on the movement of the observer. Thus, the observations of an observer may not be taken as an example of observing the objective truth or reality. The same is true for the layman's observation that the sun is orbiting planet earth: Galileo Galilei presented a theory which — counter to common sensory observation — claims that it is actually the earth which is orbiting the sun and also that it is the sun that is in the middle of our solar system. Anyway, why should we believe that Einstein's theory of relativity is the final and ultimate theory of its kind?

In conclusion, could science eventually be developed to such an extent that we have a complete insight into the way phenomena come to existence, develop, and come to maturity? Can the phenomenon of falling in and out of love ever be fully understood?

This is a philosophical question that we currently cannot answer. However, philosophy of science so far has produced two basic approaches to reality and truth.

1.2.1.3 *Only one truth exists*

The first approach asserts that only one truth exists, consequently, it only has to be uncovered. *Universal laws may be sought after, laws that may be using mathematics and formulae to present themselves.* Here, formal language, including parameters, are used. Nevertheless, although the ensuing laws are very practical — one could use them to bring a spacecraft to the moon and back — this does not necessarily constitute proof that these universal laws actually have truth in them. In a philosophical sense, they really are still laws of probability as there is no way (no external criterion) to formally determine the truth content of these laws.

However, when only one truth exists, ultimately we will have discovered everything that is there. In other words, the process of the growth of science is finite. Ultimately, all scientists are to retire as their work is done.

1.2.1.4 *Multiple truths may exist*

The second approach asserts that multiple truths may exist in the minds of all and each individual, mind you, regarding the same phenomenon. Truth, as is the experience of reality, is an elaborate construction of the human mind, which is constantly under development and which is influenced by major life events as processed by individuals. *In this way, individuals gain experience of life, as they learn over time (and as influenced by the sociocultural setting in which they were raised and live currently) how to interpret events they are confronted with. The way they learn may be described by means of the explanatory principles they adopt in the course of their lives. These principles as bounded by time and place may be sought after, principles that may be using informal language, with a plenitude of associations and intricate — often personal connotations, to present themselves.* Truth has the characteristics of a social construction, and is not governed by incontestable laws or principles. There is an absence of unchangeable verities.

This raises the question whether science itself is able to decide which approach is really true, and describes the one and only valid view on reality. The answer is that science as such is not able to make that decision. The reason is of course (as said before) that we would need an objective and absolute criterion outside our world to establish the one and only truth and reality. Halas, we are part of the same world we would like to study and so this is not possible. Compare the tale of Baron von Munchhausen who was sitting on his horse and sinking in a morass, and in order to save himself he pulled himself out by pulling up his hair.

1.2.2 *Scientific knowledge versus layman's knowledge*

So, we need knowledge and insights regarding the world. If it is true that we experience or perceive phenomena, and in this way collect knowledge and insights regarding these phenomena, why would we need a scientific approach instead of a layman's approach? The answer is simple: Where the layman just follows his drift or his "instincts" when making interpretations, the scientist chooses a formal approach. For instance, a scientist makes a deliberate and targeted choice regarding the way he defines and delineates concepts, and the specific way he chooses methods to collect and analyse data. Moreover, specific aims lead to specific methods. All of this results in more consistency of the research design. Consequently, the research design can be checked by the reader of the article in which research outcomes are presented. Finally, the research project can be reproduced, or replicated in exactly the same way as was done in the first place. Why is all of this so important? It is of prime importance because, generally speaking, scientific research is aimed at reducing uncertainty (about views of reality and truth), and we can have more confidence in the systematic, consistent, and verifiable approach of the scientific researcher as compared to the well-meaning layman.

An example to wind it all up: suppose you would be interested to know whether a certain workshop had a number of specified effects on the participants. Would you ask a layman who was around whether these effects occurred or would you have (more) confidence in a researcher who carefully included the specified effects in an experimental design in order to shed light on the actual workings of these specified effects? Indeed.

1.2.3 *Building knowledge and reducing uncertainty*

We already mentioned the reduction of uncertainty as a highly-valued yield of carrying out research. The point is that we can safely assume that in the (social) sciences still a vast amount of knowledge and insights, currently, is there to be uncovered. As a consequence, we would not say that a certain theory has been "proven". This only happens in certain advertisements recommending a brand of shampoo or a magic potion to lose weight while eating as much as you can. Instead, we would say that the outcomes of a study "lend support" to the adequacy of that theory. As a consequence, the uncertainty about the validity (correctness) of the tested theory is reduced.

As said earlier, reduction of uncertainty comes into being by creating transparency with regard to the research process that leads to the accumulation of scientific knowledge and scientific insights. The critical reader of an academic article is able to follow and judge each of the steps. Based on that he decides whether the study truly supports the theory under study.

Special attention merits the guru in this context. This person generally has a strong image with respect to a certain field of knowledge, and he or she is eminently able to create trust and confidence when, for instance, presenting interpretations and recommendations to a captive audience. However, there is no basis for determining the validity of the guru's actual knowledge and insights objectively and independently — we have to believe him, we have to accept his word for it, and that might generally not be a good idea.

1.2.4 *The process of the development of science*

One might surmise that the development of science occurs in a linear way, step by step, so to say. In that case, scientific knowledge would accumulate in small, orderly steps. The opposite seems to be true, however. On the one hand, one could observe that a theory, as published in an academic journal, has rudimentary and incomplete characteristics as it has just come into existence. Next, (fellow) researchers come into play and they tend to refine and complete the theory gradually over time, and on the basis of numerous more research projects. Here, the way to maturity of the theory under construction may occur in orderly and consecutive steps. However, in the same span of time, *rival theories* may be presented with the obvious claim that these are "better" in some ways. Then, after a period of turmoil, the international experts in the field may decide that a specific theory merits more or most attention because it is a "promising" theory. In the latter case, there is no linear development. In fact, when a rival theory suggests a major improvement with respect to the knowledge and insights concerning the explanation of a specific phenomenon (i.e., its explanatory power) we might say that the improvement (in terms of knowledge and insights) is definitively nonlinear.

On a bigger scale, these sudden changes of approaching a phenomenon to be studied occur as well. We refer to *paradigm changes* in science as they are called. Paradigms are basic general scientific approaches to study phenomena. This is a definition of a paradigm:

> A paradigm is a fundamental image of the subject matter within science. It serves to define what should be studied, what questions should be asked, how they should be asked, and what rules should be followed in interpreting the answers obtained. The paradigm is the broadest unit of consensus within a science and serves to differentiate one scientific community (or sub community) from another. It assumes, defines, and interrelates the exemplars, theories, methods, and instruments that exist within it (Ritzer, 1975).

Example: In psychology, the individual mental processes emanating both from the inner world of the individual, his outside social world, and his environment, are studied as they have an influence on his behaviour. These basic processes and relationships are not questioned as they form the starting point for all kinds of research projects. So, this is the paradigm for psychological research. In contrast, in Economics, the paradigm is cantered on maximization of utility. This principle is the starting point for carrying out economic (behavioural) research. It is interesting to compare these two paradigms when it comes to explaining donation behaviour of individuals. A psychologist would say that an individual donating to charity experiences feelings of satisfaction, and experiences himself (for a short time) to be a good person, it enhances his self-esteem. In contrast, the economic study starting with the paradigm of Economic sciences has a hard time in explaining why people would donate, as this reduces utility instead of maximizing utility. This all goes to say that the prevailing paradigm may be more suited to explaining certain behavioural phenomena while being impeded when it comes to other behavioural phenomena.

Up till now, we compared paradigms over major types of scientific fields (Psychology versus Economics). The same is true, however, when we look at the existence of multiple paradigms, and paradigm shifts, *within* one type of scientific field. In most cases, academic journals exist which only accept studies based on a specific paradigm. Thus, multiple journals exist for multiple paradigms. Now, paradigms come into existence, grow, mature, and decline, and so do the corresponding journals. A paradigm may come to the point of exhaustion, which means that, within the boundaries of the prevailing paradigm, no real expansion of the existing theories or models is possible. There are two consequences now: older and settled researchers continue to do research within this exhausted paradigm; they have invested time, money, and prestige in this line of research and they may not feel able to make a switch. At the same time, young researchers draw the inevitable conclusion and turn to new, young paradigms, or try to invent a new paradigm themselves. If successful, a new journal is created and the cycle of birth to death starts anew.

We started with the question whether the development of science, hence the development of scientific knowledge, would be linear. In view of what has been said, now it is obvious that no linear development can be expected, or maybe should be expected. Consequently, we cannot establish "how far we are" in terms of fully-grown theories with high predictive power, or predict at what point in time or after how many steps we would achieve an ultimate level of development of science. To some this conclusion may be disillusionment. When discussing various qualitative research approaches below, the corresponding paradigms will be indicated.

1.3 Research

In the realm of the social sciences, conducting research is the act of providing explanations for phenomena with a focus on the behaviour of individuals, groups or organizations. This process can be fuelled by thought processes (e.g., Introspection, Freud) or by empirical data that are collected, analysed, and interpreted to that end. Here, we only consider empirical research approaches as these approaches are the dominant approaches at this current age and day. Explanations predominantly take the form of models and theories. Both of these structures are built from concepts and relationships between concepts (i.e., the conceptual model). Again, predominantly these relationships take the form of causal relationships where a cause invokes an effect. Approaches such as Chaos Theory are not discussed here. In sum, research is aimed at ultimately finding (constructing) theories that are able to explain a phenomenon.

It goes without saying that, in order to achieve this, research is an ongoing process. During this process, the researcher attempts to improve a theory step by step by adding and deleting concepts and relationships. Alternatively, the researcher may decide to discard the theory under construction and start over again. When overviewing this process over an extended period of time, one could speak of the maturity process of science. This maturity process may be sketched as follows:

- Theoretical development may be depicted by steps such as describing, explaining, predicting, controlling;
- Facts collected during research may be converted from data to information to formal knowledge;
- The theorising process may start from a description to (conceptual) model, and may end with a (mature) theory at the explanatory level.

In view of the above, one could say that the social and management sciences generally and currently are at the formative stages of this maturity process. Also, at a certain point of the process two types of branches of research may be distinguished as based on their focus:

- **Scientific research:** Academic research which is primarily aimed at the development and elaboration of scientific knowledge as such.
- **Applied research:** Research which is primarily aimed at providing a contribution to the solution of a practical problem, for instance in the domain of business and management.

However, proponents of purely academic research may point to a model called the "Prisoner's dilemma game". This is a model from

Game Theory outlining relative advantages of cooperation versus non-cooperation. On the one hand, this is a clearly academic approach to science. On the other hand, the principles involved in this dynamic phenomenon may be applied in an attempt to solve the problems of the world where multiple parties are involved in a form of negotiation. Here, the academic insights gained contribute to the solution of a practical problem.

Prolific research projects all start with a *formal problem analysis*. The problem analysis entails the formulation of research aims and research questions, among other things (Groenland, 2014).

Research aims are formulated in such a way that it becomes clear which knowledge and which insights are sought after with respect to which party, e.g., which target groups (individuals, companies) upon finishing the study. This is the basic starting point for any study and it will determine the basic research approach.

Research questions are specifications of the research aim. The researcher asks himself which questions must be answered in order to attain the research aims, and which research questions fit the research aim. When collecting the data, the research questions are the starting point for the checklist to be used. Ultimately, the answers to the research questions build up the conclusions of the research.

Both academic research and applied research must be carried out according to certain rules, principles, and procedures. These characteristics warrant the coherence of the research process and ultimately they incite trust and credibility with respect to the outcomes of the study at hand. These are the *rules of the game and the standards to uphold* while carrying out and evaluating research:

- **Procedures and working methods**
  - *Transparency*
    - All of the steps of the research process are described in full;
  - *Verifiability*
    - Both the logic of the research (design) and the research steps can be judged by the reader of the research report;

- ○ *Consistency*
  - ▪ Starting points chosen earlier in the research process are followed consistently in consecutive research steps;
- ○ *Reasoning*
  - ▪ Assumptions are made clear,
  - ▪ Basic suppositions which are — as such — not tested are identified;
- ○ *Arguments*
  - ▪ Aspects of the problem at hand which indicate the (in) correctness of the direction of the solution are formally presented;
- ○ *Conclusions*
  - ▪ Statements about the problem, as based on the arguments presented, are spelled out.
- **General principles of validity, reliability and sensitivity**
  - ○ *Validity*
    - ▪ Measuring exactly that which you actually wish to measure;
  - ○ *Reliability*
    - ▪ Test–retest reliability; taking identical measurements on the same sample should yield essentially the same outcomes;
  - ○ *Sensitivity*
    - ▪ The precision, the level of detail that is required in order to answer the research questions.
- **Replication**
  - ○ Identical research circumstances should yield identical research outcomes when the phenomenon under study is stable in time;
  - ○ Consistency leads to acceptation.
- **Public nature**
  - ○ *Academic research*
    - ▪ The outcomes should always be available for everyone who would like to scrutinise and criticise the study;
  - ○ *Commercial research*
    - ▪ Usually the outcomes are only available to the commissioning client and not to competitors.

This concludes our overview of rules and guiding principles concerning the research process.

1.4 Theories and Models

1.4.1 *The components and characteristics of a theory*

Any formal theory is set in a paradigm, as discussed earlier, and consequently any such theories are embedded in a number of points of departure. For instance, the prevailing paradigm of psychology indicates that, generally speaking, behaviour of some kind, as expressed by a behavioural unit such as an individual, a citizen, a household or a company, is to be explained by mental processes, characteristics of the behavioural unit and forces from the environment. Needless to say that in addition to this generic process structure, many variations may occur as in the structure of the process to be studied.

Generally speaking, three types of points of departure may come into play in the context of a theory. The first is the *postulate*. This is a proposition, which is not eligible for theoretical proof; however, this proposition is to be accepted as a starting point in order to make theoretical sense of the theory presented. An example would be that psychologically sane individuals tend to keep up and protect their self-esteem in order to function adequately as a human being. Alternatively, this could be a hypothesis under study. In that case, it no longer would be a postulate.

The second one is a *presupposition*, a prerequisite, a condition, or a starting point in reasoning which is taken to be true without proof. Based on this presupposition, arguments and consequences may be studied. An example would be that ordinarily family members share common values and that this will shape their family-related behaviour to some extent. Obviously, this could also be a topic by itself to be studied. Then, it is not a presupposition anymore.

The third point of departure is the *assumption* (as a starting point). This is a supposition, i.e., a belief or a presumption of fact. For example, a researcher could take as an assumption that companies attempt to abide by the prevailing laws in their country. Again, this behaviour could be the focal point of a study itself. In that case it would not be an assumption anymore.

When comparing these three points of departure, we may conclude that the differences as to their meaning are small. In order to keep things simple, we may treat them as largely similar.

We will now turn to the *structural contents* of theories, and their *structural characteristics* in particular. In terms of structural contents, one could say that a theory is a coherent system of assertions, statements, allegations, or even claims. This is true because at any time new evidence may be brought to the fore, which might challenge these assertions. In principle these assertions are testable using empirical data. Any theory claims to be "true" when describing and explaining a designated process under well-specified circumstances, and of course, "true" refers to the claim that the processes described in the theory basically match those of the "real world".

Let's now turn to the components of a theory. What are the building blocks of a theory? A theory is built from the so-called *concepts* and *relationships* between these concepts. These two elements provide shape to its anatomy.

A concept may be conceived as a unit of thought at the most basic level. Also, a concept may be conceived of as notion, sometimes an idea, an image or a view at the basic level of understanding. They act as building blocks in order to form cognitive units and cognitions. Examples are not only Knowledge, Attitude, and Behaviour, but also Chair (or the experience of sitting on it), Money (its perception), Skies (the mood it creates). When concepts become inherently complex we replace Concepts by Construct, such as Love, Peace, and Happiness. As can be seen from the examples, a concept may refer both to concrete objects and abstract objects.

A further point of consideration concerns the unit of analysis. Does the theory describe and explain individual behaviour, family behaviour, the behaviour of teams or units working within a company? It may be conceivable that processes under study are different when individual behaviour is involved versus the behaviour of individuals within a (small) group versus the behaviour of individuals as part of masses of people (e.g., a mass panic). One could argue that each time different parts of the brain may be involved which are not fully integrated. As this would have problematic consequences for causality in the process under study, any theory must specify this unit of analysis. This should be a deliberate choice of the researcher attempting to create a theory. Moreover, the chosen unit of analysis must be the same throughout the entire theory, that is, for each of the concepts and constructs involved. An example: the concept of "corporate culture" may be initially defined at the level of the company as it may be seen as a sociological concept. When the unit of analysis is the individual employee this concept should be converted to "the (individual) *perception* or *experience* of corporate culture".

Concepts translate into *variables* when data have been collected in order to measure, or operationalise these concepts. Here, for each of the concepts under study the researcher attempts to devise specific, concrete, and unambiguous questions to be asked to the respondents of the study. Thus, a variable is an empirical entity which represents the corresponding (theoretical) concept and it varies with respect to its value or contents over the individual units from the sample from which it was collected. When no variation takes place a variable becomes a constant and it is useless for the purposes of analysis and interpretation.

Concepts are connected or related in a theory in order to signify the orderly steps of the process, which comprises the theory. Moreover, they are arranged and connected in a specific order and this order may express causes and effects. This brings us to a more formal treatment of the nature of the relations. In essence, two types of relationships may be distinguished: an association or correlation type and a causal type. It will be clear that associative relationships do not aid in explaining relationships in a theory. After all, in a philosophical sense one might assert that all things are associated with all other things, over time, over situations, and over contexts. In contrast, a causal relationship has the power of explanation in principle. This characteristic is in line with the general purpose of a theory: providing an explanation of a phenomenon. While associations will only be able to *describe* a process, causal relationships are able to bring the interpretations to an *explanatory level.*

A number of considerations, or specifications regarding causal relationships should be discussed now. First of all, and it has been said before, causality is a construction of the human mind and it cannot be observed. As a consequence, a researcher should make causal relationships plausible, and particularly at a theoretical level. To that end, the academic literature should be scrutinized regarding connecting theories or theoretical notions (Groenland, 2018a). Next, a study may be able to support the theory. This step will also guard against deciding that a relationship between concepts is causal while in reality it manifests itself as a so-called "spurious correlation". This means that two concepts are related to each other because they are both causally influenced by the same preceding factor. A classic example that says it all in one sentence is: "roosters cause the sun to rise". A formal and precise inspection of the concepts and the relationships involved will reduce this risk.

Finally, we have to take into consideration the type of causal relationship. Are we talking about a linear or a nonlinear relationship? If the latter seems to be the case, what type of nonlinear relationship should it be (logarithmic?), and what is the theoretical explanation for it? And in an idealised picture: are the strengths of the relationships within the theory about the same or are some relationships stronger or more dominant than others? And what is the theoretical explanation for this characteristic of the theory under consideration?

As said earlier, the initial development and gradual refinements in the composition of theories are mainly based on the testing of these versions of theories by means of empirical research. Of course, logical reasoning and allowing flashes of intuition have their own merits in the process. But ultimately the scientific community awaits empirical validation. To that end, the researcher formulates hypotheses to be tested. These hypotheses may both be directed at the structure, dimensionality and contents of the concepts/constructs involved and at the causal relationships as specified in the theory under study.

A theory is really a simplified cause-and-effect structure of a phenomenon, which is inherently complex in reality, or, in other words, A theory can be viewed as a *stylistic reproduction* of an inherently complex reality.

By using theories in real (business) life, man is able to take control (to some extent) of his own life, his family life, life in his country and the world. Apart from the advantages of steering processes for their own benefit, individuals experience feelings of pleasant relaxation and smoothing comfort when they feel that they are in control of themselves, their life domains and the world.

1.4.2 *Conceptual models*

A conceptual model is really a theory *in statu nascendi*, a theory in the process of formation. When formally testing a preliminary version of a theory, we need to have a representation of this theory comprising of both concepts and relationships between the concepts, as specified by the theory. A conceptual model portrays the underlying theory as a process presented from left to right and we need to have it at our disposal because it precisely specifies both concepts and relationships. By testing the conceptual model, we find support, or fail to find support, for the underlying theory in the process of formation. Based on the outcomes of the study we may formulate recommendations for testing an amended conceptual model, while expecting that we will ultimately find a conceptual model, with the corresponding formal theory, that cannot be further improved. Hopefully, the final version of the theory is useful in terms of gaining more understanding about the phenomenon under study.

Consider a process under study for which at this time no theory is yet available. We could think of a study of the category "applied science in business". There may be some provisional ideas and notions to start with. Based on that the researcher tries to further elaborate concepts and relations between concepts based on academic literature and other sources of inspiration, such as specialist and professional literature and professional journals. Now, concepts have to be selected based on their relevance for the explanation of the process under study.

It stands to reason to start with the "management problem", an issue a company encounters while doing their business (Groenland,

2014). More specifically, "something" is functioning in a suboptimal way and the study should ultimately bring about recommendations to solve this to certain extent. Let's say as an example that the productivity levels of the employees of a company are suboptimal; according to the management they could do better. This management problem is the starting point for the study. Next, a problem analysis has to be carried out which includes the creation of a conceptual model.

Based on the management problem, one or more target concepts have to be specified. A target concept is positioned at the right-hand side of the conceptual model, as this is the concept to be explained at the end of the left-to-right process. We keep things simple here and we choose "individual production level". Now that we have decided on the target concept (and its unit of analysis: individual employees) we are in the position to study the academic literature that is relevant in the sense that this literature will suggest concepts which, directly or indirectly, have an influence on the target concept. In this way we create both a target/dependent/criterion concept (amount of production) and independent/predictor concepts. When selecting these latter factors, or *determinants*, we may try and select those concepts that will have comparatively high predictive and explanatory power. That is, while focusing on the total (direct and indirect) effects on the target concept we would choose those concepts that contribute the highest to the explanation of the process under study. At the same time, each of these concepts should be different from each other, both in terms of contents and their independent effects on the target concept. Finally, these concepts should show sufficient anticipated variation over the sample when probed during, for instance, in-depth interviews using a checklist. In this context, "depth" is defined as probing as to the *contents* and *connotations* of the concept under scrutiny. By extension, the researcher attempts to find out *which considerations and thoughts are behind the specifications* of a respondent regarding the contents and connotations of the concept. In effect, one might compare this course of action with that of a young child who repeatedly (and maybe even annoyingly!) asks the why question to his parents regarding a topic. Finally, with respect to the conceptual model, one could conceive of this process of probing as moving from right to left in the model: Question: "Why do you feel about this topic the way you do (concept B)?". Answer: "Because of the following reasons ... (concept A)". In this case concept A is a determinant of concept B.

Once the conceptual model has been prepared it is ready to be tested empirically. Earlier, we said that hypotheses concerning both concepts and relationships can now be tested. For the research example, we just presented another term that may be used: *expectations*. One could have — theoretically guided — expectations in the form of conditional statements as based on the conceptual model: if the [intrinsic/instrumental] motivation of an individual employee is raised so will be his production level. And: if personal recognition/ payment levels are raised for an individual employee so will be his motivational level. Basically, a hypothesis and an expectation follow the same logic. An expectation, however, may be used for preliminary research approaches and preliminary models while a hypothesis may be used for more mature and formal models as derived from mature theories. Remember, a conceptual model is really a precursor of a full-blown theory.

We have said earlier that the general aim of a study based on a conceptual model is to establish whether the model as specified receives support from the outcomes of the study. When this is the case, we cannot say that the model has been proven to be correct in all ways and circumstances. As said earlier, we are able to reduce the uncertainty regarding the question whether the model is correct and valid but we can never be certain. In this respect, we refer to the principle of "Popperian falsifying": we can demonstrate that a model is incorrect; however, we cannot show that a model/theory is correct. According to Popperian logic in that case, we would have to test the model/theory under literally all manifestations for which the model applies in order to be one hundred per cent certain, and this is rather cumbersome, if not impossible.

As a way to round up this discussion we will provide some concluding remarks about theories and conceptual models. First, let us talk about the *scope* of a theory or conceptual model. It is obvious that this characteristic always must be specified. More specifically, the validity of the statements as derived from the theory/model must be particularized with respect to a domain (range of applications) and/or with respect to a time period. An example regarding the latter specification: when it comes to the study of the antecedents of the popularity of a politician it will be clear that there will be an expiration time. After a period of so many years (or months!) the conceptual model may no longer apply to the new situation this politician finds himself in. More generally, theories and models may vary with respect to their scopes. Some of them may be conditional on something or on *ceteris paribus* specifications (to be indicated by the researcher) while for other theories or models universal validity is claimed.

Finally, let us discuss the explanatory power a theory or a conceptual model may have. At the theoretical level, one could compare two rival theories. Let's say that both explain the same phenomenon adequately, that is both theories show similar levels of explanatory power. Interestingly, the first theory uses many more concepts and relationships as compared to the second model. Now, the *principle of Ockham's Razor* comes into play. This philosophical principle argues that in this case the theory with the smallest number of concepts and relationships should be preferred. This points to the "elegance" of a theory and a connection is made to the so-called unification theories in, for instance, (experimental) physics. Here, it is believed that when we truly have gained all of the knowledge that exists, phenomena can be explained by only a few basic forces in our world. A second consideration regards the increase in parameters (concepts, relationships) and states that an increase in parameters creates — *ceteris paribus* — more uncertainty regarding the explanatory power of the theory. This is because we currently operate at merely the level of emerging social sciences. Therefore, both concepts and relationships may be misconstrued to an unknown extent. In applied research, we attempt to move from explaining to predicting to controlling; in academic research we attempt to reduce uncertainty about truth, reality, and theories.

1.5 Positivism and Constructivism

When deciding as a researcher about a specific method of research you will face a fundamental divide. This dichotomy relates again to the two fundamental ways truth and reality are defined in the philosophy of science. When these two positions are translated into research methods they are called Positivism and Constructivism. We will now elaborate on these two outlooks.

1.5.1 *Positivism*

Positivism embraces Empiricism: in order to gain an understanding of the world around us we need to carry out strict and, in principle, objective measurements of phenomena to be followed by determining its implications for understanding reality. Reality has to be *discovered*. Positivism follows the logic of the so-called "Hypothetico-deductive" method. We will define now its basic components:

- **Theory:** A formal statement which can explain phenomena.
- **Hypothesis:** A deduction which allows finding a connection between at least two variables — if the theory is correct.
- **Operational definition:** A precise definition of that which you wish to measure in order to determine (co)variation between the variables.
- **Measuring:** Carrying out actual (mostly numerical) observations.
- **Testing:** Drawing conclusions regarding hypotheses.
- **Verifying:** Determining the implications of the theory.

1.5.2 *Constructivism*

The second approach to research methods is called Constructivism. In order to gain an understanding of the world around us we need to open up to, communicate with, observe, and live through the private and subjective experience of worlds of fellow man. This will provide the "data", the raw materials to further analyse, that is: to find patterns — strands of thought, feelings, and behaviours — which will enable us to gain a deep understanding of the truths and realities of these men and women. Their realities need to be *construed.*

An example may be found in certain forms of Phenomenology: here, the researcher is gaining an understanding of the world around us by carrying out observations and making interpretations of phenomena especially in their (psychological, social, societal) context. His starting point is collecting the idiosyncratic views of the world as his respondents experience them.

By hook or by crook, when it comes to the process of developing a *research design* there are *universal overarching principles* to follow. Research designs should, at the most general level, show connections (more precisely: consistence and coherence) between the following elements:

- **Problem analysis:** This includes background, immediate cause, management problem, intended use of the research outcomes, research aims, research questions, conceptual model, unit of analysis (cf. Groenland, 2014 for an example of this approach).
- **Sample design:** This includes population definition, any possible subpopulations, selection procedure for respondents and size of the sample or possible subsamples; an indication of the qualitative representativeness of the sample (do all of the relevant feelings, cognitions, behaviours, opinions, attitudes, preferences, etc., that exist in the population have a chance of being shown to the researcher during the scheduled field work activities?).
- **Method van data collection:** Which method, or methods, will be used to collect the relevant information?
- **Analysis strategy:** Which specific analyses are aimed at answering which specific research questions (conclusions)?
- **Recommendations:** This is based on both the intended use of the research outcomes and the actual outcomes of the study (double anchoring); a recommendation points either at *starting* some action, *stopping* some action, or *changing* some action.

In conclusion, we could rewrite all of the above in the following practical set of coherent questions:

(1) *What seems to be the problem* (either from the viewpoint of science or from the viewpoint of the commissioning client)?
(2) *What is the intended use of the research outcomes* (science, client)?
(3) *What knowledge and which insights* are desired?
(4) *Which questions have to be answered* by the study?
(5) *What is the process to be studied?*
(6) *Which units should be studied* while moving through this process?
(7) In *what way* should *which kind of data be collected?*
(8) *Which operations* should be applied to these data in order to arrive at answers to the research questions?
(9) *What are the recommendations* to science or to the client (as based on both the specified intended use of the research outcomes and the answers to the research questions)?

1.6 Qualitative Research Versus Quantitative Research: Essential Contrasts

By way of winding up these two basic approaches towards research, we now portray the essential differences regarding qualitative research and quantitative research in terms of contrasting characteristics.

1.6.1 *Quantitative research*

In quantitative research the research problem is approached by collecting and processing *numbers*.

- Knowledge and insights are acquired regarding the structure of the *concepts* and the strengths and directions of connections as depicted in the conceptual model.
- This type of research uses *large samples*, which are often aimed at being *quantitatively* representative for the underlying population.

- Data collection is *standardised and objectified*, using, for instance, questionnaires with pre-coded answering categories.
- The analysis occurs by means of (often complex) *processing of numbers*. *Numerical statistical procedures* are available.

1.6.2 *Qualitative research*

In qualitative research, the research problem is approached by collecting and processing *linguistic expressions and observations*. Knowledge and insights are acquired with respect to occurring *behaviours* and their *motives* and *determinants* as described in the conceptual model.

This type of research uses comparatively small samples, which may be aimed at being representatives for the underlying population *in a qualitative way*.

Data collection is carried out by means of interviews which are often semi-structured and less standardised. The qualitative checklists as used during the interviews are filled with broad, open-ended questions, obviously without answering categories. The analysis occurs by means of *interpretation of patterns*. Numerical statistical procedures do not apply here as numbers are not defined. However, software packages for the analysis of qualitative data are available.

Hence, one could say that quantitative research is associated with the *act of counting* while qualitative research is associated with the process of *grasping meaning*.

In that sense the two approaches may be labelled as "incommensurable paradigms". That is, the philosophical starting points of the two research approaches are essentially different, so they cannot be integrated. It is however possible to link the two types of research projects in a *consecutive* way yielding two sequences of research as part of a research project. One could either start with qualitative research and continue with quantitative research or start with quantitative research and continue with qualitative research.

An emerging research approach is called *mixed method* research. In this approach, specific combinations of qualitative and quantitative research are carried out within one research project. The question of course is: which combinations of research methods to avoid the use of incommensurable paradigms? Combinations of research methods may for instance be defined along a time line: sequential versus concurrent/parallel. When priority (dominant versus supplementary research) is added to this time line we recognize the two sequences discussed earlier. Sometimes, however, "level" is also part of the arrangement of research methods in mixed method research, meaning, for instance, that part of the study is carried out on individuals in a quantitative way and another part of the study at the group level in a qualitative way. This raises the question whether it is possible, or valid, to directly compare research outcomes acquired at two different levels of aggregation. If it were to be established that certain processes unfold at the individual level it does not follow from this outcome that these processes may unfold in the same, or comparative way, at the level of the household, the neighbourhood, the district, or at the level of an administrative entity such as a county. County statistics about, for instance, the need for health support may not be the sum of the responses of its individual residents. Generally, it is not to be expected that statistics collected at these aggregation levels describe the same reality as the reality of the individuals themselves. The corresponding semantic systems, or *experience space time continua,* simply may not manifest themselves in the same way in terms of reality.

Earlier, we discussed the unit of analysis of a conceptual model in order to be able to define the concepts at the same aggregation level while at the same time to be able to relate these concepts in a causal way. Finally, one could expect that theories defined at the individual level as compared to theories defined at a higher level of aggregation may differ substantially as to their contents and structure. As a consequence, it may be hard, or even impossible, to directly compare and connect the outcomes of two studies of this sort within the boundaries of a mixed method approach.

1.7 Views on Reality

As stated by Cameron, "It would be nice if all of the data which sociologists require could be enumerated because then we could run them through IBM machines and draw charts as the economists do. However, not everything that can be counted counts, and not everything that counts can be counted" (1963, p. 13).

Essentially, the two types of methodologies principally differ in the way they define and approach reality. Downey and Ireland (1979) contrasted qualitative and quantitative methodologies. Quantitative research attempts to remove the investigator from the investigation (Smith, 1983) using inanimate instruments — including scales, surveys, and tests — in order to be objective in the pre-determined, structured gathering of information about relations, comparisons, and predictions of pre-defined variables, using large random samples that are representative. Those who use quantitative methodology or logical positivism assume that facts are observable and measurable; only one (objective) reality exists, and the world exists even when we are not there, whereas in a qualitative approach, social reality ceases to exist when no actors are present. Hence, they make use of quantitative measures to test hypothetical generalisations (Hoepfl, 1997) and in so doing, causal relationships can be determined, answering "why?" questions. Using a deductive approach with surveys and statistical methods leads to narrow and precise findings. In both qualitative and quantitative approaches causality is a human, cognitive invention, which creates order, logic, and prediction in our lives.

1.8 Theoretical Roots

While quantitative research is rooted in positivist and logical empiricism, in contrast, symbolic interaction is one of the philosophical roots of qualitative research, emphasising the subjective meaning of human behaviour, the social process, and pragmatism, as opposed to objective, macrostructural aspects of social systems (Mead, 1934, 1938). Herbert Blumer further developed symbolic interactionism into a perspective, a way of looking at the social world and a means of gathering data about the social world; symbolic interactionism sees the mind and self as arising through social interaction with others, communicating by means of symbols (Blumer, 1969). In other words, people act towards things on the basis of the meanings that the things have for them and these meanings are a product of social interaction in society, modified by interpretation. This socialisation process modifies one's mind, role, and behaviour. Thus, researchers who are symbolic interactionists argue that there is no objective structure outside of individual experience and perception and that social life is constructed by individuals — in interaction with others. Symbolic interactionists, therefore, focus on subjective aspects. Manning and Smith (2010) revisited symbolic interactionism. This makes for a good introduction to qualitative methodologies such as ethnography, and relevant data collection methods including participant observation.

1.9 Similarities and Differences

So how are qualitative methodologies different from positivist quantitative methodologies? The answer to this question may be summarised as follows:

- **Similarities**
  - Academic approach of problem analysis, data collection, data analysis.
- **Differences**
  - Counting versus understanding;
  - Anatomising approach versus holistic approach;
  - One, objective reality versus multiple, subjective, and social realities;
  - Data collection by inanimate instruments versus an involved researcher;
  - Pre-determined data collection versus stepwise data collection with each new step based on previous outcomes;
  - Formal testing of hypotheses versus inductive search, e.g., culture and meaning.

Quantitative approaches are ideal for summarising large amounts of data and formulating generalisations based on statistical projections. So, the choice depends on the type of question the researcher would like to answer. Quantitative studies are thus ideal for testing hypotheses. Most often these hypotheses take the form of assessing the strength and direction of a causal relationship. In management studies, quantitative methodologies have traditionally facilitated the act of getting research published.

1.10 Practical Use of the Qualitative Approach

Mintzberg wrote, "While deduction certainly is a part of science, it is the less interesting, less challenging part. It is discovery that attracts me to this business, not the checking out of what we think we already know. I see two essential steps in inductive research. The first is detective work, the tracking down of patterns, consistencies. One searches through a phenomenon looking for order, following one lead to another. But the process itself is not neat…. The second step in induction is the creative leap" (1979, p. 584).

The researcher begins the scientific investigation with no hypotheses to test, in order to be open to whatever emerges from the data (Patton, 1982)[1]; analysis is inductive, i.e., done by the researcher. This said, Ahrens and Chapman (2006) noted the importance of positioning data to contribute to theory. We start from data to build theory.

Qualitative methodology must be more flexible than quantitative methodology. Qualitative methodology is an open-minded, creative process that benefits from being emergent; it evolves with a holistic focus (that is by nature the way we experience social reality), and requiring the interviewer/observer to be an integral part of the investigation (Jacob, 1998). This involves gathering detailed data by means such as open-ended questions, allowing to record direct quotations, and to describe from the perspective of the participant. Guided by the researcher's experience and accumulating knowledge, research questions are often amended, in order for issues to better be addressed. With the researcher being the primary instrument, data are subjective perceptions of participants in the study, to be interpreted by the researcher; it is assumed that values will have an impact and seek to understand people's interpretations. Reality is what people perceive it to be. As explained by Adair (1984), the subject's view is not necessarily the same as that of the investigator(s).

---

[1] One may question this approach in the sense that no scientist (or human being) can be considered to be a *tabula rasa*.

Findings are holistic as opposed to narrow. According to the paradigm of psychology, individuals' perceptions of reality will guide their behaviour, and the choices they make in (business) life.

1.11 Best Practices for Choosing a Qualitative Approach Over a Quantitative Approach

When to decide for a qualitative approach? Choose a qualitative approach:

- when you want to gain a deep understanding of the phenomenon under study instead of assessing the strength and direction of causal relationships in your conceptual model;
- when you wish to achieve a holistic understanding of the phenomenon under study;
- when you believe the phenomenon under study to be rooted in a subjective reality;
- when you believe that gaining an understanding of this subjective reality is only possible by immersing yourself as an individual and a researcher in the reality of those involved in the phenomenon under study;
- when you are ready to grasp this reality by following a step-by-step approach in asking questions, and new questions based on accumulated insight;
- when the topic you wish to study is conceptually based on facets of social reality.

1.12 When are Qualitative Methodologies Useful?

If the goal of an investigation is hypothesis testing, prediction or confirmation, quantitative methodologies are usually appropriate; if the objective is discovery, description, holistic understanding and/or hypothesis generating or theory building then qualitative methodologies can be most useful.

While quantitative methodologies are optimal for testing hypotheses, Von Bertalanffy (1968), Morgan (1983), and others have emphasised that hypotheses are value-laden; hence, in some instances (e.g., exploratory studies) a hypothetico-deductive meth-odology might cause a bias due to the beliefs and values of the researcher.[2] Hypotheses are either about the structure and contents of a concept, or about the relationship between concepts. The com-bination of concepts, and their relations, comprises a theory (defined for a specific domain, and for a specific unit of analysis).

In contrast, qualitative methodologies are ideal to understand the perspectives of participants in their words and the meaning they give to phenomena, and also to observe a process in depth; As Eisenhardt *et al.* (2016, p. 1115) say: "Inductive methods can help examine and contribute to solving grand challenges [research prob-lems] by generating novel ideas, revealing effective processes, coping with complexity such as configurations, emergence, and equifinality, unpacking subtle constructs, and exploiting extreme cases."

Subsequently, qualitative research can assist with hypothesis gen-eration and theory building, for later testing using quantitative methods. Empirical results often serve as a stimulus for new think-ing (Mintzberg and Waters, 1982, p. 467). The field of psychology uses this approach.

The selection of one methodology over another is often a function of subject matter; Conger (1998) described a qualitative approach as being central to the understanding of leadership. Beach, Muhlemann, Price, Paterson, and Sharp (2001) discuss the role of qualitative meth-ods in production management research. Qualitative methodologies are also appropriate in the research of complex or sensitive issues. Complex phenomena would require too many concepts, and relation-ships between concepts, to be modelled and to be studied in a quantitative approach, thus reaching a point where the data collection, and especially the data analysis, no longer is manageable.

1.13 Advantages and Disadvantages

Despite the advantages of quantitative methodologies, researchers seeking to answer questions about culture and meaning have found

---

[2]When the theory is well founded as per academic criteria there is less cause for expecting bias.

experimental quantitative methods to be insufficient in their attempt to explaining the phenomenon they wish to study. Where there is a gap in the literature and the objective is to understand culture and meaning or to develop new theory, inductive qualitative methodology is optimal. Culture and meaning are concepts, which may only exist in a social reality, by the very nature of these concepts. Thus, theory development and qualitative methodology are in agreement with each other.

Qualitative methodology can produce in-depth, comprehensive information by using participant observation to provide thick description (Geertz, 1973) within the natural setting, and with high levels of external validity (as opposed to experimental or statistical as is the case with quantitative methodology). In addition, the context of the variables may be studied, and also interactions of variables in the context. Through ethnographic fieldwork, for example, the result can be a more holistic comprehension of the entire scenario. And the holistic approach is congruent with the human experience of social reality. Dana and Dana summarised, "advantages of qualitative (as opposed to quantitative) research, include the ability to learn directly from the research subject, thereby reducing measurement errors common in survey studies which often need to make assumptions. The result is a deeper holistic understanding. Such an approach, because of the interaction between researcher and subject, also reduces Type III error (asking the wrong question) and Type IV error (solving the wrong problem)" (2005, p. 80).

Despite their strengths, qualitative methodologies are limited in scope due to the fact that they require time-consuming, in-depth, comprehensive data gathering approaches, and cumbersome analysis processes. Furthermore, these compromise generalisability for detail. Since qualitative methodologies are more labour-intensive than quantitative ones, they demand much time and projects are often costly. Obtaining funding can be a challenge. Furthermore, because the human person is the primary collection tool, a problem is the subjectivity of the inquiry. As a consequence, positivists can raise doubts with regards to reliability and validity as defined in quantitative approaches.

1.14 Methodologies Used in Qualitative Research

Among others, methodologies used in qualitative research include: (i) case study; (ii) critical incident; (iii) ethnography; (iv) field stimulation; and (v) grounded theory approach. As explained by Hammersley and Atkinson (1983), semantic boundaries among these can be fuzzy, and it is also possible to combine methodologies (Mingers and Brocklesby, 1997). Eisenhardt *et al.* (2016, p. 1114), in this context, point to the commonalities of inductive methods when they say: "While differences among inductive approaches exist, they share many *commonalities*. First, they all involve deep immersion over time in the focal phenomena with openness to many types of rich data — from text, observations, and surveys to, more recently, Twitter feeds, YouTube videos, and Facebook posts. Second, inductive approaches rely on theoretical sampling, which involves the selection of cases based on their ability to illuminate and extend relationships among constructs or develop deeper understanding of processes. And third, inductive methods rely on a grounded theory-building process. Although they may not use the exact steps of orthodox grounded theory building, they all use a similar process."

Jick (1979) discussed combining qualitative methodologies with quantitative ones. Journals such as *Administrative Sciences Quarterly* do publish articles based on multiple methodologies; however, some research sometimes does not get published because of the shortage of referees who are qualified in different methodologies and can therefore do justice to a manuscript based on multiple methodologies.

A current debate is about whether qualitative and quantitative approaches can actually be integrated within one study, or that sequences of qualitative and quantitative studies should be carried out, where each separate study is of only one kind. Proponents of the latter position would argue that, at any one time, you can only approach reality from one perspective. Otherwise, the question arises which of the two perspectives is the "right one", as both cannot be "true" at the same time.

Chapter 2

Case Study Methodology

2.1 Introduction

A case study is a detailed investigation of a social unit, at times one entrepreneur or a firm. The research purpose of a case study is to describe one or more cases in depth and to address research questions and issues. A case study protocol is important to assure reliability. The focus is on understanding the subject and variables relevant to it, but not necessarily on generalisation; therefore, such study does not focus on an entire population of cases. Conclusions are valid for comparable cases. A defining element is the focus on the dynamic interactions within the group (a group can be a company because all of the employees cooperate in order to achieve a company goal). Often, a case study approach is taken when, due to the inherent complexity of the phenomenon under study, a quantitative approach is not feasible.

McClintock, Brannon, and Maynard-Moody (1979) applied the logic of sample surveys to qualitative case studies. As explained by Yin (1981, 1984), it is of utmost importance to have a clear conceptual framework when conducting case investigations.[1] As expressed by Yin (1981), the most challenging aspect is that a variety of sources

---

[1] A basic notion about an effect being influenced by one or more determinants could exist at the start of any study. A business research approach (for both qualitative and quantitative studies) taking advantage of this may be found in Groenland (2014).

are relevant. The researcher is faced with a choice of sources, any combination of which may be used simultaneously. Documents are useful for verification and added reliability. A fundamental difference between data collection in qualitative research and that in quantitative research is that in the case of qualitative research, hypotheses arise from the data and are used to modify further data collection.

Eisenhardt (1989) focused on building theories from case study research. Looking to develop a methodology for doing qualitative research, Fox-Wolfgramm (1997) discussed the dynamic-comparative case study method. Beverland and Lindgreen (2010) examined a literature review spanning 35 years of case research published in *Industrial Marketing Management.* Tsang (2013) also focused on case study methodology, addressing causality, contextualisation, and theorising.

2.2 Definition and Use

A core element of the definition of case studies is in the explaining of a phenomenon from the context (e.g., a company) in which it takes place. A more formal and elaborate definition is provided by Yin (2009, p. 18): "An empirical inquiry that investigates a contemporary phenomenon in depth and within its real-life context, especially when the boundaries and phenomenon are not clearly evident. The case study inquiry copes with the technically distinctive situation in which there will be many more variables of interest than data points, and as one result. It relies on multiple resources of evidence, with data needing to converge in a triangulating fashion. And as another result benefits from the prior development of theoretical propositions to guide data collection and analysis". And already more than a quarter of a century ago, Yin (1981, p. 58) adds to this: "Experiments differ from this in that they deliberately divorce a phenomenon from its context. Histories differ in that they are limited to phenomena of the past, where relevant informants may be unavailable for interview and relevant events unavailable for direct observation". Swanborn (2003) emphasises the structural complexity of the phenomenon to be studied when he defines the aim of case studies as "Describing and explaining the origin, further changes and the entire complex structure of a phenomenon by paying attention to a large set of variables at the same time".

Obviously, the defining properties of the case study approach leaves ample space to specify its particular research design for a specific case study to be carried out. Therefore, we will further provide defining characteristics of the case study approach by elaborating on the more practical question: when to choose a case study design? So, when to decide for a case study design? Choose the case study approach:

- when the research objective indicates that the deeper insights that need to be acquired take a central position (hence, that counting or determining the strength and direction of causal relations are not the issue);
- when the phenomenon under investigation is of a social nature (there are interactions within the system and there is reciprocity with context factors) — as a result of which the grounds for explanation need to be inherently found on the system level instead of in the individual processes of participating individuals; that is, grounds for explanation are sought within the company, within the group;
- when the relations between the phenomenon and the context are too complex to examine by means of a survey;
- if little formulation of theories regarding the phenomenon under investigation has taken place, possibly in preparation of later quantitative targeted research.

Another way to assist the researcher in making the decision of what to choose for a case study design would involve two considerations. That is, a case study design may be chosen

- Depending on the type of *question*: what is the effect of the group dynamics on how group members interact?
- Depending on the type of *problem*: how can the broader context, in which a phenomenon takes place, describe this phenomenon?

Now that we have dealt with definitional aspects and core properties of the case study approach it is time to review some of the major uses of the case study method. To that end, we will present a number of its applications. In this presentation, we will focus on methodological characteristics and generic topics.

Yin (2009, p. 46) provides some broad types of case studies. He distinguishes between:

- Innovations and implementations company/institution
  - **Example:** "We wish to understand how to implement an incentive structure as applied to managers in such a way that their achievements will improve structurally."
  - **Studying problems in the context of:**
  - Reorganisation;
  - Culture change;
  - Conflict management;
  - From policy body to commercial enterprise;
  - Increase of production efficiency, or profitability.

Yin makes a comparison with management consultants in this context:

- **Example:** "After the merger we encountered all kinds of problems with regard to teamwork. We wish to find the underlying causes. The research outcomes should help us to decide how to adjust or transform both employees and processes."

There are some further uses of case studies that provide insight into both its design and the way they are applied. We will examine these in what follows.

Avenier and Thomas (2015, pp. 4–7), while reviewing the domain of field of Information systems, organisation and management research, place emphasis on the fact that every researcher who engages in case study research, explicitly or implicitly, chooses an underlying philosophy of knowledge for their study. That is, underlying any form of research is a philosophy of knowledge, also called an *epistemological framework*. The point these authors make is that a researcher should make an explicit choice here and must attempt to maintain internal consistency of the research design. Specifically, this is of paramount importance when choosing the (general) goal of the study, this goal being theory building, theory refinement or theory testing, and when choosing the research method to be used.

Tsang (2012, p. 199) also focused on case study methodology, addressing causality, contextualisation, and *theorising*. He proposes four methods of theorizing in order to build theory as part of the case study approach. These four approaches are depicted as follows:

- **Interpretive sense making:** This involves seeking an in-depth understanding of human experience embedded in a rich, real-world context.
- **Contextualised explanation:** A causal explanation in a single case is based upon a theory structured in terms of what comprises a critical realist causal explanation.
- **Empirical regularity:** This intends to identify empirical regularities from case study findings, while the outcome may or may not lead to theory creation.
- **Theory building and testing:** This involves building or testing theories based on case study outcomes in order to provide an explanation.

To this, Tsang (2012, p. 201) adds that the four methods of theorizing can be used sequentially for implementing a thorough case research programme.

Eisenhardt (1989) focused on building theories from case study research. She notes (p. 546) that "One strength of theory building form cases is its likelihood of generating novel theory".

Looking to develop a methodology for doing qualitative research, Fox-Wolfgramm (1997) discussed the dynamic-comparative case study method. She posits that the Dynamic-comparative case study method (D-CCSM) (p. 440) "capturers the interplay of historic and real time, contexts, and layers of reality to find out what is going on in more than one organization over time, in order to reveal complex mechanisms that are responsible for many of the similarities, differences, and tendencies of a particular observed occurring across organizations. A dynamic re-description of the phenomenon, in more than one organization, results in midrange theory about the phenomenon."

Eisenhardt (2007, p. 30) concludes that theory building from case studies is a "relevant research strategy" when based on a "thoughtful research design", based on "careful justification of theory building, theoretical sampling of cases, interviews that limit informant bias, rich presentation of evidence in tables and appendices, and clear statement of theoretical arguments. The result is fresh theory that bridges well from rich qualitative evidence to mainstream deductive research". Romano (1989), in the context of small business, provides an apt overview of research strategies.

Beverland and Lindgreen (2010) carried out a meta-analysis and examined a literature review spanning 35 years of "qualitative case research" published in *Industrial Marketing Management*. Specifically, they applied quality criteria (p. 57) from a positivist viewpoint to these 105 studies. These criteria included *construct validity* (correct operational measures have been established for the concepts to be studied), *internal validity* (a causal relationship has been established), *external validity* (the domain of the study can be generalised), and *reliability* (the findings from a case study can be replicated). They conclude (p. 61) that a steady improvement has been realised in the way researchers have addressed these criteria over time.

In the same vein, Gibbert and Ruigrok (2010) evaluated "case study rigor". To that end, the authors carried out content analyses on all 159 case studies published in 1995–2000 in 10 management journals. In the process, they examined what rigor types the authors reported and how they reported them. They conclude (p. 42–43) that authors should focus on reporting the concrete research actions taken (rather than abstract validity and reliability types). Also, more consideration should be given to internal validity and construct validity over generalisability, or even at the expense of generalisability.

Hoon (2013, p. 527), in the context of organisational and management research, attempts to transcend the analysis level of cases in case studies. She proposes to carry out a *meta-synthesis of case study projects* that were carried out and published in the past. To that end, she develops an eight-step procedure. In her words, a meta-synthesis is defined as an exploratory, inductive research design to synthesise primary qualitative case studies for the purpose of making contributions beyond those achieved in the original studies. Thus, a meta-study involves the accumulation of previous case studies' evidence, and more specifically its extraction, analysis, and synthesis. A meta-synthesis needs to incorporate a broad yet still manageable set of studies in which sensitivity toward the analysis and synthesis of other researchers' findings can be maintained. And, a meta-synthesis seeks (p. 544) to move a body of knowledge forward by interpreting primary qualitative evidence across different contexts to come to a higher replicability of theory.

A special word about the so-called *rival theories* is in order in closing this paragraph. A rival theory is a theory that claims to have equal explanatory power to explain the same phenomenon under study, however with a different theoretical content. Thus, rival theories come in place when research is carried out into the plausibility of alternative (rival) explanations of real-life phenomena. A research example may clarify this type of research. Suppose the following assertion is made: "Works significantly developing the infrastructure most often are more expensive than estimated and often fail to be delivered on time". And suppose that two, alternative explanations for this phenomenon are available:

"Theory A" argues that lack of project control is the cause, while "Theory B" argues that the political decision process frequently results in too low an estimate of the project. These would be called here "rival theories". A final example about the cause of realizing an optimal level of control of corporates processes: "Applying Enterprise Risk Management (ERM) results in an optimal level of control of corporate processes". However, an *alternative explanation* is available: "by applying modern theories in the field of management control an optimal level of control of corporate processes will be achieved". Again, two rival theories exist and may be tested against each other. This concludes our overview of definition and use of the case study approach.

Any methodology in research may be characterised by both advantages and disadvantages, and this is also true for the case study. In the following, a summary is presented. Now, we will discuss some advantages and disadvantages as attributed to the case study method.

2.3 Advantages and Disadvantages

No doubt, any methodology in research may be characterised by both advantages and disadvantages, so this is also true for the case study. Obviously, the case study approach, based on its defining characteristics, is a quite particular approach, well delineated from other research approaches. Therefore, its advantages and disadvantages may be deduced directly from these defining characteristics. In the following a summary is presented:

- **Advantages**
  - Complex, system-like phenomena may be studied in a holistic manner, while other methodologies would fail because of the inherent complexity;
  - Dynamic processes may be studied as they occur in real life, fostering external validity;
  - Multiple sources of data are available, so the principle of triangulation concerning data sources may be taken advantage of.
- **Disadvantages**
  - Analytical instead of statistical generalisations;
  - Theory and conceptual model for the process to be studied not always available from the academic literature;
  - Approach (with respect to theory, data collection, and data analysis) may be arbitrary to some extent, affecting the outcome of the study.

To this, we may add that the case study approach allows for a deep understanding of determinants and of the dynamics of a complex social (or system theoretical) phenomenon while statements are valid — *mutatis mutandis* — for comparable cases.

Now, it is time to focus on the steps to be taken when carrying out a case study.

2.4 Best Practices

We will start this section by highlighting some basic characteristics of the case study in order to provide the context of such studies. Earlier, we saw that a case study design is chosen when the research is located at a company or an institute. Also, most often a well-defined problem analysis is not yet available. Instead, such a problem analysis could have a provisional and loose structure. An example would be: "We wish to investigate why our system of bonuses fails to boost our profitability". Furthermore, here the employees are the information carriers and the unit of analysis is a group (company/institute). Also, explanations are being sought by studying the various different ways the employees of the company function within the company or the institute. The study is an empirical study in the sense that research and analysis are carried out on the basis of measurements (observations). Next, a case study has to connect with one or more theoretic notions. Finally, the study must be able to generalise statements as based on the sample design as it is no casuistic research in itself.

Now, let us discuss the case study set up in broad steps:

- First, check the academic literature and choose an assumed theory or theories and possibly "rival theories" (if any) in both descriptive and verifying research. As said before, a rival theory is a theory that claims to have equal explanatory power to explain the same phenomenon under study, however with a different theoretical content.
- Next, select preferably multiple cases, assuring that qualitative verification is possible (that rival theories can be examined). Remember, the group or company is the unit of analysis, not the individual.
- Then, start with the collection of data by means of conversations, semi-structured interviews, possibly questionnaires, and on the basis of supporting documentation.

- Now, perform qualitative analyses aimed at finding explanations for the phenomenon in the dynamics of the chosen context or environment. That is, take into account the (large number of) interactions between case and context and the fact that there are few data points — many variables and vice versa.
- Finally, report via text reports, dressed up with qualitative tables.

The rival theory case mentioned above may be viewed as a replication design. As such it merits some attention here. A replication design *requires* the following:

- A rich theoretical framework;
- Literal replications;
- Theoretical replications (investigation of "rival theories");
- When needed: modifications to theory;
- And this leads to generalisations to theory (analytical generalisations).

Now, let us move on to the particulars of the case study research design.

2.4.1 *Preliminary problem analysis*

The process starts with a preliminary problem analysis here, the background of the study to be carried out is of importance:

- Which (company) environment is to be selected?
- Which actors are involved?

And what is the cause of the study, that is, *which changes, or situation make(s) this research important?*

Next the "Problem", including the management problem is laid out:

- Broadly speaking, what is the problem that needs to be studied?
- And distinguish the problem to be studied from the management problem.

Based on this information now start the theoretic research or literature study.

If you're looking at a scientific publication, you're probably looking for a *theory or a model*:

- What is the set up: concepts and their relations?
- Which presuppositions or assumptions are made?
- To which domains is it applied?
- Are notions or concepts applied?
- What are the definitions?
- How has it been made operational (has it been measured)?

Also, the *method used* may be of importance:

- Which research method was used?
- Which method of analysis was carried out?
- Which analyses have been performed?
- An overview of the results may be relevant;
- Which results have been found, and which haven't?

It is advised to perform targeted searching and reading while skipping what is irrelevant.

2.4.2 *Final or formal problem analysis*

This phase of the preparatory research process starts with formally carrying out a problem analysis (for a formal treatment see Groenland, 2014):

- Research objectives
  - "to acquire knowledge and understanding regarding [subject] within [target audience]";
  - are mostly qualitative.
- Research questions
  - broad phrasing of the questions to achieve the research objective.

- Conceptual model
  - visual help tool;
  - can be adapted in the course of the study.
- Limitations/prior conditions/validity
  - depends on
    - design of the sample;
    - method of data collection;
    - analysis strategy.
- Designated use of the research results
  - to serve science;
  - to contribute to solve the client's problem.

The procedure as described above follows a general and structured approach, variations may be possible and may be necessary.

2.4.3 *Sample design*

The researcher must provide a sample design at the start of the case study. However, adaptations may be necessary during the process of carrying out the research project. A general approach would involve the following:

- Distinguish groups on the basis of preliminary aprioristic assumptions regarding answering and reaction patterns of respondents on checklist. Examples within the context of a company are:

  - Subordinate versus superior in terms of the company employee hierarchy;
  - Special interest groups;
  - Groups based on formal power and responsibility;
  - Groups based on informal power;
  - In accordance with consciously chosen variables, in the form of a hierarchic tree diagram.

  A starting point regarding the size of the sample may be four groups. However, this predominantly depends on the topic to be studied and the structure of the organisation under study.

Remember that it must be possible to generalise the research results analytically. This must always be specified in the research proposal. Let's now move on to the data collection part.

2.4.4 *Data collection*

We will start with a number of important general observations. McClintock, Brannon, and Maynard-Moody (1979) applied the logic of sample surveys to qualitative case studies. As explained by Yin (1981, 1984), it is of utmost importance to have a clear conceptual framework when conducting case investigations.[2] As expressed by Yin (1981), the most challenging aspect is that a variety of sources are relevant. The researcher is faced with a choice of sources, any combination of which may be used simultaneously. Documents are useful for verification and added reliability. A fundamental difference between data collection in qualitative research and that in quantitative research is that in the case of qualitative research, hypotheses arise from the data and are used to modify further data collection.

A more detailed examination of the data collection process provides the following description:

In general, and as said earlier, data collection is carried out by way of interviews, questionnaires (which are optional), and existing internal sources of information, such as annual reports, internal company documents, external sources, and the Internet.

(Semi-structured) interviews may be based on (semi-structured) questionnaires and presented to various groups in multiple rounds. Observations may be based on an observation schedule in order to create a form of organisation of the various aspects to be observed. Also, document research may be carried out by collecting, for instance, internal memoranda, notes, and minutes of (company)

---

[2]A basic notion about an effect being influenced by one or more determinants could exist at the start of any study. A business research approach (for both qualitative and quantitative studies) taking advantage of this may be found in Groenland (2014). Furthermore, a qualitative deductive analysis approach for the analysis of qualitative, semi-structured interview data may be found in Groenland (2018b).

meetings. Finally, questionnaires may be employed to enable using the results in a current round for a next round of data collection.

2.4.5 *Analysis*

In broad terms, the analysis strategy focuses on relations between context factors and the phenomenon under investigation. These relations are split up, and next their contrasts are brought out for distinct subgroups in the sample (see the sample design).

Yin (1981, pp. 63–64) provides a structural element of the analysis of data of a case study when he proposes, "Whether the case-survey or case-comparison approach is used, the case study researcher must preserve a *chain of evidence* as each analytic step is conducted. The chain of evidence consists of the explicit citation of particular pieces of evidence, as one shifts from data collection to within-case analysis to cross-case analysis and to overall findings and conclusions. Most case study research has failed to establish an explicit chain, and critics can rightfully question how specific conclusions were reached".

We end with a more systematic and detailed treatment of the analysis process, focusing here on the relations of the theoretical framework built earlier. Such a process would encompass the following elements:

- Analyse in detail the characteristics of the relations present in the data:
  - Select the (assumed causal) connections;
  - Establish causal chains of proof;
  - Specify the form of the relations;
  - Determine, if possible, whether the form may be linear;
  - Determine, if possible, whether the form may be conditional;
  - Establish whether connections are derived from theories that need to be tested;
  - Create a conceptual model based on the analysis outcomes.
- Find universally valid, causal relations for the coverage of the research:
  - Find connections within subdomains, that is, subgroups in the sample design;

- o (Ideally) come to an integrated process description, and include a *Leitmotiv* if possible.
- Systematically answer research questions to achieve the research objective.

2.4.6 Conclusions

The conclusions are the answers to the research questions. Conclusions may be drawn with respect to the tenability, validity, and the applicability of the investigated theories.

2.4.7 Types of recommendations

Recommendations are of two types: scientific and applied. Scientific recommendations may be aimed at follow-up research, validation of a theory or a model under scrutiny. They may also be directed at modifications of such a theory or model. Finally, different measuring methods may be recommended as based on the current research outcomes.

Applied recommendations formulate the actions to be taken by the client. When applying the Annabel approach (Groenland, 2014) for the problem analysis, the researcher may provide double anchorage for the recommendations. That is, they are based both on the conclusions of the study and the designated use of the research results, as specified at the start of the study. Finally, recommendations have to be checked against the criteria relevant in a business context. That is: feasibility, cost versus yield, speed of the result of implementation, and visibility — can the client "score points" by carrying through these recommendations?

2.4.8 Report format

In order to report the outcomes of the case study, a qualitative text report is drawn up which may include qualitative tables. As said at the start of this chapter, case study protocols must be provided in the report, which may be placed in its appendix. Apart from the considerations as specified above, the report may follow a general format as being used in scientific reports.

2.4.9 *Validity and reliability*

A final word about the issue of validity and reliability of case studies. Yin (2009, p. 41) presents a number of design tests in order to elevate both validity and reliability. Additionally, he provides four strategies that are relevant in this context:

- *Construct validity* [may be enhanced by]:
  Multiple sources of information (triangulation), test procedures regarding assumptions, hypotheses, and validation of interview reports;
- *Internal validity* [may be enhanced by]:
  Pattern recognition, searching for explanations, researching alternative explanations, documenting the reasoning followed;
- *External validity* [may be enhanced by]:
  Connecting to theories, using (theoretical) replication studies;
- *Reliability* [may be enhanced by]:
  Creating a case study protocol, and a case study database.

By spending time and effort on both the validity and the reliability issues of a case study in all of its phases, that is, setting it up, carrying it out, and providing the final report, the researcher is ultimately blessed with a study that can withstand the severest judgments of dyed-in-the-wool critics about this powerful research approach in general and the concerned study in particular.

2.5 Sample Study

In order to demonstrate how a research may employ the case study approach as a research method, an overview of the study performed by Dana (1990) is provided, and the excellent case study characteristics of this study are highlighted.

2.5.1 *Issue and relevance*

The article compares the developmental efforts of two nations that coexist on the island of St. Martin. St. Martin, at 37 square miles, is the smallest land mass in the world which is divided into two countries. Two distinctly separate governments rule the two sectors of the island: Saint Martin (French) and Sint Maarten (Dutch).

2.5.2 *Research goal*

The research goal of this study is to gain knowledge and insights regarding the ways culture, government, and policy, over the years, have differentially influenced and shaped the economic development of the two sectors of the island: Saint Martin/Sint Maarten.

As the two countries are otherwise quite similar, for instance with respect to remoteness, and with respect to their limited national resources, logic dictates that differences with respect to economic development of the two countries must be caused by these forces.

2.5.3 *Research design*

The research goal points to three broad, dynamic forces: culture, government, and policy. These forces are each inherently complex of its own, and therefore may not be easily demarcated. Moreover, the reach of these forces may not be determined exactly. For that reason, a research approach using a great multiple of well-defined concepts and variables was found not to be feasible. In view of the aforementioned characteristics, a case study design was chosen.

2.5.4 *Sample design*

In a case study design sources of information are sought for. Here, sources of information include the following: secondary sources such as newspaper articles, local publications, and journal articles; and primary sources such as government officials, Chamber of

Commerce representatives, and entrepreneurs, in both Saint Martin and Sint Maarten.

2.5.5 *Data collection*

Data were obtained from the secondary sources as described previously. In addition, primary data were collected by means of interviews with individuals listed to represent the aforementioned primary sources. These interviews were part of the field research *in situ* as they were mainly held in locations on the island. Interviews in Sint Maarten were conducted in English while those in French Saint Martin were done in French and subsequently translated by the author.

2.5.6 *Data analysis*

The data from the interviews were analysed with regard to meaningful patterns as they had influenced and shaped the economic development of the two sectors of the island Saint Martin/Sint Maarten. Specifically, the outcomes of both sectors were formally contrasted. In the general process of analysis, the outcomes of the analyses of these primary sources were functionally related to the outcomes of the analyses of the secondary source materials. The final outcomes thus obtained are presented in the chapter.

2.5.7 *Report*

The report discusses the following topics: two cultures, government, trade patterns, policy and regulation, tax structure, business culture, and tourism.

The article concludes that the two cultures are widely different. And furthermore, the two nations differ with respect to the following:

- **Sint Maarten** may be characterised by high levels of entrepreneurial activity, its government policy is supportive of new ventures, contributing to an environment conducive to a healthy, growing small business sector in the absence of excessive regulation;

- In contrast, the economy of **Saint Martin** is lagging behind, as entrepreneurs are burdened by paperwork requirements, regulatory restrictions, and the government's inability to make necessary changes in due time.

It is suggested that these clear and consistent differences between the two nations cause and explain the different states of the two economies studied.

2.5.8 *Excellent case study characteristics of the study*

For a case study to be excellent a number of conditions have to be met. These include the following: the research problem has to be clear and relevant; the research design must be functional for the research purpose; data collection must be broad, including various data sources, while at the same time being to the point and exhaustive. Here, data analysis must be carried out on various different data sources using manifold analysis strategies and the outcomes must be connected and tied together in such a way that new understanding and insights may come into being, that is, the analysis outcomes as based on both primary and secondary data sources must be functionally and creatively interweaved to that end. All of this is the case in this study.

The chapter expands, elaborates, and clearly explains each of the topics found from the analysis of the various data sources in a seemingly easy manner. Thus, the defining and characteristic differences with respect to two cultures, government, trade patterns, policy and regulation, tax structure, business culture, and tourism are contrasted in a consistent way between the two nations as they exert their influence on the economic development of the two sectors of the island, Saint Martin/Sint Maarten.

Finally, the expressive language and story-like tone of voice with which these outcomes are passed to the reader evoke clear pictures and mental images that spring from the outcomes of this evocative study.

Chapter 3

Critical Incident Methodology

3.1 Introduction

The aim of the critical incident technique is to collect, analyse, and classify observations of human behaviour. Moreover, the purpose of the critical incident technique as a methodology is in obtaining a record of specific behaviours from those in the best position to make necessary observations and evaluations.

An incident is understood to be an observable act that is complete in itself such as to permit inferences and predictions to be made about a person doing this act. To be critical, the incident must occur in a situation where the purpose of the act seems fairly clear to the observer and where its consequences are sufficiently definite to leave little doubt concerning its effects. That is, "A critical incident is described as one that makes a significant contribution, either positively or negatively, to an activity or phenomenon" (Gremler, 2004, p. 66).

3.2 Definition and Use

With roots in the late nineteenth century, critical incident methodology was an outgrowth of the Aviation Psychology Program that was established during WWII to develop procedures for the selection and classification of crews, i.e., this methodology gathers data concerning specific situations. Miller and Flanagan (1950) represented the first application of this methodology in an industrial situation. As summarised by Flanagan, this methodology "obtains a record of specific behaviors from those in the best position to make necessary observations and evaluations" (1954, p. 355).

Machungwa and Schmitt (1983) made use of critical incidents to formulate antecedents of a dependent variable, in this case motivation. Gabbott and Hogg (1996) used critical incidents to understand service evaluation in healthcare. Nowadays, critical incidents form the basis for several psychological tests and job analysis procedures. In market research, critical incident technique is used to measure ensuing service quality.

Among entrepreneurship studies making use of critical incidents is Tjosvold and Weicker (1993) who explored the potential role of an entrepreneur's network on the motivation and success of the new business venture, asking people who created a new business five years prior to the interviews to volunteer in the study; participants were asked to describe in detail a recent significant incident involving the development of their Business and 51 incidents were obtained, describing a specific interaction with another entrepreneur, financial backer, supplier, government official or other external person. Chell and Pittaway (1998) used the critical incident technique as a methodology to study entrepreneurs and the result was a prize-winning paper. Cope and Watts (2000) studied critical moments in history of firms to study entrepreneurial learning; respondents were asked to think about and discuss the first two critical events in their business history. Sullivan (2000) discussed the role of life cycle development approaches in planning entrepreneurial development, the importance of double loop learning and learning from critical incidents. Kaulio (2003) assessed 65 critical incidents in infancy biotech or IT ventures; at the end of the interview the critical event was summarised to check the validity. Man (2006) explored the behavioural patterns of entrepreneurial learning by semi-structured interviews among entrepreneurs.

Data collection methods used in critical incident research may vary. Sharkin and Birkey (1992) used a postal questionnaire to further the understanding about incidental encounters and to explore perceptions and reactions during public contact between therapists and clients; they used two open ended questions and 28 forced choice questions with a sample of directors of 350 university counselling/psychological services, and received 547 complete responses. Often, interviews are used to collect data.

3.3 Advantages and Disadvantages

Edvardsson (1992, p. 19) states that among the main advantages of CIT are its capability to generate "detailed process descriptions of critical incidents as those interviewed perceive them". The fact that the respondent uses his own words makes it possible to enter the idiosyncratic experience world of the respondent. The basic weakness of CIT is in the circumstance that the interviewer may have pre-conceived notions about the incident to be discussed, and the interviewee. This in turn may create bias in the data collection, and the interpretation of these data.

Woolsey (1986) claims, "the critical incident methodology is highly flexible. It can be used to study a wide range of phenomena, for example, relationships, decision-making, self-actualization, vocational choice, and group process. It can be modified to collect data on factual happenings (rather than restricting its use to 'critical' incidents), and on qualities or attributes; to use prototypes to span the various levels of the aim or attribute (low, medium, high); and critical or factual incidents to explore differences or turning points."

Gremler (2004, pp. 66–68), while considering applications of the critical incident technique in the service domain, discusses both advantages and disadvantages concerning the use of the critical incident technology.

Advantages are as follows:

- The data are collected from the respondent's perspective and in his or her words. Therefore, the respondents determine which incidents are the most relevant to them for the phenomenon being investigated.

- It is an inductive method that needs no hypotheses and where patterns are formed as they emerge from the responses, allowing the researcher to generate concepts and theories.
- The method can be used to generate an accurate and in-depth record of events.
- The respondent accounts gathered provide rich details of first-hand experiences. The method also provides relevant, unequivocal, and very concrete information for managers and can suggest practical areas for improvement.
- The method is well suited for use in assessing perceptions of customers from different cultures. Obviously, this is a consequence of the first advantage as mentioned in this list of advantages.

Disadvantages include the following:

- Respondent stories reported in incidents can be misinterpreted or misunderstood.
- Category labels and coding rules may present issues of ambiguity.
- The retrospective process of respondents attempting to remember details of incidents that happened in the past may induce biases because of being unable or being unwilling to produce them.

Snodgrass *et al.* (2009, p. 20) add the following elaborations to this phenomenon of biased memory workings: "The critical incident technique relies on events being remembered by users and also requires the accurate and truthful reporting of them. As critical incidents rely on memory, incidents may be imprecise or may even go unreported. The method has a built-in bias towards incidents that happened recently, since these are easier to recall. It will emphasise only rare events; more common events may be missed. Respondents may not be accustomed to or willing to take the time to tell (or write) a complete story when describing a critical incident". Obviously, the researcher will have to deal with this measurement issue. Also, the recall of incidents may be problematic as memory and recall biases may lead to a reinterpretation of the incident (Baker *et al.*, 2007). This is an issue that has to be checked thoroughly for every critical incident study.

Finally, common problems that have been identified (Usability Body of Knowledge, 2016, (http://usabilitybok.org) are as follows:

1. Respondents may be reluctant to reveal incidents that reflect badly on themselves.
2. Respondents may reply with stereotypes, not actual events (using more structure improves this).
3. A common question is "How many incidents do you need to collect?" The number will vary depending on the complexity of the system.
4. The wording of critical incident questions could influence the type of incidents reported (Flanagan, 1954).
5. The meaning of "critical incident" must be clear to participants.

3.4 Best Practices

Here, we will present the basic steps of the research process in order to elucidate the logic and workings of the critical incident technique.

Flanagan (1954) specifies five steps to be carried out in order to realise a full-scale critical incident technique study. We will present and discuss these steps as described by FitzGerald *et al.* (2008), while adding some own thoughts to these steps.

3.4.1 *Identifying general aims*

Although Flanagan uses the general label of research questions to be formulated this step is easily expanded towards carrying out a full-blown problem analysis, specifying both research aims and research questions at this point. The topic to be studied may be anything that extends to the acts of human beings as characterised by both having purpose and consequences, while the research aim is to gain deep insights into the workings and the meaning of these acts, or critical incidents. Thus, a thorough understanding of the purpose of certain behaviour, and the consequences of this behaviour, allows the researcher to answer his research questions and attain his research aim.

3.4.2 *Planning*

At this point in the preparation process the researcher needs to make two decisions. First, the "situations", or critical incidents to be studied have to be selected as they pertain to answering the research questions. These critical incidents may have both positive and negative consequences. In this way the full range of effects may be eligible to be studied.

The second decision relates to the choice of "observers". An observer generally is the researcher who already has some familiarity with the context within which the acts to be studied occur and who will collect the data by communicating with the respondents of the study.

3.4.3 *Collecting the data*

Data collection methods used in critical incident research may vary. Sharkin and Birkey (1992) used a postal questionnaire to further the understanding about incidental encounters and to explore perceptions and reactions during public contact between therapists and clients; they used two open ended questions and 28 forced choice questions with a sample of directors of 350 university counselling/psychological services and received 547 complete responses. For another example of a quantitative approach see Löffler and Baier (2013).

Data often have the characteristics of storytelling. A principal approach to data collection could therefore be carrying out semi-structured in-depth interviews with those involved in critical incidents. Edvardsson (1992, p. 19) suggests including the entries "cause", "course", and "result" in the checklist, to that end. An alternative would be presenting open-ended questions in a questionnaire, as illustrated above.

The sample design takes the critical incident as the unit of analysis. Thus, the sample design specifies which critical incidents are to be sampled in order to ultimately answer the research questions. Generally speaking, it is preferable to continue sampling critical incidents until saturation occurs. Also, a rule of thumb (Twelker, 2007) suggests 100 critical incidents to be included in the sample of critical incidents. However, one could argue that this number must be chosen in such a way that arbitrarily adding or removing a, or a few, critical incidents from the data set will not have a pertinent effect on the patterns or the structure of the outcomes as based on the analysis of the data.

As said before, individuals involved in these critical incidents must be selected in a next step. It is desirable that the incidents to be discussed have occurred recently because this will minimise memory faults, biased memory effects, or even partial memory failure on the part of the individual to be interviewed.

As regards the checklist to be used, the following generic types of questions may be asked during an interview (Hughes, 2007):

- Think of a time that (indication of the incident).
- Describe the circumstances and nature of this incident.
- Explain why you consider this incident to be significant.
- What did this person do that was effective/ineffective?
- Why was it effective/ineffective?
- Describe the outcome(s) or result of the incident.

An example of a procedure that may be followed in a critical incident study is reported in Deakins and Freel (1998, p. 149). The researchers chose to carry out the following steps in an interview process in order to collect their data:

- A semi-structured interview designed to elicit general development issues around motivation, formation, and later development.

- This initial interview served to highlight potential critical incidents and issues to be taken up with subsequent open-ended interviews.
- These critical incidents were then used to encourage the respondent (in this study: an entrepreneur) to expand on the process that led to the incident, how it was resolved, and, more important, what was learned from the incident.
- The cases built in this way involved considerable time spent alongside the entrepreneur understanding the nature of the firm, the innovation or technology process and discussion in addition to the formal and informal interviews.
- Using observation techniques, the researchers were able to identify critical factors in the entrepreneurial learning process.

3.4.4 *Analysing the data*

The analysis comprises of three steps:

1. Selecting a frame of reference that will be related to how the data will be used. As the analysis approach is inductive no pre-conceived conceptual model will be tested. Instead, a frame of reference is sketched which may be modified along the analysis process. This structure should add to finding answers to the research questions.
2. Developing a set of major area and subarea categories. Categories should evolve from the data and its structures and patterns. To that end, Grounded Theory approaches such as described elsewhere in this book could be employed. Again, systems of categories could be elaborated, expanded or dismissed in an iterative analysis process. In addition, a so-called "Inter-Judge Reliability Analysis" may be carried out (Zainol and Lockwood, 2014), which provides an "inter-judge reliability check agreement" of a certain percentage on the classification system.
3. Placing the critical incidents as discussed with the respondents into these categories and carrying out simple counts. It stands to reason to expect that the outcome analysis now shows or suggests

two types of patterns. On the one hand, the final category system suggests a pattern as to the contents of each of the categories as such, and in their connection. On the other hand, comparing the simple counts of the categories may suggest dominant versus feeble force elements in the fabric of the structure found. Kai-Chieh *et al.* (2013), while following this latter approach, use cross-tabulation comparisons in order to disclose the patterns in their study on service failure and service recovery in the context of airlines.

Alternatively, data from Critical Incident studies may be analysed by a procedure called Content Analysis. An example may be found in Bitner *et al.* (1990).

3.4.5 *Interpreting and reporting the results*

Woolsey (1986) states, "the objective of data analysis is to provide a detailed, comprehensive and valid description of the activity studied". To this end, the researcher may now consider and reconsider various different category systems, as fitting in the chosen frame of reference. The ultimate criterion would be the variation, which enables best to answer the research questions in such a way that the research aim (acquiring deep insights into the phenomenon under study) is realised. A second criterion would be to choose an interpretation, which allows for clear, effective, and executable recommendations for the commissioning client, or for the benefit of science and the scientific community.

Chapter 4

Ethnographic Methodology

4.1 Introduction

Ethnography is a research methodology that aims to describe and understand social groups and their culture. During the process of describing such a group, insights and explanations regarding the perceptions of the members of the group of themselves, their comembers, their social views, their group and individual values, and their behaviours may, or even should, occur. Ethnography is a systematic study about people and their culture from an insight perspective (as evolved primarily in the twentieth century). Ethnography is study by prolonged field experience, with the researcher immersed in the daily life of the observed.

In order to *collect the data*, the researcher acts as a participant observer, making observations, talking to members of the group, collecting documents, and collecting group artefacts which may shed light on the processes to be studied and to be understood. For an example of the methodology involved, see Dana (1995, p. 58), who describes, in a study about entrepreneurship in a remote sub-arctic community, his method of working: "Methodology involved the researcher taking temporary residence in the community under study, in order to observe and record interactions and to conduct extensive open-ended interviews with business owners, employees, and key informants. Substantial information was obtained only after a personal, trusting relationship was established. The interview guide consisted of open-ended questions to capture what people had to say in their own words, about how and why they got involved in their own business and what their entrepreneurship or small business experiences meant to them. Interviews lasted between two and five hours". As another example, Wagstaff *et al.* (2012) employed ethnographic techniques such as observation, field notes and reflexive diary, and interviews and informal communication.

The *analysis* constitutes of a largely unstructured process of trying to think of and reflect on possible reasons why the group under study, and its members, hold the specific views, beliefs, perceptions, and understandings, and exhibit certain behaviours that were observed. In this way explanations, which may be of a cultural nature, are probed, reformulated and refined in order to derive meaning from the data. Where explanatory patterns occur, these patterns may be formulated as theoretical notions, and presented ultimately as formal theories. An example of an ethnographic study may be found in Dana and Anderson (2007), who studied an indigenous community holding on to Promethean values.

4.2 Definition and Use

Hammersley and Atkinson (2007, p. 1) indicate that the roots of ethnography may be found in nineteenth century Anthropology; research was based on the accounts of travellers and missionaries visiting non-Western societies and cultures. Later on, "tribes" and communities, such as villages and towns, were studied in an effort to "document and interpret their distinct way of life, and the beliefs and values integral to it". Thus, human social life and culture were studied in various different ways. A core definition of ethnography, according to the authors (p. 3), includes the following features: people are studied in everyday contexts, data may be primarily collected by participant observation (taking field notes) and talks with the group members (without a pre-defined structure), only a few cases may be studied, and the analysis of the data is carried out through interpretations of meanings and consequences of human behaviour on the (local) living context. As a result, descriptions, explanations, and theories are produced.

Cresswell (2014, p. 496) lists the main characteristics of an ethnographic study as studying cultural themes on a culture-sharing group. This group shows shared patterns of behaviour, belief, and language. In order to acquire the data, the researcher engages in fieldwork. The analysis involves descriptions, themes, and interpretation. During the process of analysis, the researcher considers context or setting while carrying out reflective processes.

A range of paradigms of ethnography exists nowadays. Sanday (1979, p. 537) presents a typology of paradigms when he says: "Obviously, the *ethnographic paradigm* in anthropology is internally differentiated. The main differences are whether the primary focus is on the whole, the meaning, or the behaviour and the degree to which the analytic goal is diagnosis or explanation. Which mode one adopts in one's own work is a matter of taste and not of dogma". He then goes on to explain each of these three foci:

- A focus on the *whole* implies that (Sanday, 1979, p. 532) the key concepts here are process, maintenance, survival, adaptation, change, imbedded in, and integral part of. Such concepts convey the image of a dynamic system straining towards maintenance and equilibrium. Each part of the system has its function, no part can be studied without considering its relation to other parts, and each new part that is added to the system must find its accepted fit. This image of social behaviour as a dynamic system is one which most social scientists share.
- A focus on the *meaning* is explained by Sanday (1979, p. 533) by referring to a quote from Mead (1959, p. 38), "The basis for the semiotic approach can be traced to Boas' notion that the main task of the anthropologist was 'the adoption of an informant's mode of thought while retaining full use of his own critical faculties'."
- A focus on the *behaviour* means (according to Sanday, 1979, p. 536) entering the domain of behaviourism. Behaviourism in anthropological ethnography involves the formulation of deductive propositions. The ethnographic portion of such studies is not meant to uncover meaning or to diagnose the whole. Rather,

its purpose is to provide observational data on pre-selected functionally relevant categories.

Furthermore, the author notices that 'ethnoscience' as a related research approach, has developed over time, as compared to 'thick description'. In his words: "In recent years the semiotic approach has produced the highly specialised field of 'ethnoscience' on the one hand and 'thick description' on the other. These two prongs of the semiotic approach, guided by different epistemologies, have produced the usual exchange of prickly remarks".

Geertz (1973, pp. 5–6), in this context, believes that "man is an animal suspended in webs of significance he himself has spun". He continues (pp. 5–6) to state that culture is to be viewed as one of those webs and the analysis of culture to be "not an experimental science in search of law but an interpretive one in search of meaning". For Geertz, anthropological analysis requires thick description, that is, wading through the clusters upon clusters of symbols by which man confers significance upon his own experience.

By contrast, Creswell (2014, p. 492) presents 10 types of ethnographies:

- **Realist ethnography:** An objective, scientifically written ethnography.
- **Confessional ethnography:** A report of the ethnographer's fieldwork experience.
- **Life history:** A study of one individual situated within the cultural context of his or her life.
- **Auto ethnography:** A reflective self-examination by an individual set within his or her cultural context.
- **Micro ethnography:** A study focused on a specific aspect of a cultural group and setting.
- **Ethnographic case study:** A case analysis of a person, event, activity, or process set within a cultural perspective.
- **Critical ethnography:** A study of the shared patterns of a marginalised group with the aim of advocacy about issues of power and authority.

- **Feminist ethnography:** A study of women and the cultural practices that serve to disempower and oppress them.
- **Postmodern ethnography:** An ethnography written to challenge the problems in our society that have emerged from a modern emphasis on progress and marginalising individuals.
- **Ethnographic novels:** A fictional work focused on cultural aspects of a group.

In spite of this diversity, it is still possible to denote the common elements of ethnography. Originating in anthropology, the purpose of ethnography is to describe the cultural characteristics of a group and to describe cultural scenes. The researcher is the research instrument, not limited to survey or interview. The key of ethnography is for the researcher to become immersed in the everyday life of the observed. Glaser and Strauss (1967) and Denzin (1978) emphasised the role of ethnography in developing and testing theory. An appropriate data collection method in ethnographic studies is (participant) observation.

Describing the cultural characteristics of a group, and its (sub) culture, extends to the business domain as well. A specific example within this domain is the study of informal ethnic and ethnographic entrepreneurship. Ramadani *et al.* (2019, p. 2) define ethnic entrepreneurship as "a process of identifying opportunities in the market, undertaking innovative, unsafe, and dangerous activities by individuals who are not members of the majority population in a given country, to ensure prosperity for themselves, family and whole society". And, "The informal economy provides individuals with business opportunities regardless of immigration status or educational qualifications and this is especially important to entrepreneurs". The book focuses on issues such as the evolution and activities of ethnic entrepreneurship and informal business activity, and innovation and creativity as processes that occur in this domain. A content analysis of the methodologies, sampling techniques, data collection approaches, and analysis approaches, as used in this book, demonstrates that the ethnographic approach, next to other qualitative approaches, may be utilised fruitfully in this type of research.

We will conclude this review of ethnographic varieties with a comparatively new member of the ethnographic approach family. It is called *Netnography*. Here, empathic, non-obtrusive observations in existing online communities (forums and social media) are carried out. Specifically, in the areas of marketing and customer research there is a focus on listening to the "voice of customer", spotting new trends and opportunities, building emotional bonds with customers, gaining unbiased consumer insights, and creating user groups' typologies. While this approach is less obtrusive, studies adopting this approach may be costly and time consuming when compared to, e.g., interviews. Issues to be addressed here are: who is engaged on such forums? Bots? Super fans? In sum, sample issues are to be solved. And, as always, the researcher's interpretive skills need to be available to be used for the analysis.

4.3 Advantages and Disadvantages

According to Hammersley and Atkinson (2007, p. 9), a major advantage of the ethnographic research approach is that of being part of the "natural setting". External validity may be high because of this method of working. Also, learning and appreciating the culture of the group, both from within and at an external angle, produces both inside and external knowledge.

The authors (p. 7) continue by saying: In contrast, criticisms from Positivism have been voiced. That is, data, interpretation and findings are subjective, they are mere "idiosyncratic impressions of one or two cases"; the qualitative approach — called Naturalism by Hammersley and Atkinson (2007) — emphasises that specific behaviours of an individual cannot be caught in general or universal laws, and therefore questions positivist approaches to unravel general and universal laws of causality, and its determinants. Instead (p. 7), "human actions are based upon, or infused by, social or cultural meanings". However (p. 9), some form of theories may have the structure and contents that allow for explanatory power of "capturing social complexity". In this context, Tavory and Timmermans (2013) state that causality in ethnography may be based on multiple "activities", that is, embracing a mechanism-based approach to causality by tracing iterations of meaning-making-in-action, while examining forms of observed variation to distinguish regularly occurring causal sequences and temporally and spatially remote causal processes. Finally, they suggest that the plausibility of claimed causality, including assessments of explanatory fit, must be presented to a disciplinary community of inquiry. Thus, causality can never be claimed in absolute, universal, and timeless dimensions.

Summarising, *advantages* include getting in-depth insights you wouldn't be able to gather otherwise, the researcher himself functions as research instrument, data collection occurs in a natural setting, and the ability exists to verify what people say. *Disadvantages* include the notion that you might need to "get your hands dirty", the data collection is often unstructured, and these types of studies are often time consuming and expensive. Commitment and social skills are needed by the researcher, only limited generalisation is possible, and past papers can be considered racists in the present because of changed social views and values.

A final word about the noble art of interpretation, as creating adequate, rich, and insightful interpretations is a major prerequisite for a successful study in terms of academic adequacy and societal impact. Van Maanen (1979, p. 549) sketches the interpretation problem when stating: This normative discussion raises a final concern because it suggests that the expressed aim of ethnography, "to depict", in Goodenough's (1964, p. 14) terms, "the system for perceiving, believing, evaluating and acting" is a shockingly broad and preposterous one. Culture is itself an interpretation and therefore most of the facts one goes into the field to discover are themselves already known and interpreted in a particular light by the people one talks to in the setting. The results of ethnographic study are thus mediated several times over — first, by the fieldworker's own standards of relevance as to what is and what is not worthy of observation; second, by the historically situated questions that are put to the people in the setting; third, by the self-reflection demanded of an informant; and fourth, by the intentional and unintentional ways the produced data are misleading. Though most ethnographers are well aware of this irreducible dilemma, they still maintain the stance that if they spend some more time in the field to dig a little deeper and probe a little further, certain crucial facts will be revealed which will tie up loose ends and provide closure to a study in danger of infinite expansion. Ultimately, this is an illusion although, I hasten to add, it is an altogether necessary one. The world, according again to Sherlock Holmes, is full of obvious things which nobody by any chance will ever see.

4.4 Best Practices

For an overview of the steps to take in carrying out an ethnographic study we will present the suggestions given by Hammersley and Atkinson (2007), occasionally interspersed by other sources of relevance. The following steps will be presented and clarified: formulating research questions, creating the sample design, providing access to the data, collecting the data, and analysis of the data, in that order. Finally, we will present some general criteria for judging the quality of an ethnographic study.

Formulating research questions: This may imply (p. 24) a narrative description of a sequence of events, a generalised account of the perspectives and practices of a particular group of people, or a more abstract theoretical formulation. A researcher may choose between a topical and a generic research problem. During the research process the research questions may be adapted in either direction.

Creating the sample design: Generally speaking, sampling strategies have to be developed and may have to be updated several times during the research process.

Furthermore, and in particular, both settings and cases have to be chosen. A setting is a named context in which phenomena occur to be studied. Settings have to be both suitable and feasible for carrying the study. This choice may have an influence on the formulation of the research questions. Cases may be available both inside and outside the chosen setting. The selection of "typical" cases for the context of the study may enhance its generalisability. Also, the principle of "snowballing" may be applied, where a current subject suggests the next subject. Typically, a sample consists of one to a few subjects.

Sampling *within* cases is carried out along three dimensions (p. 35): time, people, and context.

- *Time* refers to the choice of which episodes of the process to study are to be selected.
- *People* refers to choosing subjects based on specific combinations of characteristics and features as decided by the researcher (observer-identified categories), or on labels used by the population under study in their natural habitat (member-identified categories).
- *Context* refers to the various settings in which the process under study occurs. Obviously, a choice must be made here that ultimately allows collecting the most relevant data for the study, and as a consequence finding the most adequate and rich answers to the research questions.

Providing access to the data: It is important to take in advance all of the steps to be allowed to enter the settings where the process to be studied is taking place. Permission may be both a formal and an informal matter. In both cases, the parties in command and with the necessary power have to be addressed. Both sacred and taboo settings may be present. Obviously, this is true for the overt participant observer; but even covert participant observers have to take care that their covert observations are not problematic, overt behaviour. Finally, the overt participant observer has to define and negotiate his role in such a way that the other parties involved in the setting agree on this role. Personal characteristics of the researcher, including the gender characteristic, may either open up the research settings, or may create problems with those who are part of the setting.

Collecting the data: *Dynamic data* may vary from (solicited or unsolicited) tales the subjects tell, to observations made by the researcher, and to informal and planned interviews. The researcher is to determine where and when to interview. It is up to the researcher to determine the value and use of each of these types of information. The researcher engages in reflexive interviewing, that is, on the one hand the phrasing and order of the questions may vary, and on the other hand, often a list of issues to be covered is present. The interview process usually takes the form of a conversation, allowing for non-directive questions.

Morgan (1997) suggests that, as part of the ethnographic research process it may be desirable to carry out focus groups. Focus groups may be employed in order to acquire an initial understanding of topics and interactions of the population to study. These insights may subsequently suggest avenues to design the ethnographic research design. Also, Kuhn and Koschel (2018) indicate that focus groups may be fruitfully combined with ethnographic research as the former may yield specific additional information about the subjects which may be utilised to improve the observation process as carried out in a next step of the research process.

Furthermore, when multiple sites are available for the ethnographic study focus groups may aid as to make an informed choice of the sites for the main ethnographic study. In the same vein, the researcher may use focus groups in order to decide on a subsequent, theoretical sample to study ethnographically.

Data may be of various sorts, as follows:

- *Static data* refer to documents and material artefacts.
- *Documents* of three kinds may be available: informal, formal, official. Informal documents may include diaries and letters, formal documents may include published biographical and autobiographical sources. Finally, official documents are publicly available documents such as rule books, and instructional and regulating publications.
- *Material artefacts* may cover material goods such as products used or manufactured at the setting, and objects such as technical equipment.

The *data* for this type of research may also include audio and video recordings, and data retracted from the Internet. Dana and Dana (2008) provide insight into the use of pictures in an ethnographic study on entrepreneurship in Morocco. Another example: Dana (2011) carried out a study about entrepreneurship in Bolivia. To that end, he studied ethnographic literature, carried out field interviews, and also presented photography of the Pueblo Indians and their culture. Finally, data may be collected from "digital spaces" (p. 137) such as virtual communities.

Analysis of the data: The analysis of the — unstructured — data of a study is of a process-like nature. This process is initiated at the start of the study and continues until the phase of report-writing. In the early phases of a study, the elaboration of the research problem already may influence data analysis and the approach to be taken. In that sense, the procedure resembles the workings of grounded theorising as carried out in the Grounded Theory approach. Furthermore, there is no general recipe, there are only guiding principles. In what follows, we will discuss each of these guiding principles:

- Ideas and data are considered in an iterative process, that is: there is (p. 157) "a constant interplay between data and ideas, throughout the research process". For that reason, moments of reflection on the process of collecting data and the way they are analysed should be made available by the researcher.
- A funnel structure is developed where over time research questions may be amended or transformed, and scope and structure of the study may be further specified or even changed.
- Starting with the description of events and processes, next steps may involve clarification and hypothesis testing. Also, typologies may be developed, and analytic categories created.
- Initial (analytical) concepts have to be looked for in the data or are constructed by the researcher. Next, relationships have to be defined between concepts. Following, and at a more general level, patterns are to be found which make sense with regard to the research questions and the broad issue to be studied. Ultimately, by developing a fabric of these patterns, an understanding of the processes under study may be unclosed that shares the characteristics of a theory.

- The analysis may follow the actions, and social actions, of those observed while attempting to analyse the reasons for these actions. The reasons take the form of (situated) "meanings" involved. The basic premise is that (p. 168), "people construct their social worlds through engagement in concerted social activities". In this way, also cultures and subcultures may come into being.

- Actions may take the form of routine behaviour. In addition, rituals and ritual behaviour may be studied as specific forms of behaviour, and their antecedents. Finally, deviant behaviour and unexpected behaviour are of importance here, as they may give rise to crises.

- Acts may also be studied in conjunction with informal rules or norms that guide these acts. In this sense, decisions that guide these acts may be studied. Finally, "spoken actions" may be analysed. That is, the analysis of talk implies that (p. 170) "social actors do things with words".

- Typologies may be developed from the data, for instance the various different ways a member of a community under study may respond to a crisis that presents itself to this community member. It is important to define the underlying dimensions of such a typology, and its subcategories, as the availability of these dimensions makes it possible to evaluate or criticise the validity of the proposed typology structure.

- During the analysis, the researcher has to be aware of the fact that receiving information from those observed always occurs within a social context. It matters what authority the observant is imputed by the subject. Moreover, this subject may decide to be honest or not. When recognising the social context, however, this information may still be valuable.

- Also, the temporal elements of the data are relevant for the analysis. On the one hand, this involves temporal processes, that is, things that happen as time goes by. On the other hand, the phase a subject is in with respect to a maturity process may be of importance. For instance, a group member may start as a novice in his eyes, or the eyes of the comembers of a tribe, or a company, while trying to reach maturity. His current position in this temporal framework, and his idiosyncratically constructed memories about the past may have explanatory power as such.

• Subjects, as information carriers, occupy a certain place in the social order of the group. As a consequence, they have certain knowledge that is based on this position. Furthermore, they have a reference framework, or perspective, that is also connected to their place in the social order of the group. While carrying out analyses the researcher has to take this into account.

The analyst may or may not decide to present draft outcomes of his analysis to the subjects involved in the study. On the one hand, this may create additional insights as they may provide new information through their feedback. On the other hand, the feedback may be biased. A researcher deciding to ask feedback should be aware of this.

The design of the study may include various forms of triangulation. In effect, this means that data from different sources are collected and compared in the analysis. In this context, we may distinguish between data source triangulation, observer triangulation, theoretical triangulation, and method triangulation. Most commonly, data source triangulation is available as the researcher routinely collects data from various sources such observation, documents, narratives, interviews, etc. The challenge here is to meaningfully relate research outcomes from these diverse sources while realising that parts of the differences of the outcomes must be attributed to the inherently differential characteristics of these sources. If successful, the study may benefit from elevated levels of validity.

The research report is a textual report. Obviously, the report presents the research outcomes and their interpretations, while moving from descriptive outcomes to outcomes and their meanings at the explanatory levels. Also, the researcher presents his reflexions on these outcomes and their meanings. At the onset of the writing process, the researcher chooses (p. 193) a "style of ethnographic writing" that both fits the type of outcomes to report and the academic audience to which the study is addressed.

At the end of this expose, the question may be raised as to how the "quality" of the reported study may be determined. While no clear-cut criteria are available that are supported by all of the members of the academic community of ethnographic researchers a number of criteria merits attention and consideration. Patton (2002, p. 544) presents general criteria "for judging the quality and credibility" of ethnographic studies and they include both *traditional scientific research criteria* and *social construction and constructivist criteria*, among others.

Traditional scientific criteria refer to the following:

- Objectivity of the inquirer (attempts to minimise bias);
- Validity of the data;
- Systematic rigor of fieldwork procedures;
- Triangulation (consistency of findings across methods and data sources);
- Reliability of codings and pattern analyses;
- Correspondence of findings to reality;
- Generalisability (external validity);
- Strength of evidence supporting causal hypotheses; and
- Contributions to theory.

Social construction and constructivist criteria refer to the following:

- Subjectivity acknowledged (discusses and takes into account biases);
- Trustworthiness;
- Authenticity;
- Triangulation (capturing and respecting multiple perspectives);
- Reflexivity;
- Praxis;
- Particularity (doing justice to the integrity of unique cases);
- Enhanced and deepened understanding, i.e., *Verstehen*; and
- Contributions to dialogue.

Obviously, the overview as presented above holds the characteristics and has the status of an objectified consideration set; it is not a formalized, logical, comprehensive, and exhaustive list of rules and criteria. Specifically, the rules and praxes are not objective, in the sense that every researcher would interpret these criteria exactly in the same way. Nonetheless, this broad set of criteria may be quite useful as such when carrying out an ethnographic study aimed at high levels of academic "quality".

4.5 Sample Study

In order to demonstrate how an ethnographic study may be carried out an overview of Dana's (2007) study is provided, and the excellent ethnographic characteristics of this study are highlighted.

Issue and relevance
The Amish form an enterprising community with their own way of living, educational process, and commercial activities, while refraining from assistance from the outside world and refraining from government help. It is of social and academic importance to acquire both knowledge and insights regarding the origin, and current existence and activities of this subculture.

Research goal
The purpose of this study is to add to the understanding of humility-based economic development and entrepreneurship among the Amish — a religious group — in the USA, whose culture values asceticism, frugality, thrift and work, as well as humility.

Research design
A classical ethnographic study based on the immersion of the researcher in the community under study in order to develop "inside" knowledge and understanding.

Sample design
The population to study was the Amish community; the sample consisted of a few Amish families and individuals.

Data collection
Data were collected using participant observation and interviews as the primary tools.

Data analysis
Data were analysed through a process of meaning-making as based on the stenographic notes of the interviews and the field notes made both by the researcher and an assistant. Thus, triangulation was carried out.

Report
A text report describing and explaining the observations and interview outcomes, thus offering meaning as to the experience world of the subjects and their behaviour. Citations were included to offer more insights to the reader.

Excellent ethnographic characteristics of the study
For an ethnographic study to be excellent a number of conditions have to be met. These include the following: the research problem has to be clear and relevant; the research design must be functional for the research purpose; data collection must be to the point and exhaustive; data analysis must involve the culture of the members of the community while providing novel and deep insights into the social world of the community. That is, above all, interpreting meaning processes as these provide an explanation of the mental processes and the behaviours of community members. All of this is the case in this study.

This is a classical ethnographic study. The research objective was clearly formulated, as based on the extensive literature.

The researcher was able to live with an Amish family for a prolonged time in order to make observations and do the chores at the farm as a truly participant observer. He devised a strategy to get acquainted with Mennonite individuals who were befriended with Amish individuals and requested the former to introduce him to the latter individuals — his target group. The Amish speak a specific form of German; however, the researcher spoke the language fluently.

Difficulties such as not being allowed to take pictures or make sound recordings were overcome by using stenography during the interviews. An assistant took field notes and assisted in checking the accuracy of the data collected. Triangulation was used for verification. The researcher focused on belief and symbolism, which are part of the subculture of the Amish, their humility expressed as simplicity, while maintaining their social fabric of brotherhood.

The analysis is a mix of description and meaning-making. Systematically, all aspects of Amish life are presented and explained in terms of the beliefs and values of their religiously inspired subculture. In that way, the reader is presented with the ways the Amish define and live in ways that are meaningful for them. Both views on life and consecutive behaviours are treated this way. Furthermore, an effort is made to tie causal factors to the empirical phenomenon where the Amish continue to exhibit a propensity for entrepreneurial behaviour within their community and in the form of self-employment or to work amongst themselves.

The report is written in such a way that the reader easily picks up life, life conditions, and entrepreneurial behaviour of the Amish. Thus, clear insights are offered into the fascinating world of this community.

Chapter 5

Field Stimulation

5.1 Introduction

Field Stimulation is also known as *contrived observation* (Webb *et al.*, 1966), "to distinguish it from observational studies in which the investigator acts as a passive recorder who avoids provoking or interrupting responses" (Webb and Salancik, 1970). For instance, Goodsell's (1976, p. 142) study used the method of *unobtrusive observation* in order to study cultural roles, but similar methods can be used to study organisational roles.

5.2 Definition and Use

Salancik (1979, pp. 638–639) defines *field stimulation* as a qualitative research methodology that "encompasses a set of research methods rather than any single instrument or form. It is an approach for researching organizations, although it has been used mainly to study individual social behavior in public places. The researcher may play himself or pose in another role. Interventions might vary from the most natural to the most contrived depending upon theoretical needs, the bounds of decency, and the limits of imagination".

An example clarifying the field stimulation approach may be found in Curry and Copeman (2005), who studied reference service to international students as delivered by librarians. They presented 20 librarians with a "proxy", that is, a (p. 409) foreign student with heavily accented English who was asking help in order to write a paper on "immigration". The librarians were unaware of the fact that they were part of a field stimulation study. The actual pattern of interactions was studied, using both a checklist and narrative reports as made up immediately after the visit to the librarian. A number of pre-conceived questions were asked, and the responses noted. In addition, observations were made regarding approachability, whether questions for clarification were asked, and whether the librarians showed awareness of language barriers, among other things. In the analysis, answering patterns and interactions were related to ratings of the proxy with respect to satisfaction and a possible return to the same librarian for extended help. Thus, a systematic research design was carried out in a real-world environment on an unknown target group, studying an interaction process between an expert and a person in need of assistance.

As can be seen from the example above, field stimulation is a type of qualitative research methodology that aims to induce a specific situation, in order to get reactions that could otherwise be hidden in a normal survey scenario. For example, Bryan and Test (1966) studied under which circumstances people stop when travelling on the road to help others with a flat tyre. Another example is a study aimed at finding out under which circumstances people may call for a repair service for a distressed motorist (Romer *et al.*, 1977).

Salancik (1979, p. 638) explains this methodology in depth, stating that field stimulation "belongs to a class of qualitative methodologies in which the respondent determines the character of the response. It differs from some qualitative methodologies by encouraging the investigator to determine the occasion for a response which is, in turn, a measure of the organization's nature and capacity". That is, this methodology is designed to discover an organization's nature without having to directly ask for the information. Another use of the field stimulation method is to select different types of organisations to stimulate. However, as said before, field stimulation may also focus on "individual social behaviour in public places". The author (p. 638), provides a broad definition of field stimulation: it is a general methodology for the study of organisational and human behaviour.

And he adds to this: the major value of field stimulation as a strategy for research is not merely in analysing the basis for responses, but in the freedom which the method allows in manipulating the conditions of a response, and hence the conditions for organisational behaviour. Furthermore (p. 645), he feels that "fewer field stimulation studies have dealt with organizational behaviour. But such methods can reveal something about an organization, its structures, its routines, what it attends to and what it ignores, and about its relations with other organizations."

He further (p. 638) recommends that field stimulation is used to study organisations by "tickling them, tempting them, and perturbing them". In his view (p. 644), "the major value of field stimulation as a strategy for research lies not merely in analyzing the basis for responses but in the freedom which the method allows in manipulating the conditions of a response, and hence the conditions for organizational behavior". And finally, as a matter of fact (p. 639): "The data we collect are assumed to be outcroppings of some underlying process and are the stuff from which the structures and processes which generated them are inferred. This naive realism notion of data assumes that data have no meaning outside of the theories which link to them."

Finally, he believes that, although fewer studies use it, the methodology of field stimulation can be also fruitful when studying organisations' internal structures, routines, focus and relations with other organisations. Understanding how firms respond to external stimuli with their actions can answer many questions about their inner behaviour and processes.

Jones (1996), as quoted in Curry and Copeman (2005), adds to the definition and use of the field stimulation approach when he indicates the conditions for a field study to be conducted:

- The research occurs in a public place.
- No possibility of identifying information is recorded.
- The interactions take little time or effort by the subject.
- Tasks required of the subject are within the range of the subject's normal experience.

Kerlinger (1986) states that, under the generic heading of "field stimulation", two types of research design may be placed: the *field experiment* and the *field study*. While discussing these research designs, he takes a predominantly quantitative approach. It is, however, entirely possible to study his descriptions from a qualitative viewpoint. When carrying out qualitative research based on the research methodologies of the field experiment or the field study as presented by this author, while analysing the data in a qualitative manner, fruitful results may be anticipated. For this reason, these research approaches are presented in this chapter.

The field experiment, as presented by Kerlinger (1986, p. 369), "is a research study in a realistic situation in which one or more independent variables are manipulated by the experimenter under as carefully controlled conditions as the situation will permit". An example would be to introduce two or more teaching methods in a school environment in order to find out which method comparatively yields the best results as defined in terms of a set of specific criteria. A typical feature of this kind of study is that the independent variables, which are supposed to exert influence on the dependent variable, can be manipulated only to a certain extent, because the process under study takes place in a real-life setting. Also, randomisation (assigning subjects to experimental conditions in a random way) may not be possible. Obviously, in a real experiment, the independent variables can be fully manipulated, as this type of research is carried out in a laboratory-like setting. A prominent, present-day application is in commercial companies, studying the effects of methods and procedures on the motivation and productive output of employees. Also, the effects of leadership styles on motivation and output of employees may be studied in this vein.

The field study (Kerlinger, 1986, pp. 372–373) is a non-experimental type of research. Its aim may be to discover "the relations and interactions among sociological, psychological, and educational variables in real social structures". No independent variables are manipulated.

A field study may either be involved with an exploration of relevant variables and relations between them or it is aimed at hypothesis testing (Kerlinger, 1986, p. 373–374). Therefore, exploratory research has three purposes here: "to discover significant variables in the field situation, to discover relations among variables, and to lay the groundwork for later, more systematic and rigorous testing of hypothesis". Thus, the *meaning* of significant variables, or concepts, may be studied by examining their dimensional structure while the *relations* among these concepts may be studied in order to find the correlates of a concept under study and thereby being able to trace back its meanings. The structure of concepts and relations that comes into existence this way may take the shape of a conceptual model from which hypotheses may be formulated and tested. Research of this type may take place in (Kerlinger, 1986, p. 372) "life situations like communities, schools, factories, organizations, and institutions".

Field stimulation is related to, but not the same as a research approach called *mystery shopping*. Mystery shopping is primarily used to uncover specific elements of the performance of companies and organizations. The researcher poses as a customer or a visitor while carrying out specific tasks (buying a product or a service, filing a complaint, or asking for information). These tasks are specified beforehand, and the same is true regarding the aspects to measure or to evaluate. Based on these data a detailed and concrete report is generated. The report is either presented to an external research agency or to the organization under study, depending on the client who ordered the research. An introduction to this research approach may be found in Suneetha and Vidhyadhara (2016).

5.2.1 *A plea for a qualitative approach to field stimulation*

As said earlier, fruitful research results may be expected when field stimulation is carried out in a qualitative way. This would preclude the use of questionnaires. Salancik (1979, p. 638) says: "this method of investigation is designed to encourage researchers to uncover the nature of organization without asking for an accounting on a questionnaire". The author claims that "a major value of field stimulation is the freedom with which the method allows to manipulate the [qualitative] *conditions* of a response, not merely analysing [quantitatively] the *basis* for responses."

He goes on to criticise (p. 641) the use of questionnaire in this context by stating the following:

- Responses obtained from a questionnaire question depend not only on the contents of the question but also on the very nature of the question asked.
- When formulating a questionnaire question, only words that can be understood by both the researcher and the respondent can be used. As a consequence, only existing knowledge may be produced.
- More generally, here only the type of knowledge can be found that can be expressed in words. And this may create a selective reduction of all of the knowledge to be uncovered.

Finally, while many times quantitative questionnaires are used to assess attitudes, he states that (p. 647) "it is also possible to study employees' attitudes through field stimulation methods", suggesting a qualitative, field stimulation approach.

Let us end this paragraph with a rather vivid expose regarding the significance of using and applying the field stimulation approach in a qualitative manner.

LaPierre (1934, pp. 8–9) observes the limitations of a questionnaire approach over techniques that enable to observe behaviour in a natural setting when he makes a distinction between attitudes and actions. He says: "The questionnaire is probably our only means of determining "[religious] attitudes". An honest answer to the question: "Do you believe in God?" reveals all there is to be measured. "God" is a symbol; "belief" a verbal expression. So here, too, the questionnaire is efficacious. But "moral attitudes" must have a significance in the adjustment to actual situations or they are not worth the studying".

That is to say: he claims that in reality no actual behaviour is measured here. And exactly this, being able to observe actual behaviour in a natural setting, is one of the forces of the field stimulation approach.

5.3 Advantages and Disadvantages

Again, any research approach has both its advantages and disadvantages. We will successively present the views of several authors on this subject in this paragraph.

Salancik (1979) presents the following overview while covering the broad field of field stimulation:

- **Advantages**
  - Approach brings curiosity and fun to research.
  - "What would happen if . . ."
  - Determines the occasion for a response.
  - Lessens historical reliance on questionnaire responses from self-selected samples in favour of unfiltered reactions by the participants.

- **Disadvantages**
  - "Instead of wondering what will happen if a firm had to face a crisis, one might consider going out and organising a crisis for it".
  - Contrived observation, created by an artificial situation.
  - Consent might not be given before the experiment; Permissions are also severe political gatekeepers (p. 641).

As discussed in Section 5.2, under the generic heading of "field stimulation" two types of research design may be placed: the field experiment and the field study (Kerlinger, 1986). For each of the two types of research design the strengths and weaknesses are summarised by this author. We will start with the field studies design.

The strengths and weaknesses of the field studies are summarised by Kerlinger (1986, pp. 374–375) and they involve the following:

- **Strengths** of the field study
  - p. 374: "Field studies are strong in realism, significance, strength of variables, theory orientation, and heuristic quality."
  - The realism of field studies is such that they are close to real life.

- o   The field study is heuristic in the sense that its design is highly methodical.

- **Weaknesses** of the field study
  - o   There is much noise when attempting to measure variables because of the life situation in which the study is carried out.
  - o   It may be difficult to control all of the variables of the study because this has to be done within the field setting.
  - o   There may be a lack of precision in the measurement of field variables because it has to fit in the field situation.

As indicated above, the second major research design of field stimulation is the field experiment.

The strengths and weaknesses of the field experiment are summarised by Kerlinger (1986, pp. 370–372) and they include the following:

- **Strengths** of the field experiment
  - o   Although the control of the experimental field situation may be difficult to achieve (independent variables may be contaminated by uncontrolled environmental variables) a field experiment has the advantage of being carried out in a realistic setting, thereby contributing to its external validity.
  - o   The design allows for complex social and psychological influences, processes, and changes in lifetime situations.
  - o   Field experiments allow both for testing theory and answering practical questions.

- **Weaknesses** of the field experiment
  - o   It may not be possible to manipulate independent variables.
  - o   The research situation may not allow for a field experiment to be carried out on a particular problem under study.
  - o   Randomization may not be possible or desirable — for instance, some subjects assigned to a control group of study in a school setting do not receive a desirable treatment according to the design of the study.
  - o   It may not be possible to fully control the conditions of the experiment during the field experiment as the researcher

may have only partial control of the research situation; consequently, concomitant variables may exert their influence inadvertently.

o   There is an inherent lack of precision. There may be a great deal of systematic and random noise, while the measurement of the dependent variable and the independent variables may be inadequate.

Finally, Salancik (1979, p. 639) discusses the **ethics** of carrying out a field stimulation study and says that an investigator requires no more permission to carry out his investigation than that required of anyone interacting with an organisation in other roles. He argues (1979, p. 648): "[The above point and counterpoint could be extended indefinitely, but] it would be [more] useful to recognize [instead] that the ethics of an action do not vary by the fact that they are part of a research project or not. Some acts are simply unethical or illegal. And others are merely indecent."

5.4 Best Practices

Field stimulation has been used to study internal processes of organisations. An example is in Barling *et al.* (1996), who studied (p. 828) the effectiveness of training branch level managers in transformational leadership. To that end, a field experiment was conducted on 20 bank managers who were randomly assigned to two groups: (1) the control (no-training) or (2) the training intervention. The results of this study (pp. 829–830) suggest the effectiveness of training managers in transformational leadership.

Hauser *et al.* (2017) propose a taxonomy of field experiments in organisational research in order to carry out a research project in accordance with a variation of the critical incident methodology. This taxonomy is based on the characteristics of the organisational process to be studied in a company or organisation. Hauser *et al.* (2017, p. 5) define "process" as "the organizational structure in place for certain purposes in the firm (e.g., hiring, on boarding, leadership trainings, employee communication, etc.)." In order to make a choice between any of the research approaches of the taxonomy, three questions have to be answered, and one of three can be answered in the affirmative:

1. "Variation of inputs into process"? Carry out an **Audit Field Experiment**.
2. "Variation of existing components of a process"? **Carry out a Procedural Field Experiment**.
3. "Introduction of new process"? Carry out an **Innovation Field Experiment**.

These three variations will be elaborated upon in what follows.

1. **Audit Field Experiments:** Here, the researcher systematically varies selected inputs into a process, while assessing whether it causes changes in the output that may be unwanted or unexpected. This method does not alter the process itself. For that reason, the experiment can be conducted without necessarily requiring consent from an organisation. One example is changing the ethnicity of applicants to a job position in their CVs and assessing whether this influences the recruiter's decision to hire or not a person based on their race (Bertrand and Mullainathan, 2004). This method may be used to identify flaws in a process, which, in a next step, could be studied through the use of Procedural Field Experiments.

2. **Procedural Field Experiments:** In a Procedural Field Experiment, parameters of the process are systematically varied without changing the input parameters. When using this method, it can be in the interest of the organisation to participate and collaborate with the research, in order to improve specific aspects of their process. Extending the example given for Audit Field Experiments, a company would give the actual CVs provided by the candidates (therefore keeping the input unchanged) but would hide their names and their ethnicity/gender in order to avoid bias from the recruiter (Hauser *et al.*, 2017). Such hiding strategies have resulted in more diverse recruitment and reduced gender bias when hiring the most appropriate applicants (Bohnet, 2016; Goldin and Rouse, 2000).

3. **Innovation Field Experiments:** Innovation Field Experiment introduces an entirely new process, aiming to solve a problem that an existing process is not able to do successfully. IFE can be used by organisations to systematically test new processes before they are rolled out, meaning the research provides a safe environment for trial that is very beneficial to the organisation. Using the same example as the previous two methods, an organisation can introduce a new recruiting process to reduce the choice bias from recruiters. Instead of "blinding" the CVs, it could actively use algorithms to identify suitable candidates and invite them to apply at equal rates across race and gender.

Salancik (1979, p. 647) describes applications of field stimulation while making a distinction between *external relations* of companies versus their *internal processes*. He says: "Studies of internal organizational processes can be done with field stimulations but require a little more doing. The analysis of participation rates illustrates analysis of internal processes. Additionally, Schwartz and Skolnick (1962) gave application folder of bogus job seekers to 100 employers and varied the presence of information about criminal records. They asked the employers if the applicant could be used in their firms". This is, in essence, an audit field experiment.

In closing, the use and application of Field Stimulation does not merely imply executing procedures as have been described in this chapter. As always, the researcher should use his imagination, creative powers, and above all, his research skills to do the job. As Daft (1983, p. 540) says: "Significant research, then, is the outcome of a way of thinking that can be called craftsmanship."

Chapter 6

Grounded Theory Approach

6.1 Introduction

Rather than starting from a conceptual model, grounded theory (GT) leads to a conceptual model; the research purpose of the GT approach is to inductively generate a GT describing and explaining a phenomenon. As explained by Glaser and Strauss (1967) GT methodology is designed to expand understanding of symbolic interactionism, pragmatism, and social psychology. Glaser (1968) pioneered GT. Miles (1979) addressed GT and Glaser (2002) focused on deriving theories using GT. Giske and Artinian (2007) provided a good overview of GT. Bruce (2007) addressed the interaction of analysis in a GT study with data collection, which shall be discussed in what follows. This chapter introduces and discusses a general qualitative research approach called "Grounded Theory". GT is widely used in academic circles around the world, and it has received widespread international, scientific recognition.

Here, we will focus on the "constructivist" version as advocated by Charmaz (2014). She designates Constructivist grounded theory (CGT) as a contemporary version of GT, adopting certain methodological strategies with respect to the process of analysis of the data. "Constructivist grounded theorists aim for abstract understanding of studied life and view their analyses as located in time, place, and the situation of inquiry" (Chamaz, p. 342). That is, the processes under study are explained by constructing concepts and constructs, and relationships between these concepts and constructs, which may be relative instead of absolute/universal. They are related to the afore-mentioned parameters of time, place, and situation. The explanatory forces constructed may have no meaning beyond the space time continuum of the study. Throughout this chapter, the book by Charmaz (2014) is taken as the basis for describing and explaining this research approach.

6.2 Definition and Use

CGT is a scientific method and a research approach for explaining perceptions, drives, emotions, environments, and actual behaviours of specific (groups of) individuals as they experience life in specific circumstances within the wider social and cultural contexts they live in. Often, the focus of a study is on a specific issue or problem they encounter. CGT researchers may interview a number of individuals who are involved, and/or make observations, while interpreting these data. The researcher here attempts to develop and take an insider's view (Charmaz, 2014: 325).

At the onset of the study a few existing theoretical concepts may be selected as a starting point to elaborate. Generally speaking, the research process starts with "a few tools and provisional concepts" (Charmaz, 2014: 22). The successive interviews are analysed on the spot and they give rise to a process of defining emergent analytic goals and foci. Next, several rounds of data collection and interpretation may take place in an iterative research process. All of this constitutes a characteristic feature of GT.

Thus, CGT takes an *inductive approach* to the research process, where individual cases are studied, and the patterns found are extrapolated to form a conceptual category (Charmaz, 2014: 343). Furthermore, the researcher does not take as a starting point existing theory, or theoretical notions. Instead, a *tabula rasa* approach is adopted where only a few existing, theoretical concepts are used to start the research process. The end result is a theory or conceptual model. In contrast, a *deductive approach* would start with a conceptual model or a theory in an attempt to find empirical support for this model.

CGT lends itself both to a cross-sectional approach and a longitudinal approach. The former approach focuses at collecting data at one point in time, or one period, while the latter approach is aimed at collecting data at consecutive periods, while treating the data of these consecutive periods as materials of the steps of a process to be studied and interpreted. The ultimate purpose of a CGT study thus is solving a theoretical or practical problem by creating new theory and new explanatory approaches.

Interestingly, a variation of GT is defined, called "objectivist grounded theory" (Charmaz, 2014: 343). Here, a form of positivist qualitative research is practiced: there is a focus on "empiricism, generalizability, universality, abstraction, and parsimony" (Charmaz, 2014: 343). Also, the researcher takes the position of an outside expert and a neutral observer while focusing on emergent theory construction.

The method describes a specific research process to be followed. The adoption of this process and its operating procedures, once carried out, results in a (grounded) theory.

Ultimately, emerging concepts are to be ordered in such a way that theoretical notions, and theories may be constructed. Through a continued process of interaction with respondents and other sources of information, high levels of external validity regarding the constructs may be accomplished. The prescribed procedures are assumed to be adequate for revealing and unveiling the universal/ local/domain-specific forces that shape the perceptions, experiences, and behaviours of the group of individuals under study. In this connection, the data truly represent the empirical *social* world of these individuals.

6.3 Advantages and Disadvantages

CGT allows for both focus and flexibility. An enormous wealth of relevant, focused, and accurate (thick) data becomes available, allowing the researcher to develop deep levels of insight into the problem at hand. Also, it is observed that CGT "retains an open-ended character of pragmatism" (Charmaz, 2014: 339) as described by Corbin and Strauss (1988); thus an "interpretive rendering of the worlds we study is constructed rather than an external reporting of events and statements". And it is the process of constructing the events under study that provides the researcher ample opportunities to gain unique types of insights into the issue at study.

The precise criteria to be used in order to evaluate the quality of a CGT study remain abstract and may lack precision. This may be, however, an inherent characteristic of this type of research approach. The same is true for the reliability of the data. Are the data as collected during the course of the study the "right" data? And is the data collection exhaustive in a theoretical sense? Next, observer biases may come into play. Can the researcher rule out the existence of subjective impressions, pre-conceived concepts, and an idiosyncratic selection and collection of the data/type of data? Finally, process and product may not be differentiated for the reader. Obviously, this can be remedied by the researcher up to a point.

6.4 Best Practices

While practicing CGT a number of particular, successive steps are to be taken. These involve the problem analysis, sample design and procedure, the data collection, and the data analysis. They will be discussed next. In the remainder of the chapter the yields of a GT study will be considered, just like the types of recommendations that may be formulated as based on the outcomes of the study. Finally, the criteria in order to assess the overall quality of the study will be presented.

Problem analysis

It is obvious that the principles of GT forego the creation and development of a full-fledged problem analysis, as is the case in deductive, qualitative research approaches. Such a full problem analysis would comprise of the management problem, the reason for the research, the research objective, and the ensuing research questions at a minimum (Groenland, 2014).

When comparing the full problem analysis with the practices in GT, the "Management problem", and the reason for the research seem to apply. Most frequently, a social issue, that is, a problem in the social sphere, draws the attention of GT researchers. When the problem carries relevance for specific societal groups the likelihood of deciding to study the phenomenon will grow.

The research topic typically is defined in broad terms. In the absence of a formal conceptual model, no pre-described goal of the study is formulated. Instead, a few existing theoretical concepts (called sensitising concepts in GT) are taken as a starting point of the study to be carried out, while the research questions remain general in nature: these questions are generic types of questions at most.

Finally, the focus of the study may shift as based on outcomes of previous steps of the study. As a consequence, new rounds of data collection, continued analysis, and interpretation will occur based on adapted, changed, dropped, or added research questions.

Sample design and procedure

Basically, the researcher makes use of a procedure called theoretical sampling. This is a flexible sampling procedure, which may be adapted multiple times in the course of the study. More precisely formulated, it is a sampling procedure where, at any stage of the research process (data collection process) new (sorts of) data elements or data entities may be chosen based on the expectation that the study of these elements will bring the process of constructing theory to a next level. Also, various different sources of information (in-depth interviews, observations, documents) may be chosen at any stage of the process of data collection and interpretation.

In conjunction with *theoretical sampling*, the principle of *theoretical saturation* may be employed (Charmaz, 2014: 345). This leads to a sampling procedure where a researcher continues to collect more information elements until it is expected that any new element collected will not provide new information that is useful to contribute to the emergence of the GT in question.

Moreover, a *CGT* approach would focus on saturating categories; here, the number of interviews may be higher depending, among other things, on the complexity of the topic to be studied, the discovery of unexpected findings, the complexity of the categories and the constructs, and the choice regarding the number of sources of information to make use of: additional sources of information may go together with fewer interviews.

Alternatively, an *objectivist* GT approach would solely focus on saturating data. Based on rules of thumb, a guideline for the number of interviews could be 12. If the research population is heterogeneous to a certain extent, higher numbers of interview, up to 15 or 18 interviews, are considered. An advantage of this approach is that the number of interviews to be carried out can be determined at the time point of the research proposal. Thus, the parameters of time and money are fixed before the study commences.

Data collection

In-depth interviews are increasingly employed in order to acquire the data for the study to be carried out. As already stated earlier, in addition, other types of sources of information may be considered, such as observations, diaries, documents, and all kinds of secondary data, including non-academic information such as company annual accounts and their websites, newspapers, and information from individuals engaged in the social media.

The CGT researcher may be vehemently in search for the so-called *rich data*: A "detailed, focused, and full" kind of data. Rich data "reveal participants" views, feelings, intentions, and actions, as well as the contexts and structures of their lives" (Charmaz, 2014: 23). To that end, *thick descriptions* are sought for: various types of data from multiple (written) sources that are to be combined in the analysis.

In-depth interviews are organised, structured, and carried out as *intensive interviews*. They encompass basic interviewing techniques with some noted exceptions and alterations. First, the respondent is the party in the interview who does almost all of the talking. Second, questions are focused on life experiences, and they may change in terms of content and nature during the course of the period in which a number of interviews is carried out. Third, the questions asked during an interview are aimed at describing and reflecting upon the respondents' experiences, including subsequent questions aimed at elaborating about these experiences.

The *interview guide (checklist)* consists of open-ended questions that cover the relevant aspects of the issue of study. The process of crafting an interview guide induces a better understanding of the problem at hand for the researcher. A number of dos and don'ts apply for the checklist.

The checklist should refrain from reflecting the researcher's own views or assumptions. No interrogation techniques should be used. Sensitive questions should be introduced and posed in an undemanding manner and softened where necessary. "Why" questions should not be asked in a direct manner. Instead, one could ask for an elaboration. At all times the interviewer must be in charge and no negotiation about the topics and questions to be asked should occur. The interviewer must be sensitive about unwanted influences during the interview as related to race, class, gender, age, or ideologies. Finally, respondents may refrain from answering confronting questions.

During the interviews, not only data are collected; in addition, the interviewer attempts to progress in constructing theory by developing abstract conceptual categories. As a consequence, rules are less formal and less strict. That is, an interviewer may decide that enough data have been collected or that a respondent should be interviewed again. Also, questions in the checklist may be skipped or questions may be added. In more general terms, respondents' words and meanings may be understood and areas of theoretical interests may shift.

A researcher may choose to only use the in-depth interview as a vehicle to collect data. On the other hand, he/she may choose to add for instance observations or focus groups as sources of information. Based on the above, constructivist interviewing is a process where the interviewer is more personally involved and interactive, while becoming part of the experience world of the respondent. This as opposed to only formally collecting opinions, preferences, and judgements regarding a topic of interest and the reasons behind it.

Data analysis

The data analysis is comprehensive, and it is a characteristic feature of CGT. We will first provide a general overview of the analysis process. Next, the three, basic elements of the CGT data process will be discussed in further detail.

A very broad and abstract depiction of the data analysis process would be to state that it is all about "Interpreting scenes and situations", attempting to find "the collective in the subjective" (Charmaz, 2014: 318). When we focus on the acts the researcher is to carry out during the analysis the following observations may be made.

Analysis encompasses both the gathering of data and their analysis as one, concerted process in time. Concepts (and theories) are construed in an emerging process through interaction between the researcher and the data. Through interaction interpretations come into existence, a "lens" is chosen. That is, a general perspective from which the data are interpreted is chosen.

Data is analysed by categorizing them by means of *coding*. That is, the things a respondent says are each converted into short statements with an appropriate label, i.e., the code. Thus, coding implies creating constructed abstractions. The best codes are both short, simple, precise, and analytic. The set of codes produced in this way may be *categorised*: some codes pertain to the same category in terms of meaning as they may suggest a common theme or pattern. For that reason, these codes may be combined into categories.

Other codes may have different meanings. In this case, new categories are formed in order to accommodate these related codes. By proceeding this way, "analytic categories are directly "grounded" in the data", as all of the pieces of data are instances of a category.

The next step of categorising pertains to abstracting common themes and patterns in several codes into an *analytic concept* (an "abstract idea", p. 342). Next, the properties of the concept are determined, the way it is influenced by certain concepts and the way it influences other concepts. In this way relationships between the analytic concepts are specified. Limitations of the categories may prompt for modifications, such as sorting and integrating categories, which subsequently may have consequences for an analytic concept.

It stands to reason to initially focus on the analysis of the sensitising concepts as mentioned earlier. Let's elaborate this a little further. Sensitising concepts are existing concepts that are used as a starting point in the data collection and the analysis, being initial but tentative starting points at the beginning of the research process. At this point the question is: in what ways do they have meaning for the issue under study as observed from the experience world of the research participants and as interpreted by the researcher?

Finally, the researcher may engage in *comparative analysis*. Now, successively comparisons are carried out between data, codes, and categories. As a result, each of the successive steps (iterations), may result in evermore abstract concepts. Finally, an emergent, theoretical framework is created. This concludes our general and more abstract overview of the process of analysis.

Now, we move to the three basic elements of the CGT data process and discuss them in a more detailed manner. These basic elements are *initial coding*, *focused coding*, and *memo-writing*, respectively. We will discuss them in that order.

The analysis (of interview data) is aimed at constructing substantive (often new) theoretical concepts and constructs that describe the processes under study. The final aim is, following an inductive approach, to define generic processes that apply to multiple settings and areas. These processes are constructed as concept/constructs, and relationships between these building blocks. *The analysis is carried out following two logical steps: initial coding and focused coding. Throughout the process of analysis, the researcher engages in memo-writing.*

1. **Initial coding:** This refers to the act of providing labels for segments of data from, for instance, interviews. To that end, the full transcriptions of the in-depth interviews carried out may be utilised. For each sentence, or short set of sentences, a name is

chosen that may describe both contents and meaning (within the setting of the research aim). Alternatively, word-by-word coding or line-by-line coding is carried out. Finally, terms used by the respondents may be coined as codes, the so-called "*in vivo* codes". The codes are written (labelled) as acts or processes, using concise terms. Often, these codes are written as gerunds. Examples are: "following the boss' directives", "being proud to finish the job in time", or "being in need of autonomy regarding life's choices". While performing initial coding the researcher aims at taking steps to begin conceptualisation of the actions and the processes ("events") the respondents are telling about.

2. **Focused coding:** This refers to the act of selecting initial codes based on their significance or frequency, while creating broader categories from them that make analytical sense of the data in terms of emerging concepts, and relationships between concepts. To that end, focused coding attempts to synthesise and integrate sets of initial codes in such a way that large amounts of data are converted into manageable codes, or broader categories, that adequately describe behaviours, processes, and social or cultural contexts. A technique which aims to relate categories to subcategories is called "axial coding" (Strauss and Corbin, 1990). Axial coding is a type of coding of the data, which allows defining dimensions of the category and allows for the specification of relationships. Thus, both properties and dimensions of a category may be specified. This approach suggests the use of an analytic frame, a pre-set structure, pointing to the building up of a conceptual model. Obviously, this would constitute a deviation of the starting point of GT where researchers try to start the research process without preconceptions, that is, pre-conceived codes and categories.

Both types of coding processes are iterative, requiring multiple analysis steps in order to reach an interpretable end result. After each cycle, the researcher may carry out comparisons in order to find similarities and differences, and in order to check whether the codes form coherent and interpretable sets. The analysis requires from the researcher to be in interaction with the respondents' experience world throughout the process.

Memo-writing refers to the act of writing informal analytic notes. This happens throughout the entire research and analysis process. These memos may on the one hand discuss what the researcher has found so far during the process of coding and speculate about their meanings for the further development of the research process ("early memos"). On the other hand, memos may focus on constructing theoretical categories ("advanced memos") at later stages of the research process. Memos are personal aids to the researcher, containing questions and ideas regarding findings and next steps. Memos may come into existence by scribbling and jotting down catchwords, while connecting these in order to catch ideas regarding next steps towards analysis or collecting more data. Alternatively, the contours of concepts may be outlined, and the ways they connect to other categories of the analysis.

Two variations of memo-writing are being used in GT approaches: Clustering and Freewriting.

1. *Clustering* involves creating a map or chart of codes as created earlier. By visualising these codes in a chart, it may become easier to appreciate how these elements form a structure or a process, as the visual memory of the researcher is invoked.
2. *Freewriting* involves a process of automated, non-cognitive writing, thus allowing free associations to enter the writing process. It is believed that this way of writing frees latent thoughts and structures from the subconsciousness of the researcher, thereby making it possible for these to become manifest in the memo.

In the final stages of the study, some form of literature review may be carried out, and its results may be processed and used in the final draft of the research report. The end result may be a textual manuscript presenting a theoretical framework. This framework assumes the form of a text, discussing both concepts and relationships between concepts, in addition to providing arguments and explanations of the positions chosen.

6.4.1 *Yields of a GT study*

Both a GT and CGT study have the potential to create types of outcomes that are unique, and that are the only ones of their kind. Scientifically sound, these outcomes are useful both for academic purposes and practical purposes.

In addition to being based on sound, analytic writing, the approach allows the express use of the wealth of words, expressing very precise semantic meanings and connotations. As a consequence, the social meanings of concepts and constructs can be used most fruitfully to generate explanations and insights.

The approach includes the use of causes, conditions, categories, and consequences (Charmaz, 2014: 338). Furthermore, it presents a conceptual analysis of "patterned relationships" (Charmaz, 2014: 322).

Finally, theories may emerge as a result of CGT studies that allow, to a certain extent, for general and abstract meaning, explanation, and insight of highly relevant, social phenomena in the world.

6.4.2 *Types of recommendations*

"Knowledge should transform practice and social processes" (Charmaz, 2014: 340). In almost all cases, next steps for future research are obvious and relevant from the outcomes of the study. Which knowledge gaps should be filled by follow-up research? The researcher should, however, specify which avenues are most promising and why.

As to the creation and presentation of practical recommendations, based on the research outcomes, there seems room for improvement. At this point, there may not be enough focal attention to create recommendations that are effective and concrete, practical, and can be implemented quickly and at low costs.

6.4.3 *Criteria in order to assess the overall quality of the study*

Criteria with respect to the quality of the data are (inherently?) unclear. Are enough data with sufficient detail available eventually?

Are there enough data of the right sort and content that allow finding patterns, categories, and comparisons? Do the data available allow for presenting multiple views on the research issue? (Charmaz, 2014: 33)

Overall criteria refer to credibility originality, resonance, and usefulness (Charmaz, 2014: 337–338). Obviously, both an open mind and a high level of professionalism are required to construct an expert opinion here.

It seems that, apart from the undeniable merits of the CGT as described above, one could also use the methodology from a positivist perspective. In that perspective, the *objectivist GT approach* was observed and discussed earlier.

Some of the differences may be a matter of degree: focusing on the creation of a theory on the one hand or focusing on the analysis of a problem using the tools of GT on the other hand. Furthermore, one could say that in all cases the researcher is supposed to be part of the interaction process with the individuals being interviewed; he or she should be involved, taking into account both the experience world of the subjects and the researcher's constructions, as being moulded by chance accidents and an idiosyncratically shaped past.

And finally, it should not be too difficult to additionally present the main outcomes of the study in the form of a conceptual model or framework. This framework could subsequently be tested empirically in a new, but quantitative study. This approach would connect to mixed method research.

A final observation about research aimed to describe and explain the world as it presents itself to us, and research aimed at changing the world in some respects.

The following viewpoints are presented:

p. 305: "Research and writing are inherently ideological activities."

p. 340: "Can grounded theory studies contribute to a better world? Yes. Should such questions influence what we study and how we study it? Yes."

p. 338: "How does your work contribute to knowledge? How does it contribute to making a better world?"

An alternative, and less pretentious view would be that the GT approach constitutes a vehicle that may be used not only to study social issues but also managerial and business issues, from a social world perspective. Thus, this vehicle may be used to "make the world a better place" as based on some private, ideological or normative beliefs. As a consequence, this research is aimed at studying how the world should be or become. Alternatively, GT may be employed to describe and explain the current world, including the business world, in order to gain forms of advantages for the commissioning client. Both of these approaches seem to have their merits and consequently, both approaches should receive scientific recognition.

Chapter 7

Content Analysis Methodology

7.1 Introduction

In his seminal publication, Krippendorff provides a short and basic definition of content analysis: "Content analysis is a research technique for making replicable and valid inferences from data to their context" (1980, p. 21). The same author uses virtually the same phrase to define again: Content analysis is "a research technique for making replicable and valid inferences from texts (or other meaningful matter) to the contexts of their use" (Krippendorff, 2004).

A more elaborate designation may be found in the paper by Hsieh and Shannon (2005, p. 1278). They define content analysis as "A research method for the subjective interpretation of the content of text data through the systematic classification process of coding and identifying themes or patterns". Nowadays, the materials that may be content-analysed may not only include data and texts but may also encompass data sources such as pictures and audio and video recordings. The basic idea is to assign codes to pieces of text, or to pieces of other data. These codes assist in finding patterns and relationships, and eventually an interpretative structure. Thus, the researcher acquires an understanding of the various meanings of the research materials.

Content analysis can be carried out both from a quantitative angle and from a qualitative angle. Both Vitouladiti (2014) and Berg (1995) point to the differences between these approaches. They bring to the fore that there are two methods for content analysis in social sciences: qualitative and quantitative. The former term refers to non-statistical and exploratory methods, which involve inductive reasoning. Conversely, the latter term refers to methods that are capable of providing statistical inferences from text data. This chapter will mainly focus on a qualitative research methodology approach. At present specialized computer programmes may assist in analysing huge amounts of data. However, the cognitive processes and processing of a human researcher are still indispensable for the analysis.

7.2 Definition and Use

Krippendorff (1980, pp. 29–31) proposes that content analysis has some distinctive characteristics: content analysis is an unobtrusive technique, it accepts unstructured material, and it is context sensitive and thereby able to process symbolic forms. Finally, content analysis can cope with large volumes of data.

Flick (2014, p. 429) favours a narrower definition when he says that content analysis is a procedure. The aim of content analysis is to analyse textual materials, in order to reduce the material. In this way the meaning of the data is sought. Preferably the main categories are derived from appropriate theories that have been validated earlier and were published in scientific journals.

Schreier (2014, p. 174) summarises the steps to be taken to carry out a content analysis study:

- Deciding on a research question;
- Selecting material;
- Building a coding frame;
- Segmentation;
- Trial coding;
- Evaluating and modifying the coding frame;
- Main analysis;
- Presenting and interpreting the findings.

The challenge of this approach is no doubt in the building of the coding frame. A coding frame is a comprehensive set of categories and subcategories based on the elements of the data materials.

In accordance with Flick's views, as expressed in the above, ideally the categories of the coding frame are theory-based categories.

Coding categories are defined by providing a suitable label, a short description of what the category entails, and decision rules for applying the category to the data (that is, text).

The research questions and the coding frame should be created before the analysis is carried out. This provides (some) assurance that these research components have been assembled in an independent way, that is without prior adjustments inspired by the contents of the material to be analysed.

Next, *analytic units* are defined. Mayring (1983) refers to three kinds of units: "A *coding unit* indicates what is the smallest element of material which may be analysed, the minimal part of the text which may fall under a category. Also, a *contextual unit* defines what is the largest element in the text that may fall under a category. Finally, an *analytic unit* defines which passages are analysed one after the other". Furthermore, a coding frame may be altered in the process. The final coding frame may be applied to a large data set to disclose its hidden meanings. The approach is systematic which sets it apart from other qualitative analysis approaches such as narrative inquiry.

As said earlier, computer software packages may be used to process large data sets. After feeding the coding frame to the analysis software such a programme can present the number of occurrences of each of the categories and the subcategories. In addition, the programme can indicate the locations or distances between categories in the text, suggesting possibly meaningful connections. Generally speaking, this kind of software is able to retrieve text and analyse it. Based (primarily) on this information the researcher may develop his interpretations of the text and ultimately formulate the answers to the research questions. For an example of a practical hands-on guide to actually doing content analysis see Erlingsson and Brysiewicz (2017).

7.3 Advantages and Disadvantages

We will present an overview of the opinions voiced in the academic literature regarding the strengths and weaknesses of content analysis. Where appropriate we will provide brief comments to the views presented.

Content analysis is capable of capturing a richer sense of concepts within the data due to its qualitative basis and, at the same time, can be subjected to quantitative data-analysis techniques (Insch and Moore, 1997). Obviously, this statement refers to the potential, or capabilities of content analysis.

Bush *et al.* (2012) list a number of advantages and disadvantages regarding the use of both quantitative and qualitative content analysis. Among the advantages are the following characteristics and features:

- **Advantages of Content Analysis**
    o   Directly examines communication using text.
    o   Allows for both qualitative and quantitative analysis.
    o   Provides valuable historical and cultural insights over time.
    o   Allows a closeness to data.
    o   Coded form of the text can be statistically analysed.
    o   Unobtrusive means of analysing interactions.
    o   Provides insight into complex models of human thought and language use.
    o   When done well, is considered a relatively "exact" research method.
    o   Content analysis is a readily understood and an inexpensive research method.
    o   A more powerful tool when combined with other research methods such as interviews, observation, and use of archival records. It is very useful for analysing historical material, especially for documenting trends over time.

When looking back on this list the main advantages would seem to be the "potential to provide valuable historical and cultural insights over time" and the potential to "provide insight into complex models of human thought and language use". If this, in broad terms, is the aim of the researcher the content analysis approach may be the right (or only) research methodology.

The authors also observe potential drawbacks which include the following:

- **Disadvantages of Content Analysis**
  - Can be extremely time consuming.
  - Is subject to increased error, particularly when relational analysis is used to attain a higher level of interpretation.
  - Is often devoid of theoretical base, or attempts too liberally to draw meaningful inferences about the relationships and impacts implied in a study.
  - Is inherently reductive, particularly when dealing with complex texts.
  - Tends too often to simply consist of word counts.
  - Often disregards the context that produced the text, as well as the state of things after the text is produced.
  - Can be difficult to automate or computerise.

Based on the above, a real risk seems to come into existence when a researcher reduces text dramatically without considering theoretical starting points such as theoretical notions or theories. These potential risks, it seems, may be overcome relatively easily by firmly adhering to a reasoned choice with respect to a theoretical point of departure.

Content analysis as a method of gathering information requires "correct" codifying of qualitative and quantitative information into pre-defined categories in order to derive patterns in the analysis and reporting of information (Thia and Ross, 2011). Thus, the way the researcher codifies the information is crucial to the ultimate quality of the study. In that sense, it is not (merely) a matter of advantages or disadvantages of the content analysis approach.

We will close this section about advantages and disadvantages with respect to content analysis by turning to the viewpoints of Duriau *et al.* (2007). According to these authors, content analysis advocates have noticed several advantages of this method over competing choices. Foremost to management research, content analysis provides a replicable methodology to access deep individual or collective structures such as values, intentions, attitudes, and cognitions. Another key element noted is the flexibility of the method.

Below are some of the key strengths and weaknesses of this method:

- **Strengths**
  - Can be applied to examine any written document, as well as pictures, videos, and situations.
  - Widely used and understood.
  - Can help decipher trends in groups or individuals.
  - It is inexpensive, and can be easily repeated if problems arise.
  - It is unobtrusive and does not necessarily require contact with people.
  - Useful for analysing archival material.
  - Establishing reliability is easy and straightforward.
  - Of all the research methods, content analysis scores highest with regard to ease of replication. Usually, the materials can be made available for others to use.
- **Weaknesses**
  - Content analysis is a purely descriptive method. It describes what is there, but may not reveal the underlying motives for the observed pattern ("what" but not "why").
  - The analysis is limited by availability of material.

A closer look at the alleged positive and negative characteristics reveals that the authors may have had in mind mainly a quantitative approach to content analysis. This becomes clear when the authors state that the "what" question can be answered, however not the "why" question. Also, they indicate that content analysis is a "purely descriptive method". Obviously, the researcher has to make up his mind here when considering the use of the content analysis methodology. That is, if the purpose of the study is to acquire deep insights into processes and to develop interpretations that explain these processes, the researcher should choose explicitly the qualitative approach over the quantitative approach to content analysis.

7.4 Best Practices

Earlier, we cited authors who urged to carry out content analysis based on existing theories. However, there seem to be no reasons to start from "scratch", that is, by carrying out the analysis process with an open mind. In that case, the researcher chooses the way he codes and categorises solely (or mainly) as based on the information characteristics of the data. Berg (2001) puts it this way: The purpose may be of a descriptive or exploratory nature based on inductive or deductive reasoning. Inductive reasoning is the process of developing conclusions from collected data by weaving together new information into theories. The researcher analyses the text with an open mind in order to identify meaningful subjects answering the research question. Deductive reasoning is the opposite. Here, the researcher looks for pre-determined, existing subjects by testing hypotheses or principles.

A content analysis study always starts with a plan, which is by defining or choosing a number of coherent steps to follow in a certain order. According to Krippendorff (2004), the following six questions must be addressed in every content analysis:

1. Which data are analysed?
2. How are the data defined?
3. From what population are data drawn?
4. What is the relevant context?
5. What are the boundaries of the analysis?
6. What is to be measured?

Moreover, in order to design a content analysis study three units have to be specified (Krippendorff, 1980, pp. 57–60): *sampling units* (as the elements of a population of sampling units, for instance a specific type of TV programme); *recording units* (the separately analysable parts of a sampling unit, for instance the characters involved); and *context units* (the immediate environments that codetermine meaning). A final point in this respect: the minimal or optimal sample size of the sampling units has not been defined conclusively as yet by the scholars of content analysis.

In the remainder of this chapter we will discuss the best practices topics of data collection, data analysis, quality criteria, and the report respectively.

In the remainder of this chapter we will discuss the best practices topics of data collection, data analysis, quality criteria, and the report respectively.

7.4.1 *Data collection*

Content analysis may be focused on various types of data. Some types of data are readily available to the researcher, such as books and other printed materials, and hypertexts from the Internet. Data such as radio and TV programmes, videos and movies may be available as well. Even drawings and paintings may be accessible. However, for spoken data the researcher has to devise a strategy to collect these data. The planning of the data collection procedures should occur at the initiating point of the study to be carried out.

7.4.2 *Data analysis*

We begin by citing Krippendorff (2013) who posits that the interpretation process may unfold according to the metaphor of a hermeneutic circle. That is, the researcher continues to reinterpret the data as new insights come into existence. This is a basic and general principle, which may be applied to the data analysis process.

Alternatively, Bengtsson (2016, p. 10) proposes that either of two types of analysis may be employed. "In a *manifest analysis*, the researcher describes what the informants actually say, stays very close to the text, uses the words themselves, and describes the visible and obvious in the text. In contrast, *latent analysis* is extended to an interpretive level in which the researcher seeks to find the underlying meaning of the text: what the text is talking about".

However, a number of approaches exist when it comes to the actual analysis of the data collected. We will present them hereunder.

Flick (2004, pp. 431–436) suggests that three techniques are being used as part of the analysis process:

1. **Summarising content analysis:** The material is paraphrased while deleting irrelevant passages and paraphrases with the same meaning.

2. **Explicative content analysis:** Now diffuse, ambiguous or contradictory passages are clarified by using context material, for
   instance definitions from dictionaries. Using narrow content
   analysis additional statements from the text are employed to
   elucidate the meaning of an ambiguous passage; wide content
   analysis uses information, which is not part of the text to analyse.
   Examples include information about the author, situational
   characteristics, and formal theories. Based on the above, an
   explicating paraphrase is formulated.
3. **Structuring content analysis:** Formal, internal structures are
   being sought and formulated based on the domains of content
   of the text.

In addition, Flick makes two observations in this context: Firstly,
the procedure allows for multiple cases (texts) to be analysed as a
whole. This is an advantage when the research design suggests a
multiple case sample design. Secondly, an advantage of content
analysis is in the systematic element of this analysis approach. At the
same time, however, it may be more difficult to explore deeper levels
of meaning that may be hiding in the text.

Mayring (2014) presents the analysis steps to take in order to
create a deductive category assignment. This general description of
a structuring content analysis can be shown in a procedural model
as follows:

- Research question, theoretical background;
- Definition of the category system (main categories and subcate-
  gories) from theory;
- Definition of the coding guideline (definitions, anchor exam-
  ples, and coding rules);
- Material run-through, preliminary codings, adding anchor
  examples and coding rules;
- Revision of the categories and coding guideline after 10%–50%
  of the material;
- Final working through the material;
- Analysis, category frequencies, and contingencies interpretation.

He continues by saying: "the procedure is deductive because the category system is established before coding the text. The categories are deduced from theory, from other studies, from previous research. Theoretical considerations can lead to a "further categories" or rephrasing of categories from previous studies, but the categories are not developed out of the text material like in inductive category formation. So deductive category assignment is the adequate procedure if there is relevant previous research."

On a similar vein, Hsieh and Shannon (2005) propose three distinct approaches to the analysis: conventional, directed, or summative. "In *conventional content analysis*, coding categories are derived directly from the text data. With a *directed approach*, analysis starts with a theory or relevant research findings as guidance for initial codes. A *summative content analysis* involves counting and comparisons, usually of keywords or content, followed by the interpretation of the underlying context." The latter approach may be taken when carrying out a quantitative type of content analysis.

7.4.3 *Quality criteria*

When overviewing the analytical process to be carried out for a content analysis, it is obvious that the final quality of such a study depends on the quality with which each of the various steps in the process have been carried out, and the consistency between these steps. This is true for any qualitative study. For that reason, we will first discuss a number of general quality criteria as specified for general qualitative approaches. Next, we will present a number of validity issues for the qualitative approach. Finally, we will discuss reliability considerations as they pertain to content analysis.

Let us start with some *general quality criteria for qualitative research*. Symon and Cassell (2013, p. 206) discuss *assessment criteria* for qualitative research. They present various kinds of assessment criteria and order them into three broad classes:

- Methodologically and theoretically derived lists
  - **Universal criteria:** Criteria comparable to both positivist and qualitative research approaches, and therefore deemed to be valid for both;

- ○ **Contingent criteria:** Research-paradigm-specific criteria pertinent to the management and organisational field.
- Empirically derived lists
  - ○ **Quality output:** Whether the research contributes to our understanding of a particular research topic and yields useful recommendations; whether it creates "new problems" to research further;
  - ○ **Quality process:** Whether all of the major steps in the research process have been carried out in acceptable or good manner;
  - ○ **Quality performance:** Whether the researcher "has created and presented a credible story of the research".

The authors ask themselves the question whether universal assessment criteria could be valid. That is, whether it would be better to evaluate qualitative studies solely based on qualitative criteria. Moreover, they conclude that specific qualitative studies may require their own, specific assessment criteria. Certainly, long and specified lists of assessment criteria are not practical for use. Also, journals (and their reviewers) should be clearer as to the assessment criteria they use. Finally, researchers presenting articles to journals should be clear themselves as to the assessment criteria they have applied to their own work.

Next, we will discuss *general validity criteria for qualitative research.* Maxwell (1992, pp. 279–300) presents five types of *validity* for qualitative research:

1. **Descriptive validity:** Factual accuracy.
2. **Interpretive validity:** How far the meaning of statement (or observation) is developed, used, and presented adequately to the participants' view.
3. **Theoretical validity:** Refers to an account's validity as a theory of some phenomenon (both validity of concepts and relations between the concepts).
4. **Generalisability (external validity):** Refers to the accounts made on the grounds of analysing the material to other fields or parts of the material.

5. **Evaluative validity:** It refers to the adequacy of the evaluative framework used for analysing or categorising a statement (or activity) in a specific category (or as "typical" or as "a-typical" for a group, for example).

Although formulated in general terms and concepts, most of these types of validity may be effortlessly applied to content analysis. Only in the case of a content analysis study that does not depart from theories this list may not be entirely to the point.

Silverman (2005, pp. 212–220) presents five approaches to address the *validation of research findings*:

1. **The refutability principle:** Instead of engaging in anecdotalism, for specific, major interpretations of research outcomes try and find outcomes which suggest refuting such an interpretation.
2. **The constant comparative method:** Find another case to test out a provisional hypothesis.
3. **Comprehensive data treatment:** Every major interpretation of a research outcome should be corroborated by all of the elements of the data set (no exceptions that cannot not be explained satisfactorily).
4. **Deviant-case analysis:** Anomalies or deviant cases should be studied in detail in order to find out the reasons for deviating from an interpretation of a specific research outcome; this approach is in a sense a specification of the one discussed above;
5. **Using appropriate tabulations:** if and when appropriate, simple counting techniques (which might take the form of tallies) may add to some extent a notion of validity of the research outcomes.

Again, this general-purpose list of validation acts to be carried out by the researcher may need little adaptation in order to apply it to concrete content analyses. Thus, the researcher may find support from this list when attempting to elevate the quality of his study.

Now, we move to reliability issues in content analysis studies. A distinct element pointing to the quality of a content analysis study is the reliability of the research outcomes. According to Krippendorff

(1980, pp. 130–131), when obtaining data through the involvement of humans, the issue of reliability of a content analysis study has three angles of approach:

1. **Stability:** The degree to which a process is invariant or unchanging over time; it refers to intra-observer reliability, or consistency.
2. **Reproducibility:** The degree to which a process can be recreated under varying circumstances, at different locations, using different coders; it refers to intercoder reliability, intersubjective agreement, or consensus among observers.
3. **Accuracy:** The degree to which a process functionally conforms to a known standard or yields what it is designed to yield; it refers to the performance of a coder or a measuring instrument that is compared to the correct performance or measure.

These reliability approaches, although framed for content analysis studies here, come from the broader background of qualitative studies.

We will wind up this topic by referencing to a specific issue concerning reliability when human coders codify the (textual) data of a content analysis study. Neuendorf (2002) suggests that when human coders are used in content analysis two coders should be used who work independently. The resulting outcomes, when comparing them, should be consistent. Obviously, he refers to the reliability of the research outcomes of a qualitative content analysis study. For a quantitative content analysis study, numerical expressions are available that determine the level of agreement among two or more human coders.

7.4.4 *Report*

The way an end report for a content analysis study is structured merits due attention. We will again discuss this structure in terms of a general format. Content analysis researchers are supposed to take up the guiding principles as presented below and translate them into a report framework containing those specific contents and structural characteristic that are beneficial for the creation of a smooth communication process with the reader of the study.

Let us start with a *hierarchical report structure*. Silverman (2005) presents a two-level reporting structure: a macrostructure and a microstructure. For the purpose of the content analysis report, the designation "story" (see below) can be meant to signify a (main) outcome of the study. In this way the suggested reporting structure can be used for content analysis reports.

The *macrostructure* addresses the report structure as a whole, that is the basic structural elements of each of the chapters. These include the following:

- **Early planning of table of contents:** Plan what to put into your data chapters and keep revising it; if problems occur scrutinise your research design.
- **Planning your story:** One of three models may be employed:
  1. **The hypothesis story:** Present your hypotheses — test them — discuss the implications.
  2. **The analytic story:** Decide on the main analytic story line and present the resulting story in a conversational way; lay out the analytic logic that carries the story.
  3. **The mystery story:** The report starts with empirical examples, to be followed by questions emerging from these, to be followed by full interpretations of the empirical data and by discussing the implications of the outcomes of the study.

The *microstructure* involves the following:

- **Introduction:** Start with an explanation of what each of the coming chapters has to say and how they are (logically) organised in order to contribute to answering the main research questions.
- **Main section:** Present one point at a time, preface each section and wind it up at its end, and convince the reader of your interpretations by discussing its limits and credibility. To that end, discuss alternative interpretations.

- **Conclusion:** Explain what the chapter has accomplished, describe the new questions it has raised, and indicate in which (subsequent) chapter these new questions will be addressed.

We will finish our overview of report structures and contents by presenting the elements that need to be addressed when reporting about a qualitative study and its outcomes. This is a general approach for all of the major types of qualitative research, including the content analysis approach.

According to Flick (2014, p. 518) the following elements and aspects of the study should be reported:

- Explain the aims of your project.
- Present your research questions.
- Explain your sampling procedure (persons or situations).
- Explain the way you collected your data.
- Explain the data collection process as it actually happened.
- Explain the ways (procedures) you employed in order to analyse the data.
- Explain what the quality assurances are of the research project.
- Explain how you condensed the findings in order to present the essential outcomes.
- Present the practical consequences (recommendations) of the research project.
- Present a text which is easy to comprehend (you may include illustrations).
- Include quotations in the text which serve the purpose of explaining and illustrating the main outcomes of the study.

A final word of warning from this author: "while it is obvious that these criteria are of paramount importance, a researcher cannot 'prove' that his study concurs at a satisfactory, or even high level with all of these criteria". However, a content analysis researcher may use these prescribed elements to his advantage.

Chapter 8

Semiotic Methodologies

8.1 Introduction

Semiotics refers to the study of signs and sign systems in various forms of communications, including texts, pictures, audio-visual materials, posters, drawings, and data from the social media. The analysis focuses on finding and interpreting the meanings of these communications.

Applications vary from theoretical studies, hermeneutics, empirical qualitative and quantitative studies, to applied studies. Applied studies can be found in the domain of organisations, in consumer behaviour, in marketing, and nowadays the Internet.

An example within the domain of marketing is in Oswald's article (2015). Laura Oswald proposes that (p. 144) "the semiotic research paradigm has broad and deep implications for brand equity management, consumer research, and advertising". In her article she builds and grounds the view that future research can and will be carried out in the areas of "the marketplace, including visual semiotics, marketing design, innovation, and consumer culture".

An example within the domain of the Internet is in Tsotra *et al.* (2004). That study aims to show *how* semiotics can be used to reveal concealed meanings in Internet marketing. As Internet marketing "makes extensive use of symbols in order to affect product awareness and cultural meaning, semiotics is a very effective and efficient tool for interpreting online marketing".

Furthermore, in order to elucidate the relevance of semiotics in the domain of marketing, Pinson (1992) analytically describes the workings of semiotics in the marketing process. In particular, he discusses the symbolic nature of consumption, and language characteristics of products. Finally, he elaborates how the meaning of symbols, and their structure, may be used in advertising in order to promote the communication process.

A last example is a very practical application of instrument semiotics. May and Andersen (2001) present and discuss the sign characteristics that are present in the domain of ship bridge instrumentation.

In this chapter we will deviate from our standard chapter structure while focusing on the quite various definitions and uses of semiotic methodologies. Specifically, we will discuss how semiotics has been connected to hermeneutic methods, to qualitative and quantitative methodologies, and to theoretical approaches.

8.2 Definition and Use

The purpose of a semiotic study is to answer qualitative research questions regarding a phenomenon from social reality. To that end, data are collected and analyses are carried out on these data, based on the signs and symbols they contain, and by taking both context and cultural surroundings into account as part of the analysis. The research outcomes are commonly presented in a text report.

Let us return to a pivotal characteristic of semiotics: the sign. A sign represents a symbol; it has a symbolic meaning. As Manning and Cullum-Swan put it: "Semiotics, or the science of signs, provides a set of assumptions and concepts that permit systematic analysis of symbolic systems" (1994, p. 466). They elaborate that signs, in addition to possessing a surface meaning or content, have symbolic meanings. These symbolic meanings depend on the more specific context (sender, receiver, those present in a location such as for instance a company), and the wider context, i.e., the (local, business, national) cultural context.

Signs and sign systems may be viewed as stemming from different origin within the context of the philosophy of science. Rastier

(2018) poses a question at the level of the philosophy of science regarding semiotics (p. 124): "Does semiotics derive from philosophy of language or from the science of language?" That is, as an example, should we be looking for universal sign systems that are globally valid for mankind? Or should we approach semiotics locally, that is: should we be looking for sign systems that are valid within the domain of a specific language, culture, and context? p. 124: "Saussurian semiotics follows the latter approach, while taking the diversity of languages and of other sign systems as its object, thereby adopting a differential and comparative perspective that is capable of identifying some general regularities without imposing some a priori universal rules". So, the question is: at what level do we expect to find the "real" sign systems — at the universal level or at the domain-specific level? It is claimed that, by turning to the empirical world, the scientific approach may be more promising in terms of knowledge, insights, and practical yields.

Language may be taken as a starting point, as in social semiotics. Andersen *et al.* (2015, p. 2) define and position social semiotics by referring to the so-called "Halliday's Social Semiotics" view. Here, language is taken to be a semiotic system, needed to be able to communicate. This system enables us to reflect, construe, and enact our reality. Accordingly, semiotics "is not done by minds, but by social practices in a community". Meaning is defined at the social level and is based on intersubjective activities. Finally, consciousness is a "social mode of being".

Nake (2002, p. 46) distinguishes, in the context of organisations, between three "correlates of a sign":

1. **Syntactics:** *How* does the sign signify?
2. **Semantics:** *What* does the sign signify?
3. **Pragmatics:** Why and what for is the sign signifying?

The semantics of signs refer to meanings agreed upon "within a social group, community, or culture". Both form and content are of relevance. According to the author, these three analytical aspects should be taken together in order to derive the full meaning of a sign. Data, information, and knowledge are now linked to the syntactic, semantic, and pragmatic dimension, respectively. The above is to show that signs may be studied fruitfully in the context of information systems.

Stamper (2001, p. 128), while discussing the properties of signs, presents a technical versus human framework showing the so-called "branches of semiotics". The human framework moves from "Semantic — meaning of sign-types" towards "Pragmatic — intention" towards "Social — shared understanding in the realm of information and information systems".

Semiotic approaches also have been directed at **organisational research**. Semiotics has attracted researchers of organisational structures (including companies and other organisations) in particular. They study signs from a semiotic angle as applied to organisations.

Defining a frame as "a mental model, a set of ideas and assumptions that you carry in your head to help you understand and negotiate a particular 'territory'" (Bolman and Deal, 2008, p. 11), to be developed and applied within organisations, Bolman and Deal (2008) suggest that framing organisations may be a means to better understand processes within it — including corporate culture. These authors state that by matching situational clues with the framework, a worker or manager will be more successful. One of these frames is called the symbolic frame. The symbols represent meanings that are not observable otherwise. Organisational highs may be celebrated in particular manners, organisational lows may be responded to in ways specific to an organisation. Companies develop their own routines and traditions, myths, rituals, ceremonies, values, vision, metaphors, and even humour; symbols represent these methods of working and responding to events. Thus, symbols, and their uses, signify the corporate identity. Work routines, such as in-company meetings may bring with them the use of signs and symbols that for a greater or a lesser part determine and steer the process and its outcomes. They convey the actual meaning that is behind these symbols to those involved. When studying successes or failures of a company it is therefore fruitful to analyse and interpret signs and symbols of processes instead of relying on that what is said and done as such.

Liu (2000, p. 19) states that "Organisational semiotics is one of the branches of semiotics particularly related to business and organisations". Also, Liu indicates that computer semiotics "studies the special nature of computer-based signs and how they function" (2000, p. 18). p. 119: Within this context the design of a computer information system may be studied, focusing on its semantic aspects for users. To that end, p. 133, the information requirements for users must be studied. In effect, the relationship between semantic models and database design may be gainfully employed to make user processes here more effective and efficient.

In conclusion of this paragraph, the views of Petrilli and Ponzio (2005) are presented. Petrilli and Ponzio view semiotics as an open-ended and interpretive system. Furthermore, it is characterised by an interconnection of networks and signs. Therefore, it has the capacity to generate and provide a large set of meanings. The authors claim to present an innovative model of semiotics. The innovation is in the expansion of the model as a result of the current global perspective. Finally, their model is based on interpretative semiotics instead of decodification semiotics.

In the introduction, a number of data materials have been presented as examples that may be part of the process of *data collection*. Now, we will elaborate on this process.

Märtsin (2017) suggests using both verbal and visual methods of data collection, the latter being concerned with inviting the participants to produce drawings on an A3 page of white paper in the form of *timeline images*. They were asked to draw a line where positive periods were represented as (p. 120) "mountains" and stressful or difficult periods were represented as "valleys". During the analysis process "semiotic tensions and clashes" (p. 127) between the two sources of information may occur which, eventually, result in complementarity in terms of the end interpretations of meanings. As a result of this approach, both meanings of the participant and of the researcher will come to the fore.

Simao *et al.* (2016) discuss various general forms of collecting the data. When carrying out a qualitative research project data collection may take various forms. Apart from the well-known single interviews, data may be collected through multiple interviews with the same participant, or through participating in processes with one or more respondents while making observations. Generally speaking, the researcher and the respondent take part in a communication process in various different settings, which may be extended over time. This communication process works two ways: it can be typified as a prolonged interaction process during which the researcher and the participant develop a unique relationship. This process may be conceived as partnership construction, based on an interdependence communication structure. Obviously, the two participants have different roles, and knowledge: the participant holds private perceptions, images, and interpretations of the events under study; the researcher has general, and scientific knowledge about these events. The participant presents information while the researcher attempts to interpret this information. The final interpretations and conclusions may be the end result of a process of joint or coconstruction of knowledge.

Summarising, as both parties live in their own private worlds of idiosyncratic experiences, and both relate and interact with the outside or external worlds, information exchange and data collection proceeds through "self-other-world" relationships. As a consequence, the interpretations of the information collected, or exchanged, take the form of joint knowledge construction.

Törrönen (2002) suggests that "stimulus texts" (such as photos, films, adverts, sketches, news, historical sources) may be used effectively as a means to foster the interviewee's responses during the interviews.

He goes on to propose three "strategies" for selecting and using these stimulus texts. Stimulus objects may be one of the following (p. 343):

- **Clues:** "We build the interview session so that the texts, together with the interview questions, induce our interviewees to extrapolate how the texts stand for the whole (metonymy)."
- **Microcosms:** "We pose the interview questions so that our interviewees compare their worlds and identity positions against those of the stimulus objects (mimesis, identification)."
- **Provokers:** "The researcher chooses cultural products that challenge, with the aid of provocative questions, the interviewees to

deal with the established meanings, conventions and practices (symbolic dimension, naturalness, normality) of the phenomenon under examination."

As said before, the field of semiotics and its applications is vast and varied. However, the semiotic starting point is (should be) always there. Silverman (2005) poses that qualitative research never is carried out in a "neutral" way; instead, it is always carried out based on an implied model of the workings of social reality (p. 112). Gubrium and Holstein (1997) suggest four models:

1. Naturalists who focus on understanding subcultures.
2. Emotionalists who focus on understanding experience.
3. Ethnomethodologists who focus on interaction.
4. Post-modern theorists who focus on sign systems (semiotics).

Obviously, while a researcher is free to make his own choice as regards the model to take as a starting point, it is highly recommendable to make this choice known to the reader. Generally speaking, various different models may fit, or fail to fit, a specific research problem, including the research questions to be answered and the recommendations to be presented. Finally, for a detailed history of the onset, development, and scientific growth of the discipline of semiotics, with a foregrounded use of signs in Mesopotamian divination tablets (third millennium BCE), see Manetti (2010).

Semiotics is a research domain including many methodologies. These include hermeneutics, qualitative and quantitative empirical methodologies, and theoretical approaches among others. This chapter will introduce and consider each of these methodologies from a practical point of view, again focusing on signs, data collection, and in addition practical data analysis.

8.2.1 *Hermeneutic methods and semiotics*

Hermeneutics is a scientific approach aimed at interpreting texts. Its origin is in the interpretation of biblical texts. Nowadays, hermeneutics is involved in interpreting both verbal and non-verbal communication, which may be approached from the semiotic angle. There is a focus on the words and the grammar of the text under scrutiny.

The principal approach to the process of analysis also highlights its basic premise as a scientific discipline. It is called the *hermeneutic circle*. The principle of the hermeneutic circle suggests that (Avenier and Thomas, 2015, p. 18) "all human understanding is achieved by iterating between considering the interdependent meaning of parts and the whole that they form. This principle of human understanding is fundamental to all the other principles".

Patterson and Williams (2002) define hermeneutics as, p. 102, "the study of human behaviour and meaning based on the belief that understanding humans and society was more like interpreting texts than like gaining empirical knowledge of nature" (Olson, 1986, p. 160) (quoted from Patterson and Williams, 2002). They distinguish four different branches of hermeneutics: (i) hermeneutic divination; (ii) hermeneutic reconstructionism; (iii) hermeneutic reenactment; and (iv) productive hermeneutics (Nicholson, 1984; Patterson and Williams, 2002; Russell, 1988).

Following the approach of productive hermeneutics, Patterson and Williams state that "the interpreter plays an active role in creating the interpretation of a text. In essence, the interpreter or researcher helps "produce" meaning in the process of analysis. Thus, rather than reflecting an objectivist perspective, this hermeneutic tradition reflects a constructivist viewpoint that an interpretation of a text is not simply there waiting to be discovered, [but] is constructed in the process of reading" (Patterson and Williams, 2002). We will once more follow the insights provided by Patterson and Williams (2002), now regarding *data collection* and *data analysis*.

8.2.1.1 *Data collection*

Multiple alternatives may exist when it comes to the way data may be collected. However, generally the in-depth interview is the approach used most likely. Other approaches to collect the data include the use of photographs, advertisements, personal diaries or narratives, and participant observation. Hermeneutic data analysis centres on the development of what Tesch (quoted from Patterson and Williams, 2002) described as an organising system. The purpose of an organising system is to identify predominant themes through which narrative accounts (interviews) can be meaningfully organised, interpreted, and presented. The process of developing an organising system is the analysis, while the final organising system is the product of the analysis. This organising system approach is fundamentally different from a content analysis approach that proceeds by developing a system of categories into which data are coded — an approach frequently associated with qualitative analysis.

8.2.1.2 *Data analysis*

The process of developing an organising system proceeds according to the following steps:

(1) Recording of the data of (for example) an in-depth interview and transcribing the responses of the interviewee.
(2) Developing an index system in order to be able to retrieve the units of reference: the smallest unit of text that may be retrieved; usually this is a key sentence.
(3) Reading the transcriptions of the interviews in their entirety in order to get acquainted with their contents.
(4) Identifying and marking meaning units within the transcript. Meaning units are segments of the interview that are comprehensible on their own.
(5) Developing thematic labels under which the individual meaning units can be grouped.
(6) Understanding the relationships among themes; to that end, creating a visual representation of the themes and their relationships (a visual organising system).
(7) Providing interpretations (not mere descriptions) of the themes' contents and relationships.
(8) Developing an understanding of individuals and their experiences as based on their interviews (idiographic level of analysis);

next, identifying and interpreting themes that are relevant across a group of individuals, or even the entire sample of respondents (a nomothetic — across individual — analysis).

It is clear from the above that the analysis revolves around retrieving the units of reference, the meaning units, the thematic labels, the themes, and a final organising system, in that order. When meaning units are inspired by semiotic signs, and organising systems by a sign systems architecture, a meaningful connection between hermeneutics and semiotics may be laid, so it seems.

8.2.2 *Qualitative methodologies and semiotics*

Let us elaborate on the relationship between qualitative methods and semiotics. Feldman (1995, p. 4) states that, in her view, a distinction should be made between surface manifestations and the underlying structure that gives meaning to these manifestations. Words have both denotative and connotative meanings. The denotative meaning of a word is formally described in dictionaries whereas the connotative meaning may be interpreted as the symbolic, implied meaning. Here, the word acts as a sign to be interpreted. The meaning of the connotation depends on the context in which it is used, and it may furthermore be dependent on the broader context of the culture within which the word is used. A coherent set of connotations forms the underlying structure of the manifestation. It gives meaning to the denotations used.

She elaborates, "Semiotics is aimed at identifying signs and understanding the processes by which they come to have meaning" (p. 22). Mechanisms producing meaning include metaphor, metonymy, and opposition. "Metonymy involves a relationship between the sign and the signified in which both are in the same domain (example given: Crown and king are in the same domain of meaning). When these two elements are not in the same domain it is designated as metaphor (example given: a rose as a sign of love or a crown as a sign of quality). Finally, with opposition the sign has meaning because of what it is not". She gives as an example the "Exit sign" placed in a certain spot. This only makes sense if there also is an entrance to that spot.

Feldman presents three ways of *analysing the data*. The first one is called **Semiotic Clustering.** Here, a table is drafted containing three columns. The first column describes all of the various ways people use a particular concept of interest during, for instance, an interview. The next column lists all of the connotative meanings of that particular word. To that end, both metaphor, metonymy, and opposition, as discussed above, may be utilised. The researcher may use these in order to capture the connotative meanings. The third column of the table identifies issues of interest to the researcher, as pointed to by the research questions of the study. These issues are expected to be related to the connotations found in the previous step.

The next one, p. 30, is designated **Semiotic Chains.** This analysis technique produces a map showing how the underlying structure is produced in everyday signs. The map relates the collected denotations to the connotations as interpreted by the researcher.

Finally, **Semiotic Squares** is presented as a semiotic analysis technique. "A semiotic square describes a system of rules or a grammar through which meaning is produced" (p. 33). The technique may be fruitfully utilised when for instance exploring the differences between sets of rules at different levels or in different parts of an organisation.

A specific analysis strategy may be employed when it comes to analysing "mute materials" including documents. In this context, mute materials are materials that contain information. However, one cannot communicate with these materials, such as by asking questions to these materials as a researcher. Taking this as an example, documents (as patterned materials) may be compared as to a time dimension (past and present), spatial distance, or between different sets of documents, making analogies between them.

Generally speaking, three areas of evaluation may be employed: First of all, the contexts of the documents may be of importance. That is, did they have similar meaning? Secondly, which are the similarities and differences? Finally, these outcomes should be corroborated by appropriate social and material culture theories. Confirmation of the researcher's interpretations may be further strengthened by coherence ("the parts of the argument do not contradict each other, and conclusions follow from the premises"). In addition, correspondence (between theory and data) is an evaluative measure here.

As always, the researcher should make well-considered choices with respect to the analysis strategy chosen. Also, these choices should be fully explained to the reader of the report.

8.2.3 *Quantitative empirical methodologies and semiotics*

Basically, a broad field of applications may be recognised when it comes to a combination of semiotics and quantitative methods of analysis. Notably, research approaches have been developed in the *field of sensory sciences and semiotics* (Spinelli, 2018). We will now discuss this field of application, as based on her work.

Sensory sciences "deal with the measurement, interpretation and the understanding of human responses to product properties as perceived by the five senses". Initially restrained to food products, these studies nowadays extend to all kinds of other consumer products.

A main question revolves about the meaning of the language individuals use in describing product characteristics. When pretesting new products (or testing existing products) this information is highly relevant for the producers and marketeers of these products. Here, semantic and linguistic knowledge may provide a key in positioning, and repositioning, a product under scrutiny. The methodologies used in this field are grouped in the following manner (Lawless and Heymann, 2010):

- **Descriptive methodologies:** They are used to find sensory differences among product variants.
- **Discriminant methodologies:** These are used to establish whether products are perceived as different by consumers.

- **Affective methodologies:** They attempt to establish to what extent the products are liked by the consumer, and to measure emotional responses with regard to the products.

In all cases words are being collected as the data to analyse. From a semiotic point of view, one may observe "the need to objectify the unobservable subjectivity". Factors contributing to the meaning and interpretation of the words used are the object that has to be described and the situation, or context, in which the data are collected.

A classical method is to expose assessors (of the product) to a number of actual products and ask them to generate terms to describe the sensory characteristics of the product including intensity perceptions. Next, consensus is reached regarding these terms by discussing apparent discrepancies found. In this way, a sensory lexicon of terms is generated. The results are analysed by a quantitative analysis called Principal Components analysis. This analysis yields sets of descriptors where the terms within a set are statistically connected while the sets themselves are independent from each other. Thus, the so-called sensory profiles are crafted. These profiles form the basis of the questions asked to a panel of assessors. As can be seen from this procedure, these sensory profiles are the result of a quantitative analytic procedure, hence its outcomes are analytic-driven. However, semiotics plays an important role in reaching a consensus regarding the use of the attributes (and of a rating scale) and in developing a (local) context-specific metalanguage.

A more general approach aimed at finding out how people perceive and describe products may be based on an alternative procedure such as a (quantitative) questionnaire with rating scales. The semiotic contribution here is in the check whether all possible descriptors are included and whether the words and concepts used are clearly unambiguous. In this context, a qualitative pilot research project addressing these issues while carrying out semiotic analyses on the data (as generated in interviews) may be viewed a necessity.

Other approaches include well-known methods such as the Repertory Grid Method (RGM) and the Free Sorting Task. Following the RGM, respondents are confronted with objects arranged in groups of three. Basically, each time they are asked to describe the similarities between two of the objects, and how these two differ from the third object. These descriptions, when analysed statistically, allow for creating spatial configurations; in addition, the verbal descriptions may be analysed.

The Free Sorting Task prompts the respondent to sort objects into classes, and subclasses, while explaining the reasons behind their sorting decisions. As they use their own criteria in the process, the explanations provide valuable information as to how they perceive the objects and why they structure the objects in a particular way. The statistical analysis provides a spatial map as based on similarities and differences. From a semiotic point of view, the organisational principles of the so-called natural semantic categories may be studied effectively in this way.

The use of open-ended questions in questionnaires also provides an opportunity to use semiotics in the process of analysis. A semantic-assisted analysis may make use of text mining tools and text analysis tools. However, many times the researcher himself will still carry out the analyses manually in order to be more precise. A combination of semantic (qualitative) and statistical (quantitative) analyses may still be preferable.

Finally, the EmoSemio approach may be noted as an integrated method for developing questionnaires to measure emotional responses to products while avoiding the ambiguity of emotional words. A characteristic of this procedure is carrying out in-depth interviews using a version of the repertory grid method, whose data are subsequently analysed in accordance with a semiotic approach. Based on these outcomes, a specific questionnaire is constructed.

As can be observed, from the above, the approach as presented above seeks to follow the basic principles of semiotics, i.e., seeking the meaning and interpretation of words, while at the same time making use of established methods and procedures from the quantitative empirical research tradition, i.e., attempting to objectify these meanings and interpretations. That is, an attempt to combine the best of both worlds.

8.2.4 *Semiotics and theoretical approaches*

A general principle for doing qualitative research points to using, or refraining from using, existing scientific knowledge. This is an important issue as it creates a genuinely different starting point for qualitative researchers. We hand the floor over to Miles *et al.* (2014, p. 67): "Earlier textbooks on the methodology of qualitative research suggested that the qualitative researcher should not start a research project based on existing literature." Instead, one should employ a mental state of 'tabula rasa', that is, one should 'forget' all of the theoretical knowledge pertaining to the topic under study." It was expected that this would open new avenues toward discovering genuinely new knowledge and insights. Today, however, for almost any research topic solid theoretical knowledge is available. Also, research topics for management studies are almost never aimed at discovering truly new scientific knowledge or insights. Consequently, at present researchers should acquire the relevant and appropriate scientific knowledge at the start of a research project, in order to benefit from substantial theories, theoretical notions, and constructs that have proven their worth in earlier studies. The same is true for proven methodologies. As Miles *et al.* (2014) write: "[One should use] the theoretical and empirical literature to contextualize, compare, and generalize your findings." The same authors review the value of triangulation when it comes to the general quality of semiotic methodologies. Miles *et al.* (2014, p. 183) suggest, "any type of research may benefit from applying a principle to a study called triangulation. Triangulation entails including additional steps in the research design in order to avoid possible biases in the data, the methodology, the analysis, or the theory used in the study. When these biases are overcome the end results of the study bear more general value, because they can be trusted more; in addition, the research outcomes have more potential for theory construction". Four types of triangulation may be distinguished according to the cited authors:

1. **Data triangulation:** The use of different data sources in a study; ideally, phenomena should be studied at different dates and places and from different persons.

2. **Investigator triangulation:** Different observers or interviewers are employed in order to be able to detect and minimise biases resulting from the researcher as a person.

3. **Theory triangulation:** Various theoretical points of view should be considered in order to extend the possibilities for producing knowledge.

4. **Method triangulation:** Within-method triangulation would involve an attempt to collect data regarding the same topic twice and make a comparison. Between-method triangulation involves collecting data regarding the same topic by means of multiple data collection methods (such as interview and observation). In both cases, the basic idea is that ideally the method of data collection does not have a (decided) influence on the contents, structure, and stability of the outcomes.

To recapitulate, while citing yet another source (Denzing, 1989, p. 236): [the] "triangulation of method, investigator, theory, and data remains the soundest strategy of theory construction."

8.3 Sample Study

Ogilvie and Mizerski (2011) used semiotics in consumer research to understand everyday phenomena.

In order to demonstrate how a hermeneutic and qualitative empirical research may be carried out, an overview of the Ogilvie and Mizerski (2011) study is provided, and the excellent semiotic characteristics of this study are highlighted. As much as possible we will use the language and terminology of the original text of the article.

8.3.1 *Issue and relevance*

This study explores the semiotics of visible face make-up in Australian Caucasian women. It aims to understand why women wear make-up and how they experience the signs of make-up and appearance in everyday life.

8.3.2 *Research goal*

The study introduces a new method of studying consumer phenomena by combining two different semiotic philosophies.

8.3.3 *Research design*

The study comprises two phases: The initial phase adopts a communication model extended from Saussurean semiotics, while the second employs a triadic semiotic philosophy as proposed by Charles Sanders Peirce.

8.3.4 *Sample design and data collection*

Among others, observations of women's face make-up in nightclubs, restaurants, on public transport, in the street, and in other everyday settings, were employed.

In-depth phenomenological interviews were conducted with 33 female Caucasian women aged 30 and above over a 15-month period. This group was selected from the cosmetic maps developed in phase 1 and was identified as being a unique market whose make-up routine was often established and who were also large consumers of visible make-up.

Participants were given disposable cameras and asked to take photos of their faces in four different settings:

1. A night out or special occasion;
2. Work or normal daily activity throughout the week;
3. Relaxing at home on day off;
4. Shopping for groceries.

Respondents were also asked to take photos or find a newspaper/magazine clipping of someone they perceived to be "different" from themselves and someone they considered to be similar or the same as themselves.

During an in-depth interview, respondents' feelings, attitudes, perceptions, and experiences about make-up were explored. A "focused" interview format was used, characterised by a general question outline to guide the interview, but allowing for the flexibility to adapt and probe with each interview situation.

8.3.5 *Data analysis*

The observational data were analysed and sorted into three code categories: *residual, dominant,* and *emergent.* Residual codes represent remnants of earlier cultural values still evident within society, but gradually weakening as they become increasingly out-dated and replaced by newer codes. Dominant codes represent the present and are visible everywhere, while emergent codes are new and developing, and not quite fully formed.

8.3.6 *Report*

A text report with tables and figures.

8.3.7 *Excellent semiotic characteristics of the study*

Again, as much as possible we will use the language and terminology of the original text of the article.

In Phase 1, a semiotic framework of metaphor and metonymy was used to examine the cultural context of face make-up within Western Australian society. An approach based on an adaptation of Levi-Strauss's theories on myth was combined with the use of bipolar axes to interpret sign communication. Using this method, observation techniques were used to identify the codes (or patterns) of facial make-up from the discourse within the culture. This technique stems from the Sausurrean school of thought, which focuses on the sign as a form of language. Integral to this philosophy is that culture enables communication through signs, and signs are a language that can be identified and interpreted through the analysis of codes within the culture.

The results provide an analysis of the culture using an "outside-in" approach, which is overlaid with a deeper understanding of how individuals experience this culture from an "inside-out" perspective.

The second phase of the study employed a Peircean semiotic framework to gain insights into the significance of visible face make-up from the individual's perspective, with particular emphasis on the icon, index, and symbol. Peirce's triadic philosophy of the sign involves three elements: the representamen — a vehicle that conveys an idea to the mind; an interpretant — another idea that interprets the sign; and object for which the sign stands.

In Peirce's philosophy these three elements are overlaid against the categories of *firstness, secondness,* and *thirdness.* Firstness is defined as "it is what it is" without relation to anything else. Secondness is defined as relating the first to the second in terms of comparison, action, time or space. Thirdness relates the second to the third, and includes memory, habit, synthesis, and semiosis in the form of communication.

Thus, this paper demonstrates how, by combining two semiotic perspectives, the researcher is able to gain greater depth and understanding of an everyday phenomenon. By examining the phenomenon from an "outside-in" approach, researchers, marketers, and social policy makers can explore the social influences of behaviour and understand why people behave the way they do. By adding an "inside-out" approach to the research, this overlays an insight into individuals' experiences within the culture. As such, the researcher is able to understand not only the shifting cultural paradigm, but also how individuals experience the culture.

All of these characteristics make this study exemplary of its kind.

Chapter 9

Narrative Inquiry Methodology

9.1 Introduction

As a way of introducing narrative inquiry methodology, here, we will provide an overall sketch of what it is, where it came from, and how it operates in general terms. In the next section more detailed definitions and uses of this methodology will be provided and elucidated. Narrative inquiry is a research methodology which is focused on the "detailed histories or life experiences of a single event or a series of events for a small number of individuals" (Elliott, 2005). Its philosophical background resides in a view where individuals as such, or individuals who are employed at a company, tell each other stories for specific purposes. These may include establishing their identity, or ordering their retrospective memories regarding important life events, or expressing their views about how "things should be" in life, in their company, or in society. As Geertz (1973) puts it: "narratives are integral to human culture because culture is constituted through the [...] ensemble of stories we tell about ourselves". And Fisher (1997, p. 314) states that "humans are essentially storytellers".

Hyvarinen (2007, p. 449), while discussing analysing narratives and storytelling, provides an apt description of the genesis of narrative inquiry. He marks the 1980s as the transition point (a narrative turn) with respect to the use of narrative inquiry in the social sciences: "The narrative turn in *social sciences* began later, in the early 1980s and encompassed entirely different issues: positive appraisal of narratives as such, a general anti-positivist and often humanist approach to the study of human psychology and culture". It is focused on the detailed stories or life experiences of a single event or a series of events for a small number of individuals (Creswell, 2007).

The aim of a narrative study is to describe in detail the understanding and meaning of the experiences from the participants perspective. Two varieties of narrative inquiry exist (Petty *et al.*, 2012): narrative research may be (1) biographical following the life of individuals, while an (2) oral history explores the personal reflection of events from one or more individuals. In order to collect the narratives both observations techniques and document search techniques may be used. Data analysis may be carried out by "reorganizing the stories into chronological order, identifying key aspects and may include interpretation and thematic analysis".

Generally speaking, the analysis is not carried out according to precise and objective instructions; instead heuristics are applied in order to arrange the data and find meaning in them. Also, participants of a study may be allowed to provide feedback on the interpretations of the researcher.

The end product is a text report, which contains the story, or stories, as construed by the researcher.

9.2 Definition and Use

Denzin (1989, pp. 183–185) poses that the aim of narrative inquiry is to present the *experiences and definitions held by one person, group, or organisation and the way they interpret those experiences*. To that end, life history materials are collected that may include records or documents of any kind, such as autobiographies, letters, newspaper messages, court records, notes, and film and pictures. Transcribed interviews may also be used for the purpose of the study. Thus, insights are created regarding the inner world and the interpretations of a person, a group of persons, or an organisation about a life, or a segment of a life.

These kinds of studies take the *perspective of the persons involved as the basic principle* while trying to make interpretations as related to social relationships. The persons studied move across various different situations and thereby create a history of events over time. The personal experiences of these persons studied, and the idiosyncratic way they interpret these experiences, form the backbone of this research approach.

The "life history" approach may be viewed as one of the varieties of the general biographical method. Other varieties include life story, personal history, and case history, among other things. Three variations of the life history approach may be distinguished: the *complete life history*, the *topical* (only one life phase) *life history*, and the *edited* (including comments, explanations, and questions by someone else) *life history*.

Furthermore, Mitchell and Egudo (2003, p. 5), while discussing the definition and use of narrative inquiry, advance the view that "the narrative approach of analysing interviews is posited to have the ability to *capture social representation processes* such as feelings, images, and time. Narrative offers the potential to address ambiguity, uncertainty, complexity and dynamism of individual, group, and organisational phenomena. Narrative analysis can be used to record different viewpoints and interpret collected data to identify similarities and differences in experiences and actions. *Stories are presumed to provide a holistic context* that allows individuals to reflect and reconstruct their personal, historical, and cultural experiences. Stories are essentially individual constructs of human experience and have limitations that may affect objectivity in presentation. The use of other approaches to complement the storytelling technique has been recommended".

Narrative inquiry is not limited to one standard form. Creswell (2014, p. 532) offers a typology of narrative research forms. These research forms include biographies and autobiographies, life writings, personal accounts and personal narratives, personal documents, documents of life, life stories and life histories, oral histories, and more.

Barkhuizen (2013, pp. 6–9), while developing dimensions of narrative analysis, relates content to reflection. He describes "content" as what narratives are about, what was told, and why, when, where, and by whom. *The combination of content and reflection of the researcher is called narrative inquiry.* Furthermore, *content and context* may be explored with respect to three dimensions: *temporality* (the times — past, present, and future — in which experiences unfold), *place* (the place or sequence of places in which experiences are lived), and *sociality* (personal emotions and desires, and interactions between people).

Pentland (1999) relates *narrative properties* to Organizational Theory and specifically connects sequence to pattern of events; focal actor(s) to role, social network and demographics; voice to point of view, social relationships, and power; moral context to cultural values and assumptions; and other indicators to other aspects of context. Thus, features of narrative can be useful as indicators for certain kinds of questions.

Bruner (1997, p. 277) concludes that *narrative structure* "emphasizes order and sequence, in a formal sense, and is more appropriate for the study of change, the life cycle, or any developmental process". And: "on the one hand, a story is experienced as a sequence, as it is being told or enacted; on the other hand, it is comprehended all at once — before, during, and after the telling. [Thus] a story is static and dynamic at the same time".

And finally, Elliott (2005): "Narratives (stories) in the human sciences should be defined provisionally as discourses with a clear sequential order that connect events in a meaningful way for a definite audience and thus offer insights about the world and/or people's experiences of it".

Based on the above, it is obvious that many variations do exist under the heading of narrative inquiry and that all of these may have merits of their own. The common element is describing in detail the understanding and meaning of the experiences from the participants viewpoint. As a consequence of the definitions presented and the point of departure chosen, generalising the idiosyncratic outcomes of narrative studies to other domains proves difficult or even impossible.

One may wonder whether *causality* plays a role in narrative research. Elliott (2005, p. 98) contends: "as regards causality in the narrative approach, two modes of explanation may be in order.

Causal explanations, following the logical-scientific heritage of the natural sciences, attempt to describe cause and effect relationships as a formal system for prediction. Narrative explanations, in contrast, are aimed at providing meaning. The former type convinces by providing arguments, while the latter type convinces by providing stories. Furthermore, causal explanations refer to multiple cases while narrative explanations refer to the individual case, and the context of this case. As a consequence, causal explanations are more generalizable while narrative explanations point to the particular. This distinction is termed 'ideographic versus nomothetic explanations'".

So far, definitions and use have been discussed from a qualitative angle. It is claimed, however, that narrative inquiries may also be carried out using a quantitative approach. As Elliott (2005) states: "This methodology comes from the humanities and social sciences and can follow a qualitative or quantitative approach. Researchers can construct narratives from quantitative evidence". And: "The majority of longitudinal data take human subjects as the unit of analysis, and therefore longitudinal data commonly record change at an individual or "micro" level" (Ruspini, 2002, p. 47). Finally, Elliot (2005) says: "Once the in-depth comprehensive nature of the data collected in many longitudinal studies is recognized, it is clear that some quantitative research may contain more detailed information about individuals than many qualitative studies".

Today, however, the mainstream approach to narrative inquiry is based on qualitative principles and procedures.

9.3 Advantages and Disadvantages

An advantage of this research approach is that the researcher is easily able to connect to the social reality of the subjects, their language, their culture, their work settings, and their life circumstances. Disadvantages include the difficulty to check the analysis approach taken by the researcher, and the risk of personal views of the researcher having an unwanted influence on his interpretations of the data materials. Finally, these studies cannot be replicated.

Elliott (2005) provides an overview of strengths and weaknesses. They include the following:

- **Strengths**
    - Provides a voice for those unheard. Empowers them.
    - Is aware of the diverse points of view and experiences that people can have of the same situation.
    - Allow for emotions to be expressed.
    - Explores a natural ability of humans to tell stories.
    - Develops in the audience a closer connection with the topic.
    - Can be used both in qualitative and quantitative approaches.
- **Weaknesses**
    - Are stories authentic? Are participants contributing with fake data?
    - Do the researchers have permission to tell the story?
    - Does the researcher gain at the expense of the participants?
    - Misinterpretation of the stories by the researcher.
    - Too much detail can shift the focus from the topic being addressed.
    - Can take extensive time in case of longitudinal studies.

However, while choosing a contrasting view, Polkinghorne (2007) resolutely presents the proposition that "it is the readers who make the judgment about the plausibility of a knowledge claim based on the evidence and argument for the claim reported by the researcher. The confidence a reader grants to a narrative knowledge claim is a function of the cogency and soundness of the evidence-based arguments presented by the narrative researcher."

Strengths and weaknesses may be further generalised by formulating *quality indicators*. According to Creswell (2007, p. 214), for a study to be evaluated as "good", attention must be given by the author of the study to seven aspects.

"The author:

- Focuses on a single individual (or two or three individuals)
- Collects stories about a significant issue related to this individual's life

- Develops a chronology that connects different phases or aspects of a story
- Tells a story that 'restories' the story of the participant in the study
- Tells a persuasive story told in a literary way
- Possibly reports themes that build from the story to tell a broader analysis
- Reflexively brings himself or herself into the study."

Etherington (2009), in this context, specifies a number of criteria. These include:

Does the work make a substantive contribution to my understanding of social life? Does the writer demonstrate a deeply grounded social science perspective and demonstrate how it is used to inform the text?

Does the work have aesthetic merit? Does the writer use analysis to open up the text and invite interpretive responses? Is it artistically shaped, satisfying, complex, and interesting?

Is the work reflexive enough to make the author sufficiently visible for me to make judgements about the point of view? Does the author provide evidence of knowledge of post-modern epistemologies that convinces me of their understanding of what is involved in telling people's lives? Am I informed how the author came to write the work and how the information was gathered? Have the complexities of ethical issues been understood and addressed? Does the author show themselves to be accountable to the standards for knowing and telling participants stories?

What is the impact of this work on me? Does it affect me emotionally, intellectually, generate new questions, move me to write or respond in any other way?

Does the work provide me with a sense of lived experience? Does it seem to be a truthful, credible account of cultural, social, individual or communal sense of what is "real"?

While all of these elements and characteristics of a narrative study make sense, it is obvious that these criteria are *objectified criteria* at best. Nevertheless, this need not keep us from making good use of them. Or, as Czarniawska (2004, p. 69) says, "they interrogate a text", and the way he does it is up to the researcher, it is a matter of what he (p. 72) "finds agreeable, that suits him or her".

9.4 Best Practices

9.4.1 *General approaches*

We will start with two general approaches. While the structure of the two general approaches to present roughly tend to correspond, the two authors add their own characteristics to the specific content of the steps taken. Here are the suggested general procedures.

Denzing (1989, p. 205): While setting up and carrying out a research project of this sort the following general steps are to be followed:

- Carrying out a problem analysis that is suitable for answering the research questions and creating "tentative operationalisations" of the main concepts.
- Creating a sample design suitable for the study and which suits the form of the life history to be studied.
- Record the objective events and experiences in the subject's life that pertain to the problem to be studied.
- Obtain the subject's interpretations of these events as they occurred in their chronological, or natural, order.
- Check measures of validity and make corrections or alterations where necessary.
- Begin testing hypotheses or propositions and modify them where necessary.
- Writing an initial draft of the entire life history and presenting the draft to the (core) subjects in order to receive feedback from them.
- Rework the report in its natural sequence after processing the feedback.
- Presenting hypotheses and propositions that received support from the study.
- Conclude with the relevance of the report for theory and future research.

Creswell (2007, pp. 55–57) also describes general procedures for conducting Narrative Research. In effect, he suggests a five-step approach:

1. The research problem or research question should fit the narrative approach. That is, there is an *ex ante* expectation that the answers to the research problem can be derived from the detailed stories or life experiences of a single life or the lives of a small number of individuals.
2. Select the respondent(s) who are able to tell their life stories. Next, collect the data. To that end, the researcher speaks extensively with the respondents, and/or he may use written (journal, diary) versions of the life stories, make observations of the individuals involved and record field notes. Also, letters sent by the individuals under study may be collected, or documents or correspondence about the individuals. In addition, photographs and social artefacts may be collected, in order for the researcher to interpret.
3. Next, the context of the stories must be ascertained. This context may include participants' personal experiences (their jobs, their homes), their culture (racial or ethnic), and their historical contexts (time and place).
4. Now, the life stories of the participants must be analysed. The analysis begins with collecting key elements of the story. Examples of such key elements are time, place, plot, and scene. The next step is to rewrite the story to place them within a chronological sequence. This is called "restorying". Now, the story makes sense in terms of chronology: it has a beginning, a middle, and an end. Also, some form of causality regarding the subsequent steps of the rewritten story (i.e., the notion of a plot) is established. Finally, themes that emerge from the story may be outlined and elaborated. The focus on chronology in his method of working is a distinguishing characteristic of the narrative approach.
5. Finally, the researcher and the respondent negotiate the meaning of the stories, adding a validation check to the analysis in this

way. This includes pointing out epiphanies or turning points that make the story change dramatically while it develops towards its end.

Finally, Kim (2016, p. 27) proposes a *theoretical approach* which is based on the *ex ante* choice of a theory. The author proceeds as follows. The process of Narrative Inquiry may start with a formal theory of some sort, or a philosophical paradigm. Examples are Critical Theory ("examining class relations of domination and subordination that create inequality in society"), Phenomenology ("examining the essence of one's lived experience through the meaning given by one's own subjectivity") or Feminist Theory ("placing gender at the centre of analysis to explain how gender inequality and sexism are pervasive in society") (pp. 301–305). Alternatively, one might decide to choose theoretical notions from the domain of the social sciences. This also may be a fruitful approach for tackling management problems.

9.4.2 *Data collection*

We will present three approaches as to the ways data may be collected. Both Flick (2006), Fraser (2004), and Kim (2016) will elaborate on this theme, and in that order.

Flick (2006) tells us that the principle method of data collection is the narrative interview. Basically, the interviewee is asked to tell his or her story (a life story, a story about a significant event, a situation narrative, etc.). To that end, the interviewer is asking the "generative narrative question". This question defines the issue and the period the narration should address. From this point in time during the interview, the interviewer refrains from asking other questions until the narration has been finished by the interviewee. By following this procedure, the narration cannot be influenced in terms of contents or structure or emotion by the actions of the interviewer. Upon finishing the narration, the interviewer may ask subsequent questions regarding elements of the story told.

Narratives are stories (p. 199) with a beginning, a middle, and an end. Generally speaking, the stories are about events and processes. The interviewee typically often may not follow a temporal dimension and (s)he may jump from and towards multiple points in time. Also, the story may contain both facts, personal experiences, idiosyncratic interpretations, and various sorts of emotions. Many times, an analysis of the story discloses a particular theme or common characteristic (perhaps a Leitmotiv) which makes it possible to understand the inherent, global structure of the story, as experienced by the interviewee. This global structure of the story should guide the interpretation of the interviewer.

A two-way distinction can be made (p. 294) regarding data to be collected. On the one hand, one may be carrying out interviews with a person of interest to the study and collect documents related to the topic of the study. On the other hand, the researcher may decide to be part of the everyday practice of the person of interest and may observe what happens. This is called participant observation, and more recently ethnography. Thus, both direct data (e.g., by observation) and indirect data (e.g., by interviewing) can be collected, from the viewpoint of the researcher.

Finally, other types of data (pp. 296–297) may be collected additionally. Examples are informal conversations, focus groups, images and photographs, diaries, organisational documents, newspapers, audio and visual recordings, and communities on the Internet. Anything goes, as long as the data are functional for providing answers to the research questions.

Fraser (2004) suggests the following procedure:

- Prepare for the interviews by studying the socio-historical contexts of participants' lives.
- Respond to different communication styles.
- Avoid "mining" interviewees for information or "cross-examining" them.
- Demonstrate sensitivity to the time frames of participants as well as our own.
- Facilitate a climate of trust.
- Allow participants to ask questions of their own, as well as how we might respond to any questions they raise.
- Reveal our own investment in the research.

- Share some of the interpretations we make.
- Appreciate the politics involved with making knowledge.

Kim (2016, p. 166) starts with providing the designation of the basic interview. In his view, the basic type of interview is "the Life Story Interview, also called the Biographical Interview. It has an unstructured, open-end format. It is based on the concept of one's life story being a social construct comprising both social reality and a personal, experiential world".

Next (p. 167), he says that two distinct phases may be distinguished: "the narration phase and the conversation phase". During the narration phase the interviewee is encouraged to tell his story without interruptions from the interviewer. Thus, the interviewee gets the opportunity to involve in his own narrative thinking processes.

During the narration phase the interviewer is both listener and observer. The interviewer is now sensitive to story elements such as sequence, coherence, continuity, meaningfulness, and transformation. Observations may relate to the way the interviewee talks, the use of body language, emotional expressions, feelings, and pauses.

Also, in order to get a good start of the process the so-called Two-Sentence Technique (p. 170) may be employed. This technique suggests starting with two combined sentences: a statement and a question about this statement. For instance: you have been in the military army for four years. Can you tell me what the biggest challenge was during that period?

During the conversation phase, the interviewer asks semi-structured, in-depth questions. Also, he may ask questions of clarification regarding utterances during the narration phase. Now, the focus is on the creation of meaning.

During both phases the interviewer makes observations about verbal and non-verbal utterances of the interviewee.

And, in addition of interviews carried out at a place that is convenient for the interviewer, fieldwork can be carried out. That is, the interviewer carries out the interviews at the natural site of the interviewee, for instance, schools, or the company of the interviewee.

The advantage would be that the setting of the interviews is a natural setting for the interviewee. As a consequence, it may be easier for the interviewee to remember issues, actions, and emotions, as these are activated by their declarative memory, which includes both episodic and semantic memory.

Episodic memory represents our memory of experiences and specific events in time in a serial form, from which we can reconstruct the actual events that took place at any given point in our lives. It is the memory of autobiographical events (times, places, associated emotions, and other contextual knowledge) that can be explicitly stated. Individuals tend to see themselves as actors in these events, and the emotional charge and the entire context surrounding an event is usually part of the memory, not just the bare facts of the event itself.

Semantic memory, on the other hand, is a more structured record of facts, meanings, concepts, and knowledge about the external world that we have acquired. It refers to general factual knowledge, shared with others and independent of personal experience and of the spatial/temporal context in which it was acquired. Semantic memories may once have had a personal context, but now stand alone as simple knowledge. It therefore includes such things as types of food, capital cities, social customs, functions of objects, vocabulary, understanding of mathematics, etc. Much of semantic memory is abstract and relational and is associated with the meaning of verbal symbols.

This concludes our overview of the process of data collection.

9.4.3 *Data analysis*

The analysis of the materials collected may proceed in a number of related, but varied ways.

Riessman (2008), for instance, while describing models of narrative analysis, provides a typology-like description which includes "Thematic analysis" (*What* is said across a number of cases), "Structural analysis" (the *Way* a story is told); "Interactional analysis" (Storytelling as process of coconstruction); and "Performative analysis" (Storytelling as performance — beyond the spoken word).

Czarniawska (2004) takes as a starting point (p. 72) the "choice of a theory of reading" by a researcher. The way data should be analysed is a consequence of this choice and defines the domain for which the outcomes are valid. As a consequence (p. 139), a philosophy and theory of interpretation comes into existence, and the researcher engages in interpreting, construing, theorising, and expounding on theory. Basically, the aim of the analysis is to formulate a structure — organising principles — and to expose the functions of (complex) narratives.

Finally, three types of "reading" the text are available (p. 139): *explication*: what does this text say; *explanation*: why and/or how does this text say what it does; and *exploration*: what do I, the reader, think of all this?

Symon and Cassell (2013, p. 494) present three major analysis approaches:

1. **Thematic analysis:** The content of a story is explored while focusing on what is actually said rather than the way it is said; the aim is to identify key themes, using as data both interviews and documents. In organizational research, often, multiple narratives are studies in order to find theme communalities across all or within subgroups of stories as taken from (subgroups of) interviewees selected from different parts of the organisational structure of the organisation such as managers versus employees.

2. **Structural analysis:** Not so much the content of a story is focused on but the way in which a story is told. Language used to persuade in commercial settings, and the internal organisation of the story are both focal points in the analysis and interpretation of sometimes-different stories. Also, finding the same simple structure of many, seemingly different stories may be a research aim here.

3. **Dialogic/Performance analysis:** This type of analysis combines the two above analysis approaches. That is, it combines both thematic and structural elements. In addition, however, the way narratives are coconstructed between teller and listener are explored. Moreover, the exploration takes the social, historical,

and cultural context into account in which the conversation takes place. Specifically, the roles of both the narrator and the researcher are studied in order to arrive at an understanding of how these roles influence the narrative by the social interactions between the actors involved in this way. For example, team meetings may be studied effectively using this type of analysis.

However, also more elaborated procedures are suggested. In the following, the writings of Denzin and Kim, will be presented, respectively.

Denzin (1989, pp. 195–198) proposes that the analysis of the materials collected is focused on comparing these materials. The analysis may proceed according to two broad strategies: objective approaches and interpretive approaches.

The *objective approach* may be sketched in the following way:

- Experiences are lined up while connecting these to life course stages.
- Narrative accounts of these experiences are assembled.
- Narrative segments and categories are created.
- An analytic abstraction of this case is written.
- A second case is selected and all of the above are repeated.
- Comparisons are made between the two cases.
- Theoretical interpretations are generated.
- Theories are built and test, and revised when deemed necessary.

The *interpretative approach* includes four varieties:

1. **Sartre's method:** A pivotal event in a subject's life is chosen, next data are selected that pertain to phases earlier than the pivotal event, and data that refer to phases after the pivotal event; this method is also called progressive–regressive method.
2. **Paul Thompson method:** Three strategies are presented:
   o Focusing on single life story narratives emphasising a single case;
   o Focusing on the collection of several life stories grouped around common themes;
   o Focusing on a cross-case analysis of oral and life story materials aimed at building theories;

3. **Dolby–Stahl method:** Focusing on the development of a literary folkloristic methodology mains steps and principles involve the following:
   - Selecting a generic social category in which the subject fits;
   - Identifying the salient themes and experiences in the subject's life;
   - Connecting the subject's life history and life story to larger, social meanings.

4. **Denzin method:** An amalgamation of the methods above, the following steps and principles may be recognised:
   - Isolating critical experiences and locating them in the subject's social world;
   - Isolating the critical others in the subject's life;
   - Securing personal experience narratives from both the subject and from his significant others;
   - Using these stories to fill in the subject's life and bring the subject alive;
   - Connecting life history with life stories and self-stories and the oral history of the subject;
   - Comparing the "case study" of this subject with those of other subjects;
   - As a consequence of this procedure, "lived time" is not linear, it is both circular and interactional.

Kim (2016, p. 198), on the other hand, contends that the analysis of the data (a story told by an interviewee) may be carried out according to one or more of the "Mishler's models" of Narrative Analysis. This approach is characterised by proposing specific types of analyses for specific types of research problems.

One type of analysis is called: "Reference and temporal order — the telling and the told". Here, the "told" is the story delivered by the interviewee. The "telling" is the story delivered by the researcher in the final research text. A major focus is in the attempt to rewrite (analyse) the temporal sequence of events and actions events as told by the interviewee (told) into the temporal sequence of events as they occurred in the real world, as analysed by the researcher (the telling). Variations of this method are presented and introduced (p. 200), such as reordering a storyline, identifying a story pattern, and inferring a story.

Alternatively, an analysis approach may be chosen which is called Narrative functions: Contexts and Consequences. Here, narratives are interpreted from the angle of experience (cognition, memory, self), or the interpretation takes cultural element into account, or institutional contexts, or power, conflict, and resistance are taken as a frame of reference, based on a suitable theoretical framework. Research issues from the management domain may be fruitfully researched using one of these approaches.

Finally, Kim (2016, p. 196) discusses Polkinghorne's Analysis of Narratives and says this may be an analysis alternative. This approach is also called the Paradigmatic Mode of Analysis. It aims to organize experience as a set of ordered and consistent elements, based on the data available from storytelling. Furthermore, the features and characteristics of these elements are used to classify them into different (types of) categories. Thus, cognitive networks of concepts are created that point to common themes, and the relationships between these themes. The concepts could be derived from existing theories and conceptual models (deductive approach), or they could be inductively derived from the data (Grounded Theory approach). By comparing multiple stories from multiple interviewee's commonalities may be found and general knowledge may be produced.

9.4.4 *Reporting the results of a qualitative study*

Miles *et al.* (2014, p. 91) describe the story-line function of the narrative as follows: "[] the story-line function of narratives enables the researcher to outline the plots of human action and how participants (or "characters") changed throughout the course of the study. Prosaic representation and presentation of our findings are essential ways to communicate to readers how the social action we witnessed and synthesized unfolded and flowed through time".

Symon and Cassell (2013, p. 195) present a more elaborate discussion regarding reporting styles. They distinguish between five styles of reporting the results of a qualitative study:

1. **Hiding qualitative research:** The qualitative component of the study is minimised or not reported at all. Reasons for this decision may include maintaining the story line of the paper, the journal to publish the paper will not allow this information. or when the target audience has biases or reservations regarding qualitative research.
2. **Mimicking the deductive reporting of qualitative data:** The study is presented, structured, and written as if it were a deductive, quantitative study. The reason may be that the researcher experiences pressure to make the paper appear "more conventional".
3. **Factor-analytic reporting:** It reduces large amounts of qualitative data into "meaningful factors" which may be generalised to other contexts. By doing this the researcher may hope to add value to the current study as this study may act as a prelude for carrying out a subsequent, quantitative study.
4. **Non-traditional reporting:** Relocating elements of the text such as theory and data; employing a post-modern approach where for instance poetry and storytelling may be utilised in the paper. The reason for this choice is a notion that traditional views of reporting styles may be too formal and non-fitting to the message to be told to the target audience.
5. **Essayistic reporting:** Here, the focus is on the exposition of the argument. The reason is that forceful arguments may be more important than traditional, academic rigor on which the other reporting styles rely.

In the end, Symon and Cassell (2013) break a lance for allowing authors of qualitative studies more space to make their own choices in this matter.

Chapter 10

Data Collection Methods

This chapter serves as a short introduction to a number of data collection methods which may be useful to the researcher who wishes to carry out a qualitative study while using one of the research methodologies as presented in the previous chapters.

The first question to be answered here relates to the following:

What is the difference between research methodology and research methods?

A research methodology is a strategic plan of action, whereas research methods are the techniques used in research. Petty, Thomson, and Stew defined methods as "techniques used to acquire and analyse data to create knowledge" (2012, p. 378).

Selecting the appropriate methods

Patton suggested, "If you want to know how much people weigh, use a scale. If you want to know if they're obese, measure body fat in relation to height and weight and compare the results to population norms. If you want to know what their weight means to them. How it affects them, how they think about it, and what they do about it, you need to ask them questions, find out about their experiences, and hear their stories" (2002, p. 13).

When conducting qualitative research, useful data collection methods include, in alphabetical order: (i) the Delphi method; (ii) document analysis; (iii) focus groups; (iv) interviews; (v) elicitation techniques; and (vi) observation and participant observation. These methods will be introduced in the following chapters.

Chapter 11

The Delphi Method

11.1 Introduction

The Delphi Method is aimed to "obtain the most reliable consensus of opinion of a group of experts through a series of intensive questionnaires interspersed with controlled opinion feedback" (Dalkey and Helmer, 1963, p. 458). The Delphi Process was developed by the Rand Corporation during the cold war to forecast the impact of technology on warfare. It is a systematic interactive forecasting method based on independent inputs of selected experts.

The key purpose for using the Delphi method remains the collection of informed judgment on issues that are largely unexplored, difficult to define, highly context and expertise specific, or future-oriented (Helmer, 1967; Ziglio, 1995). This indicates (Fletcher and Marchildon, 2014, p. 14) that the Delphi method is not only suited to quantitative and consensus-building research but can also be applied to qualitative, participatory research.

Dalkey and Helmer (1962) present a classic use of the Delphi method from the early stages of its development, thus showing the logic of the basic Delphi method. They present both the research question to be answered, the sample design of experts who are invited to answer the questions, and the steps of the data collection, using both questionnaires and interviews. Next, they present for each round the data collected, the analyses, and key statistics. Based on that, the research question is provided with an answer.

Grisham (2009, p. 125), concludes that "The Delphi technique is a qualitative survey technique that is well suited for the research of complex issues. It does not offer the rigor of clinical testing or quantitative analysis, but it provides a scientific methodology that is well suited to issues that require the insights of subject matter experts (SMEs)".

11.2 Definition and Use

Let us first review a number of *definitions* of the Delphi technique.

Delbecq *et al.* (1975, pp. 83–86) define the Delphi technique as "a group process which utilizes written responses". And: "It is a means for aggregating the judgments of a number of individuals in order to improve the quality of decision making". The authors continue and say the following: These individuals do not meet face to face, instead, a series of questionnaires are sent out in order to address a specific problem. The responses of the first questionnaire are summarised and fed back to these individuals, accompanied by a subsequent questionnaire. This process is repeated until the moment arrives that enough information has been collected or consensus is achieved. Upon finishing the data collection phase, final analyses are carried out on the data and solutions to the problem at hand are presented. The participants are often experts who are unable to meet physically. In principle, they remain anonymous during and after the process. This feature is viewed as a strength of the method as dominant or hostile participants have no means to exert unwanted influence on the process of data collection.

The technique has been used for forecasting purposes. However, it can easily be utilised to study complex social, societal, and global issues where certain forms of expertise of participants are needed in order to describe, understand, and explain issues and research problems. Often solutions to these problems may originate as well from this data collection approach.

Linstone and Turoff (1975, p. 3), broadly define the Delphi method as follows: "Delphi may be characterised as a method for structuring a group communication process so that the process is effective in allowing a group of individuals, as a whole, to deal with a complex problem". And they continue by saying that "to accomplish this structured communication there is provided:

- Some feedback of individual contributions of information and knowledge
- Some assessments of the group judgment or view
- Some opportunity of individuals to revise views
- Some degree of anonymity for the individual responses."

Generally, three parties are involved in the process: the client who is to receive the recommendations upon finishing the project, the researcher who is in charge of the projects and writes and analyses the series of questionnaires, and the respondents who fill out these questionnaires and thus provide information such as judgments and possible solutions to the problem at hand.

A number of *aspects*, or *characteristics* of the Delphi process are critical to the success of its implementation. Let us review these aspects now.

Linstone and Turoff (1975, p. 6), sum up a number of ways why a Delphi may fail:

- Not allowing for multiple perspectives as related to the problem at hand.
- Assuming that for every research problem regarding human communications Delphi is the best and only method.
- Applying poor techniques of summarising and presenting the group response while ensuring common interpretations.
- Ignoring and not exploring disagreements so that discouraged dissenters drop out and an artificial consensus is generated.
- Underestimating the demanding nature of Delphi and the fact that the respondents should be recognised and treated as professionals throughout the research process; and should be compensated for their time and effort.

Obviously, the above list may be turned around into positive actions which actually enhance the methodological quality of a Delphi study.

Linstone (1975, pp. 582–583) lists a number of threats to the sound execution of a Delphi study. In his words, a "sloppy execution" from the *perspective of the analyst* involves the following:

- Poor selection of participants in such a way that they all tend to agree on the topic to be studied as a group of like-thinking individuals.
- Poor interaction between participant and analyst where the participant is not treated seriously in his eyes; as a consequence, the participant may feel that he is not learning anything himself while he is educating the analyst for free.
- Formulating Delphi statements in a too vague or too specific way. As a consequence, the information produced by the respondents may be reduced.
- Superficial analysis of responses, thereby introducing false results. For instance, agreement among respondents may not be based on the same, underlying reasons.
- A basic lack of imagination by the designer where he fails to conceptualise different structures for examining the problem, and where he fails to perceive how different respondents may view the same problem differently.

Threats to the sound execution of a Delphi study may also arise from the *perspective of the participant*. This would involve lazy and impatient participants, providing quick and ill-considered answers to boring questions of a long and seemingly pointless questionnaire. Here, one could take the position that it is the analyst who is to be blamed if such things happen.

Obviously, again, the above list may be turned around into positive actions, which actually enhance the methodological quality of a Delphi study.

Finally, in order to use the Delphi technique successfully, there must be adequate time available to carry out the process, participants should be skilled in written communication, and have high motivation in order to remain committed to the data collection process.

The definition of the Delphi technique may also involve the use of *qualitative data processing software*. Thus, Fletcher and Marchildon (2014, p. 14) observe that *classic* Delphi studies engage in the quantitative analysis of questionnaire responses in order to arrive at a consensus among the experts who participate in a study. However, data processing methods used between rounds are qualitative by nature and this points to the possibility to process these qualitative interview data by using qualitative data processing software. In any case, Delphi researchers should be careful to provide a detailed description of the process occurring between the first and second rounds of Delphi, wherein data are often converted from open-ended to survey or questionnaire format.

Delphi may be used for various different *applications*. Hsu and Sandford (2007, p. 1) describe the following major application domains of the Delphi method:

- To determine or develop a range of possible programme alternatives;
- To explore or expose underlying assumptions or information leading to different judgments;
- To seek out information which may generate a consensus on the part of the respondent group;
- To correlate informed judgments on a topic spanning a wide range of disciplines;
- To educate the respondent group as to the diverse and interrelated aspects of the topic.

The last part of this section discusses *variations* of the Delphi technique. Fletcher and Marchildon (2014, p. 3) present a "classification of three main variants of Delphi:

(a) conventional Delphi, which follows the format of the original RAND study (i.e., an open-ended exploratory phase followed by multiple consensus-seeking rounds) and usually seeks to prioritize issues or find solutions
(b) "real-time" Delphi, in which multiple rounds are temporally compressed to occur within a single meeting

(c) policy Delphi, which creates a forum in which ideas are presented to decision-makers, who ultimately choose a solution from among a number of options."

A variation of the classic Delphi process has been developed by Bolognini (2001, Chapter 4.7). Here, for instance, two panels may be created that represent two different groups. While one panel is an expert panel, the other panel is composed of members who are no experts as such with respect to the topic under investigation, but are still able to provide answers to the questions posed. The results from this non-expert group may be shown to the expert panel, and the expert panel may be invited to respond to this information.

Linstone and Turoff (2002, p. 5) present two distinct forms of the Delphi process: The first form is the common paper-and-pencil version, which they call "Delphi Exercise", or conventional Delphi. The second form is a computer-controlled version which they call "Delphi Conference". Here, the computer has been programmed to "carry out the compilation of the group results". Obviously, "this latter approach has the advantage of eliminating the delay caused in summarizing each round of Delphi, thereby turning the process into a real-time communications system. However, it does require that the characteristics of the communication be well defined before Delphi is undertaken, whereas in a paper-and-pencil Delphi exercise the monitor team can adjust these characteristics as a function of the group responses". Thus, this feature provides more latitude when carrying out a Delphi process.

Finally, Gnatzy (2011) carried out an empirical comparison between a conventional Delphi survey with a real-time (internet-based) Delphi survey. In both approaches, the four main characteristics of the Delphi method were present (p. 1682): (1) anonymity in the process, (2) controlled feedback, (3) statistical aggregation of group response, and (4) iteration.

It was shown (p. 1692) that the internet-based, real-time Delphi works as effectively as the conventional, round-based Delphi method. The comparison analyses showed no significant differences between conventional and real-time Delphi survey methods. Therefore, the author argues "that the results of the real-time Delphi survey tool are as robust as the results generated by a conventional Delphi survey".

11.3 Advantages and Disadvantages

Let us first review a number of scientists who have pointed to the *advantages* of using the Delphi technique. Rotondi and Gustafson (in: Adler and Ziglio, 1996, pp. 41–42) describe a number of advantages of the Delphi method from the perspective of the participants, and they include the following:

- The method allows for assembling a group of high-quality experts because face to face group meetings need not be organised and the experts can provide their contributions to the process in the time and place of their choice.
- Participants have the opportunity to think through their ideas and have to write them down first before these are conveyed to the group; as a consequence, they have ample time and opportunity to think and rethink their responses.
- Participants have enough time to absorb and analyse the group responses before they are to send their own response.
- All of the responses are put on record and can be reviewed as needed.
- Because participants are anonymous in the context of the data collection process, they feel to be at liberty to voice provocative or unpopular new ideas as this cannot harm them in their formal, professional positions.
- There is a record of successful previous studies employing the Delphi method, which suggests that the current application of the Delphi method may be successful as well.

Also, Green *et al.* (2007, pp. 4–5) discuss the advantages of Delphi, now as compared to an alternative procedure called "prediction markets". Comparatively, they signal a number of advantages. We will present these advantages in more general terms here, as they have general relevance in this context:

- Delphi can be used for a broad range of problems since for many problems broad judgments may be acquired from the respondents.
- Delphi reveals opinions, which may be found more generally among the respondents;
- It is easy to address complex issues and to obtain predictions by asking direct questions of a Delphi panel.
- Delphi makes it easy to maintain confidentiality; therefore, sensitive issues may be addressed that are unaffected by power relationships within the group.
- A Delphi administrator can choose panellists who are likely to reveal their true beliefs; as a consequence, the outcomes of the Delphi process may adhere to higher quality standards.
- The opportunity to provide comments or reasons for judgments allows Delphi participants to introduce new ideas into the discussion. And the transparent exchange of knowledge allows experts to learn while participating in the Delphi process.
- The transparent exchange of knowledge reveals information that has already been taken into account. This makes the Delphi process more efficient.
- Delphi requires only 5 to 20 experts who have agreed to participate, which makes it practical and easy to set up and carry out a Delphi process.

The authors end with the following statement: "In sum, we believe that Delphi should be much more widely used than it is today. It should replace many traditional meetings."

Goodman (1987, p. 733) concludes that "the Delphi technique as a research method seems to have much to offer as a means of structuring a group's communication and decision-making processes. It is a survey approach which would be very useful for initiating discussion on a particular issue"... "the Delphi technique is an alternative to the committee process or one-off questionnaire although its ability to produce a convergence and consensus of opinion on a given topic should be viewed with caution".

Negative evaluations of the Delphi techniques have been uttered as well. In contrast with the above, Woudenberg (1991, pp. 145–146) finds no evidence that the quantitative form of Delphi is able to "remove the negative effects of unstructured, direct interaction". He reports that no evidence was found to support the view that Delphi is more accurate than other judgment methods or that consensus in a Delphi is achieved by dissemination of information to all participants. When a slight increase in accuracy of rounds is found (as based on a quantitative analysis) the author poses that this can be ascribed partly to mere repetition of judgment (which gives room to reconsider earlier responses), and to the effects of group pressure to conformity.

Sackman (1974), based on a comparison between the *Delphi methodology* and, among other things, the *questionnaire instrument*, i.e., questionnaire design, administration, application, and validation, concludes (p. 70): "The evidence adduced in this study clearly indicates that the massive liabilities of Delphi, in principle and in practice, outweigh its highly doubtful assets". Of course, the question remains whether this type of comparison can be made in a valid way. That is: are the data collection approaches of Delphi and questionnaire instrument comparable? Or do they belong to different methodological domains because they have arisen out of different/incomparable research paradigms? A study carried out by Rowe and Wright (1999, p. 372) shows on the other hand that, in general, accuracy tends to increase over Delphi rounds, and hence tends to be greater than in comparative staticised groups, while Delphi panels also tend to be more accurate than unstructured interacting groups. But also: "The technique has shown no clear advantages over other structured procedures".

Powell (2003, p. 381) adds to this: "In conclusion, the findings of a Delphi represent expert opinion, rather than indisputable fact. Goodness criteria rest on the justification of detailed decision-making and rigour in the execution of the study. Further inquiry to validate the findings may be important."

Hsu and Sandford (2007, pp. 4–5) point to possible short-comings and weaknesses when they indicate that *response rates* may be low as the respondents have to deal with a *lengthy process* and are asked to carry out *a lot of work*. As a consequence, participation is time-consuming. Furthermore, the procedure allows for potential *moulding opinions* as based on the feedback received, or on "subtle pressure to conform with group ratings". Finally, because the participants may differ with respect to relevant knowledge and experience regarding the topic studied, mostly *general statements* may be identified, while statements based on in-depth knowledge may fail to be handled adequately by those participants lacking the level of knowledge and experience as required for this task.

All in all, it seems that, in order to gain advantage of the Delphi technique, the researcher needs to spend due time on all of the features and characteristics of the Delphi technique in order to carry out a methodologically sound, effective, and successful Delphi study.

11.4 Best Practices

In this section, we will present a number of *procedural approaches* to the Delphi technique. Also, alternative approaches, or *variations* of Delphi will be discussed.

The procedure to carry out a Delphi project may be summarised in the following steps (Delbecq *et al.* 1975, pp. 86–106):

- **Develop the Delphi question:** The initial, broad question to be addressed.
- **Select and contact respondents:** They should be knowledgeable and motivated.
- **Select the sample size:** 10–15 participants are often enough, while the sample size normally should not exceed 30 participants.
- **Develop questionnaire number 1 and test:** This questionnaire allows participants to write responses to a broad problem issue.

- **Analysis of questionnaire number 1:** This should result in a summary list of items identified and comments made;
- **Develop questionnaire number 2 and test:** The items in this questionnaire should be based on and connected to the answers of the participants of the first questionnaire;
- The previous step may be repeated as necessary; normally three questionnaires are produced and processed.
- In the final phase of the projects, resulting themes and possible solutions may be forwarded and participants may be asked to cast votes on these solutions.
- **Prepare a final report:** Summaries regarding goals, process, and results are provided where results pertain to the knowledge gained in the process; finally, ensuing actions or decisions may be presented and explained.

Rowe and Wright (2001) provide a succinct and practical overview of the steps to take in order to carry out a Delphi process. These steps are comparable to those of Delbecq *et al.* (1975), but also slightly different:

- Use experts with appropriate domain knowledge;
- Use heterogeneous experts;
- Use between 5 and 20 experts;
- For Delphi feedback, provide the mean or median estimate of the panel plus the rationales from all panellists for their estimates;
- Continue Delphi polling until the responses show stability; generally, three structured rounds are enough;
- Obtain the final forecast by weighting all the experts' estimates equally and aggregating them;
- In phrasing questions, use clear and succinct definitions and avoid emotive terms;
- Frame questions in a balanced manner;
- Avoid incorporating irrelevant information into questions;
- When possible, give estimates of uncertainty as frequencies rather than probabilities or odds;
- Use coherence checks when eliciting estimates of probabilities.

In conclusion, we will present the way Hsu and Sandford (2007, pp. 2–4) describe the preparation and execution of the consecutive steps of the Delphi process as a data collection technique:

- **The Delphi process:**
  - ○ **Round 1:** An open-ended questionnaire is presented to the participants; the information thus collected is converted into a well-structured questionnaire.
  - ○ **Round 2:** This questionnaire is presented to the participants, and they are invited to rate or rank order the items of the questionnaire; sometimes the participants are asked to provide an explanation concerning their rates or rank orders.
  - ○ **Round 3:** A questionnaire is presented to the participants that includes the items and ratings as summarised from the second round by the researchers; the participants are invited to revise their judgments when deemed necessary and provide further clarifications when they deviate from the consensus.
  - ○ **Round 4:** "The list of remaining items, their ratings, minority opinions, and items achieving consensus" are distributed among the participants. They are now given a final opportunity to change their minds regarding their ratings of the various topics.
- **Subject selection:** Individuals to invite for participation in the Delphi process must be experts in the domain of the issue under study, they should have somewhat related backgrounds and experiences concerning the issue. Furthermore, they are "capable of contributing to helpful input". Finally, when necessary, they are "willing to revise their initial or previous judgments for the purpose of reaching or attaining consensus". It is suggested that a number of 10–15 or 15–20 respondents is often sufficient.
- **Time requirements:** A minimum of 45 days for the administration of a Delphi study is necessary, while the respondents should be given a period of two weeks to respond.
- **Data analysis:** "Decision rules must be established to assemble and organize the judgments and insights provided by Delphi

subjects". Criteria for establishing consensus on a topic could be an outcome where "a certain percentage of the votes falls within a prescribed range" (see Duffield, 1993, p. 236, for a successful example). Alternatively, one could define consensus to be achieved when "80% of subjects' votes fall within two [adjacent] categories on a seven-point scale". Or, one could define consensus when "at least 70% of the Delphi participants need to score 3 or higher on a four-point Likert-type scale and the median has to be at least 3.25 or higher". Finally, one could "measure the stability of subjects' responses in successive iterations" in order to establish consensus.

Alternatively, Rotondi and Gustafson (in: Adler and Ziglio, 1996, pp. 34–55) provide what they call a "toolbox" of elements and procedures which may be incorporated into the general Delphi technique. The choice is based on (p. 35) "the purposes and needs of a particular Delphi exercise". This toolbox is filled with the following elements:

- **Developing a synergistic or group perspective:** It may be desirable to develop such a perspective in order to enhance the group members' insight and creativity, thus producing more and better results. This is accomplished by facilitating an in-depth conversation among the participants.
- **Promoting mutual understanding in a group:** In order to promote the group perspective as described in the previous entry, a process of enhancing mutual understanding in the group, two procedures may be considered: team building and reduced participant anonymity.
- **The motivation to participate:** Motivation levels of the participants may be increased by fostering a "tension to change" (the current situation is dissatisfactory, and the Delphi process must remedy this). Also, levels of motivation will rise when the participant feels that he needs the help of the group to solve the problem. Next, participants need to feel that this is the moment and the opportunity that the group can solve the problem, it is

the right time for this group to do so. Another motivating factor is the consideration of the participant that this is an opportunity for personal and professional growth. As is the notion that the group, and its members, will gain respect both from group insiders and group outsiders and that participation in the process will foster their reputation as far as these parties are concerned. Finally, the participants should feel confident that they are capable of carrying out the tasks required.

When comparing the procedural approaches to the Delphi technique one may observe that on the one hand its basic steps and characteristics are highly comparable, while on the other hand slight variations and focal points may differ to some degree.

In terms of *variations of the Delphi technique*, Rotondi and Gustafson (in: Adler and Ziglio, 1996, pp. 42–53) propose an *extension of the basic approach of the Delphi technique*. They make the suggestion (p. 42) of "developing a straw model to unify perspectives". A straw model is a conceptual model of a group's task. It may be constructed by first providing the participants with a common background of the issue or the problem. Next, the participants are asked how to deal with the issue or the problem. Based on the answers to this question the straw model is constructed by the researcher, or research group. Now, it is evident to the participants which positions are taken by fellow-group members, and the angles they choose *vis-à-vis* the problem at hand.

The straw model may contain areas which are incomplete, and may contain inaccurate assertions and important omissions. As such, however the straw model provides a unified group perspective which may serve as a common starting point for the group members.

The resulting straw model may take, for example, the form of a flow diagram or a decision tree and serves as the starting point of the Delphi process.

It is allowed, or even encouraged to start side-conversations between two group members apart from the general process of information exchange. The outcomes of these side-conversations could go through a facilitator and thus ultimately find their way to the main information process involving all of the group members again.

At any one time in the process, current outcomes may be fed back to the group members. The outcomes may be restructured in one of the two ways. Different ideas on the same topic may be presented as such, or similar positions regarding the topic may be combined into a single summary idea. Alternatively, the so-called conversation histories may be assembled and made available for all of the group members. A conversation history is a full and complete record of all that has been said so far in the process regarding an issue. Making this available to the group may promote group synergy, and this may result in better and higher quality group responses and decisions.

Finally, the aforementioned facilitator may at will communicate with individual group members at any stage of the process in order to enhance their continued participation. Here, the aim is to strengthen and maintain continued interest of the participants in the topics studied. The ultimate goal is to keep the group members sufficiently motivated to continue to participate actively in the process up to its conclusion.

This concludes our review of best practices of the Delphi method. Upon reading this chapter the reader may come to the conclusion that this method of data collection pairs multiple interpretations as to the way Delphi may be set up and carried out with a rich array of applications and a high potential for obtaining results that have both academic and practical value.

11.5 Sample Study

In order to demonstrate how the Delphi method is applied in its classic form, an overview of the study by Dana and Wright (2009) is provided, and the excellent application of the Delphi method in this study is highlighted.

11.5.1 *Issue and relevance*

The global business environment is changing dramatically. Traditionally, competition in international markets was the realm of large companies, while smaller businesses remained local or regional in scope. But nowadays, because of technological advances among other things, even the smallest firms are able to access customers, suppliers, and collaborators around the world.

One consequence of the aforementioned changes is the emergence of a new academic discipline — *International Entrepreneurship* (IE). The emergence of IE as an identifiable academic field positioned at the intersection of the international business and entrepreneurship disciplines raises the question: which current research priorities should be chosen and given time and attention? Specifically, the issue is addressed of how this new academic discipline should develop itself by carrying out theoretical and applied research on topics that are relevant for both business and society, and by finding and defining a unique position *vis-à-vis* adjacent, already mature, academic fields.

11.5.2 *Research goal*

The purpose of this study is to conduct an assessment of the development and current state of research in the evolution of IE; and specifically, to ask: What are the critical questions on which we should be focusing our research in the years ahead?

11.5.3 *Research design*

A Delphi Process was used, a procedure designed to synthesise diverse perspectives towards a consensus on research priorities; followed by a plenary session to assess the results of the Delphi process and to further refine and operationalise the emerging set of priority research proposals.

11.5.4 *Sample design*

A panel of recognised experts from the fields of entrepreneurship, international business, and IE was formed. More specifically, a panel of 23 experts representing the Americas, Asia, Europe, and Australia-Oceania was created.

11.5.5 *Data collection*

Data were collected using the Delphi method. As a first step, a question was asked to identify (and elaborate upon) up to five questions or five challenges in IE that participants felt are most in need of research. Next, each of the panellists was sent the full set of responses from Round 1, without identification of the authors. Panellists were then instructed as follows: "We would ask each of you to reconsider your own ideas about research priorities, which you submitted earlier, in the light of any further thoughts or insights you have gained from the submissions of the other panellists".

11.5.6 *Data analysis*

Content analysis was used to group the responses into categories.

11.5.7 *Report*

A text report describing a foreseeable shift from the stand-alone entrepreneur to increased networking and cooperation, resulting in an internationalisation that involves a multipolar distribution of control. Suggestions from the participants involved researching partners, alliances, networks, and cooperation; no other focus received more interest.

11.5.8 *Excellent Delphi characteristics of the study*

For a Delphi study to be excellent a number of conditions have to be met. These include the following: (1) The research problem has to be clear and relevant. (2) The research design must be functional for the research purpose. (3) Data collection must be to the point and exhaustive. (4) Data analysis in-between the rounds of the data collection process must be adequate.

All of this is the case in this study.

This is a classic Delphi study. The research objective was clearly formulated, as based on extensive literature. The composition of the sample involved purposefully chosen experts from the fields of entrepreneurship, international business, and IE with clearly defined, relevant expertise for the task to be carried out.

When executing the Delphi data collection process, the researchers adhered, in a well-behaved manner, to the four main characteristics of the Delphi method: *anonymity in the process, controlled feedback* as based on a step-wise execution of the data collection process, a form of *aggregation of group responses*, and finally, allowing for *group consensus* while obtaining and synthesising the opinions of the experts. These four characteristics are elaborated as follows:

1. *Anonymity* in the process was secured: "At this stage (first step) we did not let participants know who else was participating, in order to minimize socially-desirable responding".
2. *Controlled feedback* was accomplished by following a procedure where each of the panellists was sent the full set of responses from Round 1, and correspondence was done electronically via e-mail.
3. *Aggregation of group responses* was accomplished by carrying out content analysis to group the responses into categories.
4. *Consensus* was allowed, but not forced upon the panellists. As the authors explain "The objective of Round 2 was to gain more focus". And the instruction to the panellists was: "We would ask each of you to reconsider your own ideas about research priorities, which you submitted earlier, in the light of any further thoughts or insights you have gained from the submissions of the other panelists".

In conclusion, and as a bonus to the research process, Round 2 was followed up by a baseline workshop, to further refine and operationalise the emerging set of priority research proposals. Discussion was tape-recorded and transcribed.

The report provides a full account of the methodology used and provides detailed outcomes in the main text, and in three elaborate appendices.

Thus, although a flawless execution of the Delphi method provides no guarantees regarding the usefulness of its outcomes, it may not come as a surprise that this study yielded many useful ideas, suggestions, and research proposals.

Chapter 12

Document Analysis

12.1 Introduction

Where documents exist, document collection and analysis can be a very effective qualitative research method; this includes unpublished and published documents. This method is seldom used in isolation. Dana and Galbraith (2006) produced a review of empirical research that resulted in a holistic understanding of poverty, developing entrepreneurship, and aid economics in Mozambique. Dana, Manitok, and Anderson (2010) was based on documents spanning 185 years. A specific form of document analysis is content analysis (Kassarjian, 1977), focusing on a specific configuration of characteristics (statements, beliefs, values) in documents, annual reports, or web sites, as relevant for a study at hand. Cartoons and television advertisements lend themselves well to content analysis. Kassarjian (1977) explained objectivity, systematisation and quantification in content analysis. It is all about the system of categories that the researcher/analyst, creates; this is the challenge. Krippendorff (1980) provided a user-friendly introduction to content analysis. Among the countless studies that successfully used content analysis are Bristor, Lee, and Hunt (1995) and Taylor and Stern (1997). Ahuvia (2001) noted a rise in the use of content analysis and argued that content analysis should be used as a method for counting interpretations of content and seeks to explain why replicability may be a better term for objectivity. Neuendorf summarised content analysis as the "systematic, objective, quantitative analysis of message characteristics" (2002, p. 1).

In this chapter, we will primarily discuss document analysis and thematic analysis as methods of data collection. This is followed by a short introduction to netnography. (See also Chapter 4, Section 4.2, page 70.) A brief and basic positioning of these methods would involve the following:

Document analysis is aimed at a broad and thorough review of all kinds of documents, involving both its examination, reading, evaluation, and interpretation in an empirical research setting.

Thematic analysis is directly aimed at finding patterns and themes in the documents.

Finally, *netnography* is a form of document analysis, however now aimed at a broad review of documents, which are found online.

Let us now turn to more thorough definitions and uses of these research methods.

12.2 Definitions and Use

Document analysis is a method of qualitative research in which documents are reviewed. O'Leary (2014, p. 250) defines document analysis as it refers to the collection, review, "interrogation", and analysis of various forms of written text as a primary source of research data. Bowen (2009, p. 38) says: "Document analysis is a low-cost way to obtain empirical data as part of a process that is unobtrusive and nonreactive. Often, documentary evidence is combined with data from interviews and observation to minimise bias and establish credibility". Obviously, these definitions stress that document analysis is a research approach of its own.

Document analysis may, however, also be defined by means of a defining characteristic. Thus, document analysis is often used in combination with other qualitative research methods as a means of triangulation, that is "the combination of methodologies in the study of the same phenomenon" (Denzin, 1970, p. 291). Bowen (2009) confirms this when he says that document analysis is an invaluable part of most schemes of triangulation.

Finally, Bowen (2009, p. 27) takes a broader perspective which also includes online materials. He defines document analysis as a "systematic procedure for reviewing or evaluating documents — both printed and electronic (computer-based and Internet-transmitted) material. Like other analytical methods in qualitative research, document analysis requires that data be examined and interpreted in order to elicit meaning, gain understanding, and develop empirical knowledge".

12.2.1 *Definition of thematic analysis*

We will use the highly informative Braun and Clarke (2006) article to define thematic analysis.

Braun and Clarke (2006, p. 6) provide the following definition: "Thematic analysis is a method for identifying, analysing, and reporting patterns (themes) within data. It minimally organises and describes your data set in (rich) detail. However, it also often goes further than this, and interprets various aspects of the research topic". They continue and explain (p. 8): "Thematic analysis differs from other analytic methods that seek to describe patterns across qualitative data — such as 'thematic' discourse analysis, thematic decomposition analysis, IPA [interpretative phe-nomenological analysis] and grounded theory". While elaborating the defining properties of the method they pose (p. 9) that "Thematic analysis can be an essentialist or realist method, which reports experiences, meanings and the reality of participants, or it can be a constructionist method, which examines the ways in which events, realities, meanings, experiences and so on are the effects of a range of discourses operating within society. It can also be a 'contextualist' method, sitting between the two poles of essen-tialism and constructionism".

The authors conclude by emphasising (p. 9): "However, it is important that the theoretical position of a thematic analysis is made clear, as this is all too often left unspoken (and is then typically a realist account). Any theoretical framework carries with it a num-ber of assumptions about the nature of the data, what they represent in terms of the 'the world', 'reality' and so forth. A good thematic analysis will make this transparent".

12.2.2 *Types of documents*

As the documents to be analysed are the essentially same for both document analysis and thematic analysis, we will present types and categorisations of documents for both data collection methods below.

Three essential **types of documents** can be classified as follows (O'Leary, 2014):

1. Public records (e.g., newspapers, statements of purpose, annual reports, strategy manuals, handbooks, etc.);
2. Personal records (e.g., reflections/diaries, Facebook posts, etc.);
3. Physical Evidence (e.g., posters, agendas, etc.); These include published as well as unpublished documents.

Webb *et al.* (2000, p. 90) define three "sources of unobtrusive measures" that are relevant for document analysis. They indicate that "all three are potential substitutes for direct observation of behaviour". These three sources include the following:

1. **Sales records:** An example given (pp. 91–92) is a study about passenger anxiety as produced by air crashes. In order to find out the onset, the duration, and the level of anxiety, the volume of air passengers (ticket sales), and the number and dollar value of trip insurance policies (insurance sales) were analysed while applying various correction factors. Another example is studying the construction of networks within a company by tracing back and analysing the names of previous senders on the company envelope that is to be used multiple times before ultimately destroying this envelope.
2. **Institutional records:** Within institutions and companies (pp. 99–100), "amount and quality of output [regarding individual employees and departments] are probably the most frequently used behavioural measures".

3. **Personal documents:** Classic examples are (p. 105) a study of Polish peasants sending letters between Poland and the United States and (pp. 106–107) "letters and diaries captured from German soldiers", "studying the impact of propaganda on these troops".

Bowen (2009, pp. 27–28) provides a rather complete overview of the types of documents that may be subjected to document analysis. He says: "Documents that may be used for systematic evaluation as part of a study take a variety of forms. They include advertisements; agendas, attendance registers, and minutes of meetings; manuals; background papers; books and brochures; diaries and journals; event programs (i.e., printed outlines); letters and memoranda; maps and charts; newspapers (clippings/articles); press releases; program proposals, application forms, and summaries; radio and television program scripts; organisational or institutional reports; survey data; and various public records. Scrapbooks and photo albums can also furnish documentary material for research purposes. These types of documents are found in libraries, newspaper archives, historical society offices, and organisational or institutional files".

On the other hand, O'Leary (2014, pp. 245–246) focuses on *types of text*. He lists the following types of texts that may be scrutinised:

- Official data and records — international and national data, local government data, archival data, legislation, and policy documents.
- Organisational communication, documents, and records — websites, press releases, meeting agenda and minutes, memos, human resource records, client records.
- Personal communication, documents, and records — letters and e-mails, diaries, poetry, medical records, household records (cheque-book stubs), mobile phone texts.
- The media/contemporary entertainment — websites, newspapers, commercials, biographies, and autobiographies.

- The arts — paintings, drawings, photography, music, plays, and films.
- Social artefacts — any products of social beings.

The author provides an illustrative example in this context: a researcher could use all of these documents when he wishes to determine the level of civilisation and cultivation of a country by studying the ways this country deals with mentally or physically disabled individuals.

Finally, Bowen (2003) provides *examples* of document types and data analysed. Examples of the documents selected and the data analysed are given in the table below. The second column either indicates the study's research question or points to statistics relevant to the study. The Human Development Report (UNDP, 2003), for instance, contains the Human Development Index, a measure of standard of living and quality of life, which was used for cross-national comparisons between Jamaica and other Caribbean countries.

Documents selected	Data analysed
Community Participation in Projects Funded by the Jamaica Social Investment Fund: "Making Your Project More Participatory" (JSIF, n.d.)	Importance of equitable citizen participation in decision-making processes
Millennium Development Goals: A Compact among Nations to End Human Poverty — *Human Development Report* 2003 (UNDP, 2003)	Human Development Index and related data
Jamaica Social Investment Fund's Annual Report 2002–2003 (JSIF, 2003)	List of approved subprojects

(*Continued*)

(*Continued*)

Documents selected	Data analysed
Jamaica's *Survey of Living Conditions* [STATINJA/PIOJ, 1998)	Relationship between poverty and sanitary facilities, specifically the use of latrines
Letter from a High School Guidance Counsellor to the Assistant Youth Coordinator at a local Mediation Center (11 April 2003)	Data on Peer Mediation Program in schools, a JSIF-financed subproject
A Review of Children's Homes and Places of Safety (Ministry of Health, May 2003)	Contextual data for the research on a girls home (a refuge for young, female wards of the state), which was supported by the Social Fund
Update on the National Poverty Eradication Programme 2001–2002 (JSIF, n.d.)	Data on Jamaica's Social Fund as an anti-poverty strategy
"A Week that was Strong" (*The Gleaner*, 4 December 1999)	Role of the St. Elizabeth Homecoming Foundation, a local subproject sponsor, which organised Homecoming Week activities
World Development Report 2003: Sustainable Development in a Dynamic Economy (The World Bank, 2003)	Demographic and economic statistics

This ends our overview of types of documents that may be scrutinised in the context of document analysis and thematic analysis. We will now proceed to the various ways these research approaches may be used in general research practice.

12.2.3 *Use of document analysis and thematic analysis*

In the following, both the uses of document analysis and thematic analysis will be discussed, and in that order.

12.2.3.1 *The use of document analysis*

Earlier, we pointed to one of the defining characteristics of document analysis: Bowen (2009, p. 28) pointed out that "Document analysis is often used in combination with other qualitative research methods as a means of triangulation. Therefore, the qualitative researcher is expected to draw upon multiple (at least two) sources of evidence; that is, to seek convergence and corroboration through the use of different data sources and methods. Apart from documents, such sources include interviews, participant or non-participant observation, and physical artifacts". Referring to its uses, he continues with (p. 29): "As a research method, document analysis is particularly applicable to qualitative case studies — intensive studies producing rich descriptions of a single phenomenon, event, organisation, or program. Non-technical literature, such as reports and internal correspondence, is a potential source of empirical data for case studies; for example, data on the context within which the participant operates". Furthermore (p. 118), "Documents of all types can help the researcher uncover meaning, develop understanding, and discover insights relevant to the research problem".

Bowen (2009, p. 29) furthermore notes that "It is important to note here that qualitative research requires robust data collection techniques and the documentation of the research procedure. Detailed information about how the study was designed and conducted should be provided in the research report". He ends his exposition by saying (p. 29): "Whereas document analysis has served mostly as a complement to other research methods, it has also been used as a stand-alone method".

Documents may be used in different manners. That is, documents can serve a variety of purposes as part of a research undertaking. Bower (2009, pp. 29–30) specifies five specific functions of documentary material. These will be considered in what follows.

1. As indicated earlier, documents can provide data on the context within which research participants operate — a case of text providing context, if one might turn a phrase. Bearing witness to

past events, documents provide background information as well as historical insight. Such information and insight can help researchers understand the historical roots of specific issues and can indicate the conditions that impinge upon the phenomena currently under investigation. The researcher can use data drawn from documents, for example, to contextualise data collected during interviews.

2. Information contained in documents can suggest some questions that need to be asked and situations that need to be observed as part of the research. For example, Bower cites a study where document analysis may be carried out to help generate new interview questions as they conducted a longitudinal ethnographic study of service use among families living in poor urban communities. This research demonstrates how one method can complement another in an interactive way. That is, "interview data helped focus specific participant observation activities, document analysis helped generate new interview questions, and participant observation at community events provided opportunities to collect documents".

3. Documents provide supplementary research data. Information and insights derived from documents can be valuable additions to a knowledge base. Researchers should therefore browse library catalogues and archives for documents to be analysed as part of the research process. In order to illustrate this, Bower cites a number of studies. In one study of closure of technology teacher education programmes, a university-based scholar used newspaper reports, university policy documents, and department self-evaluation data to supplement data gained through interviews. Similarly, Bowen cites a study where journal entries and memos written by participants were analysed, as a supplement to interview data, in a study of technology teachers in training. In a final example, the researchers separately employed document analysis in their investigations of the social milieu within organisations. They used document analysis to supplement data from other sources, such as semi-structured interviews and observation, as they developed a number of case studies.

4. Documents provide a means of tracking change and development. Where various drafts of a particular document are accessible, the researcher can compare them to identify the changes. Even subtle changes in a draft can reflect substantive developments in a project, for example. The researcher may also examine periodic and final reports (where available) to get a clear picture of how an organisation or a programme fared over time.

5. Documents can be analysed as a way to verify findings or corroborate evidence from other sources. Sociologists, in particular, typically use document analysis to verify their findings. If the documentary evidence is contradictory rather than corroboratory, the researcher is expected to investigate further. When there is convergence of information from different sources, readers of the research report usually have greater confidence in the trustworthiness (credibility) of the findings.

This concludes our overview of the use of document analysis. We will proceed with the use of thematic analysis.

12.2.3.2 *The use of thematic analysis*

The specific uses of thematic analysis are guided by a number of decisions. We will give the floor to Braun and Clarke (2006, p. 9–14) to elucidate on these decisions, or choices the researcher has to make. Specifically, five choices will be presented:

1. What counts as a theme?
A theme captures something important about the data in relation to the research question and represents some level of *patterned* response or meaning within the data set. An important question to address in terms of coding is what counts as a pattern/theme, or what "size" does a theme need to be? This is a question of prevalence both in terms of space within each data item, and prevalence across the entire data set.

2. A rich description of the data set, or a detailed account of one particular aspect

It is important to determine the type of analysis you want to do, and the claims you want to make, in relation to your data set. For instance, you might wish to provide a rich thematic description of your entire data set, so that the reader gets a sense of them pre-dominant or important themes.

An *alternative use* of thematic analysis is to provide a more detailed and nuanced account of one particular theme, or group of themes, within the data. This might relate to a specific question or area of interest within the data, or to a particular "latent" theme across the whole or majority of the data set.

3. Inductive versus theoretical thematic analysis

Themes or patterns within data can be identified in one of two pri-mary ways in thematic analysis: in an inductive or "bottom-up" way, or in a theoretical or deductive or "top-down" way.

Inductive analysis is therefore a process of coding the data *without* trying to fit it into a pre-existing coding frame, or the researcher's analytic preconceptions.

In contrast, a "theoretical" thematic analysis would tend to be driven by the researcher's theoretical or analytic interest in the area and is thus more explicitly analyst-driven.

4. Semantic or latent themes

Another decision revolves around the "level" at which themes are to be identified: at a semantic or explicit level, or at a latent or inter-pretative level. A thematic analysis typically focuses exclusively or primarily on one level. With a semantic approach, the themes are identified within the explicit or surface meanings of the data and the analyst is not looking for anything *beyond* what a participant has said or what has been written.

In contrast, a thematic analysis at the latent level goes beyond the semantic content of the data, and starts to identify or examine the *underlying* ideas, assumptions, and conceptualisations — and ideologies — that are theorised as shaping or informing the semantic content of the data.

5. Epistemology: essentialist/realist versus constructionist thematic analysis

As has been argued, thematic analysis can be conducted within both realist/essentialist and constructionist paradigms.

With an essentialist/realist approach, you can theorise motivations, experience, and meaning in a straightforward way, because a simple, largely unidirectional relationship is assumed between meaning and experience and language.

In contrast, from a constructionist perspective, meaning and experience are socially produced and reproduced, rather than inhering within individuals. It seeks to theorise the socio-cultural contexts, and structural conditions, that enable the individual accounts that are provided.

We will end this paragraph by pointing to a broadening of the document analysis approach as we have discussed previously. Figueroa (2008, p. 2) presents the so-called AVO-approach: "Audio-Visual data as an Object of analysis". Here, audio-visual "texts" are treated as an object of analysis. This could include a collection of narratives such as conversations, interviews, other sounds, and visuals. What is unique about the AVO-approach is that the audio-visual data consists of the narratives of multiple stakeholders. For instance, stakeholders related to the phenomenon of disasters (e.g., survivors, offender of violence, local and political leaders, etc.). Also, the use of camera work may help here to understand the nuances of verbal and non-verbal communication as well as the living conditions of the survivors.

A general description of the AVO-approach would involve the following:

(a) **Explication of researchers' standpoint and interpretive framework:** AVO closely follows the basic tenets of new paradigms of qualitative research because it asks for an explication by the researcher about one's position and interpretive frameworks used for the purpose of analysis besides emphasising the socio-historical context in which the audio-visual material was generated.

(b) **Considering audio-visual material as a "whole" for initial analysis of data:** AVO entails a close study of the whole audio-visual material by watching its contents several times to understand the context in which the events are embedded, the perspective of the filmmaker and the broad themes or "macro propositions" that emerge from the initial repeated viewing of the whole story.

(c) **Use of grounded theory procedures for the purpose of data analysis:** The macro propositions are further developed or refined with the help of the coding procedures (initial, focused, and axial coding) as prescribed in the grounded theory methodology.

This ends the description of the AVO-approach. We will now turn to the advantages and disadvantages of document analysis and thematic analysis.

12.3 Advantages and Disadvantages

In this section, the advantages/disadvantages of both document analysis and thematic analysis will be presented in succession.

- **Advantages of document analysis**
Bowen (2009, pp. 31–32) lists the following advantages of document analysis:

  o Documents are a very accessible and reliable source of data (in most cases!).
  o Documents are manageable and practical resources (they don't become offended and run away).
  o Documents contain background information and "don't forget".
  o More cost efficient and time consuming than ethnography.

o Document analysis can be used in many different fields of research, either as primary method of data collection or as a complement to other methods.

o Documents contain text (words) and images that have been recorded without a researcher's intervention. Therefore, no biases exist in this respect.

According to Patton (1990), triangulation helps to defend against the accusation that a study's findings are simply an artefact of a single method, a single source, or a single investigator's bias.

- **Disadvantages of document analysis**
Bowen (2009, p. 31–32) also lists the following disadvantages of document analysis:

o Not all documents can be assumed as good resources for research, as they may be incomplete, or their data may be inaccurate or inconsistent.

o Some documents may not be available or easily accessible (e.g., sensitive or touchy topics, as politics).

o There is a potential presence of biases, both in a document and from the researcher (Bowen, 2009; O'Leary, 2014).

When using documents, bias cannot occur as a consequence of a researcher's intervention, as already signalled above. In this context, Webb *et al.* (2000, p. 12) elaborate on this feature when they point to the fact that biases regarding the "reactive measurement effect" cannot occur with respect to this kind of data, which is an advantage over, for instance, interview data. For when a subject is being interviewed, he will be aware of this artificial situation and this may introduce unwanted mental and behavioural responses.

We end with Bower (2009, p. 29), who summarises the *profound value* of document analysis when he states: "The rationale for document analysis lies in its role in methodological and data triangulation, the immense value of documents in case study research, and its usefulness as a stand-alone method for specialised forms of qualitative research. Understandably, documents may be the only necessary data source for studies designed within an interpretive paradigm, as in hermeneutic inquiry; or it may simply be the only viable source, as in historical and cross-cultural research. In other types of research, the investigator should guard against over-reliance on documents".

We will now continue with an overview of the advantages of thematic analysis. As concerns the disadvantages, we refer to the list presented above that relates to document analysis.

- **Advantages of Thematic Analysis**

Braun and Clarke (2006, p. 37) provide a list of advantages of thematic analysis. These include the following features:

- o Flexibility;
- o Relatively easy and quick method to learn and do;
- o Accessible to researchers with little or no experience of qualitative research;
- o Results are generally accessible to educated general public;
- o Useful method for working within participatory research paradigm, with participants as collaborators;
- o Can usefully summarise key features of a large body of data, and/or offer a "thick description" of the data set;
- o Can highlight similarities *and* differences across the data set;
- o Can generate unanticipated insights;
- o Allows for social as well as psychological interpretations of data;
- o Can be useful for producing qualitative analyses suited to informing policy development.

In addition, Braun and Clarke (2006, p. 36), in their excellent nuts-and-bolts article, provide a 15-point checklist of criteria for "good" thematic analysis.

This concludes our overview of pluses and minuses of the research approaches as discussed in this chapter. In the following, best practices of document analysis, and thematic analysis, will be reported, again in that order.

12.4 Best Practices

We will start with the *process* of carrying out document analysis. O'Leary (2014) provides the following, consecutive steps:

(1) Create a list of texts to explore (e.g., population, samples, respondents, participants).
(2) Consider how texts will be accessed with attention to linguistic or cultural barriers.
(3) Acknowledge and address biases.
(4) Develop appropriate skills for research.
(5) Consider strategies for ensuring credibility.
(6) Know the data one is searching for.
(7) Consider ethical issues (e.g., confidential documents).
(8) Have a backup plan.

Furthermore, a number of *checks* on the documents should be carried out:

- When are the documents made?
- Where are the documents made?
- By whom are the documents made?
- Who are the intended receivers of the documents?

Bowen (2009) adds to this:

- Quality comes before quantity of the papers (e.g., duplicates in public media).
- Researchers must evaluate the original purpose of the document, such as the target audience.
- Was the author witnessing the events first-hand or second-hand?

Finally, a number of quality control criteria must be applied and these criteria refer to the following issues:

1. **Authenticity**
   - Does the document make sense, or has it obvious errors?
   - Are there internal inconsistencies in terms of style, or content?

- Are there different versions of the same document?
- Is the version available derived from a dubious, suspicious or unreliable secondary source?
- Has the document been in the hands of a person with vested interest in a particular reading of the text?

2. **Credibility**
   - Is the evidence free from error and distortion?

3. **Representativeness**
   - The evidence of the paper has to be typical for its kind (e.g., articles about manufacturing cars should be found in engineering journals, rather than in social sciences).

4. **Meaning**
   - The evidence of the paper has to be clear and comprehensible (e.g., date, journal, author);
   - Exploring background information is crucial — e.g., tone, style, purpose — (O'Leary, 2014);
   - Asking questions about document helps to interpret the content — e.g., who produced it? Why? When? Type of data? (O'Leary, 2014).

Finally, we will discuss various approaches to the **analysis procedure**. This is what Bowen (2009, p. 28) has to say regarding the analysis procedure: "The analytic procedure entails finding, selecting, appraising (making sense of), and synthesising data contained in documents. Document analysis yields data — excerpts, quotations, or entire passages — that are then organised into major themes, categories, and case examples specifically through content analysis". And he continues (p. 32): Document analysis involves skimming (superficial examination), reading (thorough examination), and interpretation. This iterative process combines elements of content analysis and thematic analysis. And, importantly, (p. 32): "Thematic analysis is a form of pattern recognition within the data, with emerging themes becoming the categories for analysis. The process involves a careful, more focused re-reading and review of the data. The reviewer takes a closer look at the selected data and performs coding and category construction, based on the data's characteristics, to uncover themes pertinent to a phenomenon. Predefined codes may be used, especially if the document analysis is supplementary to other research methods employed in the study. The codes used in interview transcripts, for example, may be applied to the content of documents. Codes and the themes they generate serve to integrate data gathered by different methods. The researcher is expected to demonstrate *objectivity* (seeking to represent the research material fairly) and *sensitivity* (responding to even subtle cues to meaning) in the selection and analysis of data from documents".

And (p. 33): "The researcher as analyst should determine the relevance of documents to the research problem and purpose. Also, the researcher should ascertain whether the content of the documents fits the *conceptual framework* of the study. It is necessary, as well [as said earlier], to determine the authenticity, credibility, accuracy, and representativeness of the selected documents".

And (pp. 33–34): "Document analysis, then, is not a matter of lining up a series of excerpts from printed material to convey whatever idea comes to the researcher's mind. Rather, it is a process of evaluating documents in such a way that empirical knowledge is produced and understanding is developed. In the process, the researcher should strive for objectivity and sensitivity, and maintain balance between both".

What happens when document materials include sound and film? How are these materials to be analysed? Rapley (2007) poses that the analysis of *documents* also entails in a broader sense the analysis of audio or video recordings of naturally occurring interactions and documented field observations.

The analysis starts with the research question that has to be answered. This is the leading perspective to any analysis, thus also to the analysis of these types of data. Just reading or viewing or listening to the data is an unfocused act. Instead, the key analytic question is: how will these sources of information contribute to answering the research question? Rapley (2007, p. 97) refers to this as a specific local context from which the analysis takes place. Following these considerations, the contents of a document (including video and audio recording) under scrutiny are interpreted while focusing on the reason it exists (has been produced, and by whom), and to who it was targeted. Next, its structure and length, its (hidden) messages, its arguments (if any), its use of stereotypes, its choice of words, the composition of its sentences, the use of images and metaphors, and its tone of voice are examined. Finally, the outcomes are placed in a framework of local context and the broader cultural context as deemed applicable to the document.

In conclusion, Fairclough (2003, p. 191) discusses *textual analysis*. He produced a checklist in the form of broad questions. In this checklist, he summarises the main issues in textual analysis. As an illustration, a selection of three issues is presented. For each issue the corresponding label is presented, followed by the first question of the checklist:

- **Social events:** *"What social event, and what chain of social events, is the text a part of"?*
- **Assumptions:** *"What existential, propositional, or value assumptions are made"?*
- **Discourses:** *"What discourses are drawn upon in the text, and how are they textured together? Is there a significant mixing of discourses"?*

Now, we are ready to discuss best practices for thematic analysis. These are discussed in what follows.

Braun and Clarke (2006, p. 35) lay out the consecutive phases of *thematic analysis*. Below, we present a slightly adapted version while preserving its contents. Each phase is denoted, to be followed by a short description of the process:

1. **Familiarising yourself with your data:** Transcribing data (if necessary), reading, and rereading the data, noting down initial ideas.
2. **Generating initial codes:** Coding interesting features of the data in a systematic fashion across the entire data set, collating data relevant to each code.
3. **Searching for themes:** Collating codes into potential themes, gathering all data relevant to each potential theme.

4. **Reviewing themes:** Checking in the themes work in relation to the coded extracts (Level 1) and the entire data set (Level 2), generating a thematic "map" of the analysis.
5. **Defining and naming themes:** On-going analysis to refine the specifics of each theme, and the overall story the analysis tells; generating clear definitions and names for each theme.
6. **Producing the report:** The final opportunity for analysis. Selection of vivid, compelling extract examples, final analysis of selected extracts, relating back of the analysis to the research question and literature, producing a scholarly report of the analysis.

In this context, Braun and Clarke (2006, pp. 25–26) also provide a warning about *potential pitfalls* to avoid when doing thematic analysis. We will present these potential pitfalls in abridged form.

The authors state: "However, there are a number of things which can result in a poor analysis. In this section, we identify these potential pitfalls, in the hope that they can be avoided.

- The first of these is a failure to actually *analyse* the data at all! The extracts in thematic analysis are illustrative of the analytic points the researcher makes about the data and should be used to illustrate/support an analysis that goes beyond their specific content, to make sense of the data, and tell the reader what it does or might mean.
- A second, associated, pitfall is the using of the data collection questions (such as from an interview schedule) as the "themes" that are reported. In such a case, no analytic work has been done to identify themes across the entire data set or make sense of the patterning of responses.
- The third is a weak or unconvincing analysis, where the themes do not appear to work, where there is too much overlap between themes, or where the themes are not internally coherent and consistent. All aspects of the theme should cohere around a central idea or concept.
- The fourth pitfall is a mismatch between the data and the analytic claims that are made about it. In such an (unfounded)

analysis, the claims cannot be supported by the data, or, in the worst case, the data extracts presented suggest another analysis or even contradict the claims. The researcher needs to make sure that their interpretations and analytic points are consistent with the data extracts.

- The fifth involves a mismatch between theory and analytic claims, or between the research questions and the *form* of thematic analysis used. A good thematic analysis needs to make sure that the interpretations of the data are consistent with the theoretical framework.
- Finally, even a good and interesting analysis which fails to spell out its theoretical assumptions, or clarify how it was undertaken, and for what purpose, is lacking crucial information and thus fails in one aspect".

This concludes our discussion of best practices with respect to thematic analysis. We will move on to an introduction to netnography.

12.4.1 *Netnography*

Netnography is an empirical research method that uses online data such as public conversations that are published on the Internet. It is aimed at studying social interactions of individuals and group through the analysis of these data. It originates from ethnography, which uses offline data. Netnography may be seen as on online observation method.

Specifically, existing online communities, such as forums and social media, provide empathic, non-obtrusive observations. Applications may be found in marketing and customer research where the research is aimed at:

- Listening to the "voice of customer".
- Spotting new trends and opportunities.
- Building emotional bonds with customers.
- Gaining unbiased consumer insights, or creating user groups' typologies.

The research method of netnography may be type casted as comparatively less obtrusive, less costly, and less time consuming than e.g., interviews. Issues can be noted as well. For instance, which types of individuals are engaged on such forums? In what ways do they compare with non-line samples? Which topics are, and are not, discussed online? And also, the method requires considerable interpretive skills from the researcher.

A more formal definition is provided by Kozinets (1998). In essence, he says that netnography is an empirical research method that aims to interpret online interactions and experiences from individuals, and from members of an online group, as these interactions and experiences manifest themselves in online messages and communications (Kozinets, 1998).

In order to position this type of data collection (and analysis) method, we will briefly relate it to the broader research procedure called *text mining*, which involves a quantitative approach to the collection and analysis of online materials.

Talib *et al.* (2016, p. 414) provide an overview of **text mining**. "Text mining is a process to extract interesting and significant patterns to explore knowledge from textual data sources. Text mining is a multi-disciplinary field based on information retrieval, data mining, machine learning, statistics, and computational linguistics. Several text mining techniques like summarization, classification, clustering etc., can be applied to extract knowledge. Text mining deals with natural language text, which is stored in semi-structured and unstructured format. Here, pattern analysis is implemented by Management Information System (MIS)".

The authors continue and explain (pp. 415–416) that different text mining techniques are available that are applied for analysing the text patterns and their mining process, such as:

- **Information Extraction:** Extracting meaningful information from large amount of text.
- **Information Retrieval:** Extracting relevant and associated patterns according to a given set of words or phrases.
- **Natural Language Processing:** The automatic processing and analysis of unstructured textual information.

- **Clustering:** An unsupervised process to classify the text documents in groups by applying different clustering algorithms.
- **Text Summarisation:** Collecting and producing concise representation of original text documents.

Text mining is thus a quantitative approach to the analysis of text in the broad sense. A significant feature is that all of the analyses are carried out by means of algorithms. Although these algorithms are designed by human beings, they cannot replace the researcher as a living person who is part of the social experience world of individuals who produce their texts as social human beings. This is only possible by using a qualitative approach to the analysis of documents.

Moving back to *netnography*, obviously, this is a method that can be viewed of as the qualitative variation of text mining. Netnography emphasises the cultural contextualising of online data. These characteristics are demonstrated in the article by Roth and Dana (2016) we will now introduce, which is an *example of a netnographic study*. This article presents as a research technology a netnography of an online conversation of self-designated self-made expats. The authors explain this research approach in their own words (p. 495): "Netnography is a qualitative research method that uses publicly available information produced by participants in online forums or produced by the use of internet search engines. The method is first choice for the analysis of textual behaviours and interactions and has been praised for its ease of use and its unobtrusive nature. In fact, one major and clear advantage of the method is its allowance of the analysis of content that is not produced in a particular research setting. Observational influences can therefore be considered minimal, which is particularly true with regard to the analysis of online conversations that have ended before the actual research starts."

The key *research question* of the present article therefore is as follows: *"How do self-designated self-initiated expatriates define themselves as self-initiated expatriates"*?

The data consisted of the entire thread of an "internations.org" discussion entitled *Self-Made Expats?* — comprised of 194 contributions posted between the initial post in January 2008 and the final post in October 2012.

The analysis of these data occurred as follows. First, the authors made a copy of the entire thread and they read it several times. In the course of reading, codes emerged and were altered in order to arrive at selective categories. Topical codes were complemented by frequency codes.

The results showed, among other things, that considerable numbers of self-initiated expatriates form enterprises after expatriations. Also, they refer to entrepreneurial metaphors — or even the term itself — in order to define themselves and others as self-initiated expatriates.

The authors *conclude* that "entrepreneurship" should be added as an additional dimension to the concept of self-initiated expatriates.

This concludes our discussion of document analysis, thematic analysis, and netnography. In all three cases, *documents*, published in whichever form and on whatever medium, prevail as monuments that hold forever the manifestations of the experience worlds of individuals that once were. By considering place, time, and context, for the engaged researcher these documents may serve as everlasting tokens in an ever-changing social world of mankind and its individual members.

12.5 Sample Study

In order to demonstrate how a study employing document analysis may be carried out an overview of the study performed by Dana *et al.* (2010) is provided, and the excellent document analysis characteristics of this study are highlighted.

12.5.1 *Issue and relevance*

The purpose of this journal article is to provide an account of the enterprising Aivilingmiut people of Repulse Bay (Naujaat), Canada, formerly a hub of the now-defunct whaling industry. The authors provide an apt description of the changes that took place in their territory in the course of time: "Travelling throughout the area, the Aivilingmiut traditionally lived from caribou, polar bears, seals, walrus and whales; as elsewhere among Inuit, food was shared.

The region has a rich history of whaling and trading with the Europeans. As the whaling industry declined, whalers diversified into trading for furs, and walrus ivory.

As the Hudson's Bay Company faced increased competition from traders in the south, the enterprise moved north and promoted white fox trapping among the Inuit, an activity not considered traditional among these people.

Economic activity tends to be traditional self-employment and includes fishing, hunting, sealing, and trapping as well as the carving of stones, mammal bones, and walrus ivory, given the existence of walrus in the surrounding waters. Walrus sink when shot, so the traditional harpoon is still used, attached to a float."

12.5.2 *Research goal*

The purpose of this study is to describe, understand, and explain how the Aivilingmiut people have developed their culture, their ways of earning an existence, and their entrepreneurial structure over time, while facing both losses as to the ways to earn a living, and facing the necessity to adapt to new circumstances.

12.5.3 *Research design*

A classic document analysis approach based on documents which dated from the period under study, and which were publicly available from various sources, all pertaining to the Aivilingmiut people, and their territory, in a broad sense.

12.5.4 *Sample design*

Documents pertaining to the Aivilingmiut people and their dominion between the years 1825 and 2009.

12.5.5 *Data collection*

This paper is based on the literature spanning 185 years.

In total, 38 documents were collected; to that, three published, academic articles were added describing:

- Indigenous organisations for development in the Canadian North: native development corporations;
- Entrepreneurship in Coral Harbour, Nunavut;
- A study of enterprise in Rankin Inlet, Nunavut: where subsistence self-employment meets formal entrepreneurship.

In addition, various purpose-made pictures were taken.

12.5.6 *Data analysis*

The documents were analysed chronologically and meticulously by employing a thorough process of interpretation in order to elicit grand meaning and to gain full-scale understanding.

Triangulation was carried out by analysing the pictures taken in order to cross-validate the findings of the documents. Findings were also triangulated by communicating with a representative of a governmental body and local experts.

12.5.7 *Report*

A text report describing and explaining the findings of the data analysis as they characterise and typify the chronological developments of the Aivilingmiut people and their changing home ground. These findings show that, throughout history, these people appear to have been an enterprising community, adapting well to change. Nowadays, however, the absence of business infrastructure may be a significant barrier to the development of small business opportunities in Repulse Bay.

12.5.8 *Excellent document analysis characteristics of the study*

For a document analysis study to be excellent a number of conditions have to be met. These include the following: (1) The research problem has to be clear and relevant. (2) The research design must be functional for the research purpose. (3) Data collection must be to the point and exhaustive. Here, data analysis must involve the culture of the members of the community while providing novel and deep insights into the social and entrepreneurial world of the community. All of this is the case in this study.

This is a classic document analysis study. The research objective was clearly formulated, and utterly workable. The research design clearly called for documents to be analysed and interpreted which were relevant for the target group to be studied. The data collection resulted in an abundance of documents and pictures that could be well-combined. The pictures that were presented communicate meaning, life conditions, atmosphere and mood, spirits, and state of mind, all adding to the interpretation of the documents involved.

The end result is both crystal clear and overly convincing. As the authors report: "regardless of how enterprising a community is, the absence of business infrastructure can impede entrepreneurship".

Chapter 13

Focus Groups

13.1 Introduction

The context of a focus group may be thought of as a conversation among five to seven respondents managed by a leader of the discussion or moderator; duration: 2–2½ hours. Generally speaking, focus groups, as a method of data collection, may be chosen in cases that quickly require a *broad inventory* of opinions, attitudes, or behaviour regarding a policy product, a service or an activity. It is felt that the group dynamics leads to higher input of the participants and to more pronounced and detailed insights, based on the interactions that will occur. Finally, the type of outcome of focus groups consists of a broad, extensive inventory of relevant aspects in the eyes of the target audience. Insight is acquired into which opinions, ideas, backgrounds, and motivations exist. The information obtained is more detached from the individual (the respondents), as it is derived from a group process. Ideally, the universe of a policy product, policy organisation, consumer product, service, brand, gets to a level that really can be observed: all opinions, attitudes, judgments, preferences, and actions are known upon completion of the focus group study.

13.2 Definition and Use

We will start with a brief outline of *traditional* focus groups. Normally, a focus group session is held with 8–12 participants, under direction of a *trained* moderator. The on-going conversation during the session may be characterised as formal, directive, and structured. A session takes 60–150 minutes of time. All that is said during that space of time is recorded. The session may furthermore be observed by a team of experts or scientists by means of a one-way mirror. This may be supplemented by field notes about what is said and what happened during the session.

Morgan (1988) pioneered the use of focus groups as a means to collect data. More recently, online focus groups have also been used. By employing focus groups, the researcher attempts to use the dynamic forces that are unleashed within the group to get a rich variety of answers and precise reasons for the positions that are taken with respect to the issues under study. In market research, the focus group approach is commonly taken to get a swift and efficient inventory of opinions, beliefs, and behavioural responses. Moreover, some content-focused themes include the following:

- Fundamental image or (policy) brand research: Identity/image, brand/core values, employer
- Description of the strategic market: Target audience profiles, needs
- Communication research: Strategy development, pre-test, concept test
- Product and concept development (policy)
- Behaviour of citizens or consumers or professional choice behaviour: (sleeping) needs, awareness, choice, decision, acceptance policy, product purchase
- Satisfaction and well-being of citizens
- Client and employee satisfaction
- Generating ideas or aspects: Brainstorm, followed by development of a quantitative questionnaire

Furthermore, it is important to distinguish between group interviewing and carrying out a focus group session, the difference being whether there is a focus on *interaction* in the process. As Morgan

(1997) puts it: "Focus groups are a form of group interviewing but it is important to distinguish between the two. *Group interviewing* involves interviewing a number of people at the same time, the emphasis being on questions and responses between the researcher and the participants. *Focus groups* however rely on *interaction within the group* based on topics that are supplied by the researcher."

Krueger and Casey (2015) add to this a focus on understanding *feelings*. In their words: "A focus group isn't just getting a bunch of people together to talk. A focus group is a special type of group in terms of purpose, size, composition and procedures. The purpose of conducting a focus group is to better understand how people *feel* or think about an issue, idea, product or service."

Finally, Kitzinger (1995, p. 299) summarises the defining elements of the focus group when she says: "Focus groups are a form of group interview that capitalizes on communication between research participants in order to generate data. Although group interviews are often used simply as a quick and convenient way to collect data from several people simultaneously, focus groups explicitly use group interaction as part of the method. This means that instead of the researcher asking each person to respond to a question in turn, people are encouraged to talk to one another: asking questions, exchanging anecdotes and commenting on each other's experiences and points of view. The method is particularly useful for exploring people's knowledge and experiences and can be used to examine not only what people think but how they think and why they think that way."

Focus groups may be used for various different purposes. Krueger and Casey (2015) provide an overview of the *goals* of a focus group as follows:

- Attitudes and priorities and framework of understanding;
- Group norms and cultural values;
- Explore and clarify people views;
- Group social processes;
- Reach parts that other methods cannot reach;
- Embarrassing subjects.

In addition, focus groups may also be used for broader purposes:

- Generating hypotheses;
- Early prototyping;
- Brainstorming.

Kitzinger (1995, p. 299) provides other uses of the focus groups when she says: "The idea behind the focus group method is that group processes can help people to explore and clarify their views in ways that would be less easily accessible in a one to one interview. Group discussion is particularly appropriate when the interviewer has a series of open-ended questions and wishes to encourage research participants to explore the issues of importance to them, in their own vocabulary, generating their own questions and pursuing their own priorities. When group dynamics work well the participants work alongside the researcher, taking the research in new and often unexpected directions."

To this she adds an additional use (Kitzinger, 1995, p. 300): "Focus group methods are also popular with those conducting *action research* and those concerned to "empower" research participants because the participants can become an active part of the process of analysis. Indeed, group participants may actually develop particular perspectives as a consequence of talking with other people who have similar experiences."

As becomes clear from the above, focus groups may be employed as it is, for instance as a data collection method to study attitudes and experiences. The outcome of such a study may represent — in a qualitative manner — the attitudes and experiences of a population underlying the sample of respondents. That is, while the contents and dimensions of these attitudes and experiences are known we do not know about the proportions of these characteristics in this population, as this would require quantitative follow-up research.

In addition, however, the instrument of the focus group may be used as part of a more elaborated research approach in which the focus group may have specific functions. An example was given earlier where focus groups were employed within the broader context of *action research* as the primary research approach.

13.3. Advantages and Disadvantages

Focus group methodology has both strengths and limitations. In a general sense, one could say that it is only as useful and as strong as its link to the underlying research question and the rigour with which it is applied. More specifically, the following strengths and limitations apply to the use of focus groups:

Strengths
- Provides concentrated amounts of rich data, in participants' own words, on precisely the topic of interest.
- Interaction of participants adds richness to the data that may be missed in individual interviews.
- Provides critical information on the development of hypotheses or interpretation of quantitative data.

Limitations
- Small number of participants.
- Limited generalisability (depending, however, on the rigour of the sample design).
- Group dynamics can be a challenge
  o Particularly if moderator is inexperienced.
- Interpretation
  o Time-consuming;
  o Requires experienced analysts.

Lamnek (2005, pp. 84–85) presents a number of general **advantages** of the focus group. Most importantly, the focus group enables the researcher to acquire an overview of the breadth of opinions, views and beliefs, and differences of opinion regarding the topics under study. Also, the focus group allows for a deep understanding of both structure and processes regarding positions both individuals and group members may have about the issues discussed. Finally, as association processes occur and develop during a session, the focus group opens up avenues to latent knowledge the participants may possess.

Kitzinger (1995, p. 300) presents some potential **sampling advantages** with focus groups by pointing out that focus groups:

- Do not discriminate against people who cannot read or write.
- Can encourage participation from those who are reluctant to be interviewed on their own (such as those intimidated by the formality and isolation of a one to one interview).
- Can encourage contributions from people who feel they have nothing to say or who are deemed "unresponsive patients" (but engage in the discussion generated by other group members).

Other **advantages** include the following:

- Less expensive than some other research (versus interview) because of time.
- Fast way of gathering a lot of insights as participants stimulate each other and create ideas that won't occur maybe on a single interview.
- High interaction between participants; also, interaction between consumer/customer and client.
- Group dynamic stimulates conversation and reactions.
- Additional materials may be used during the sessions, such as specific stimuli (for instance pictures, and flipcharts, and film clips).

Disadvantages that must be mentioned are:

- Unnatural social setting that may introduce bias in the answers of the participants.
- Group dynamic forces may distort a participant's authentic point of view. That is, a dominant participant may overrule less-dominant participants while creating peer group pressure. As a consequence, less-dominant participants may not utter their personal views and feelings about an issue under study, thus avoiding group conflict.
- *Polarising* (taking more extreme positions) and/or *amplifying* (want to please each other and or the moderator).
- Focusing on one single solution or viewpoint by the participants. The moderator may not always be successful in turning the discussion to focus on multiple solutions, or viewpoints.

- Influence of the researcher on the results (moderator's personal background may influence the discussion).
- Incapacity to register and react on all the verbal and non-verbal (body language, silence) information.

Finally, Morgan *et al.* (1997), while citing Merton *et al.* (1990), list four criteria to employ in order to arrive at an **"effective" focus group**. The focus group should:

- Cover a maximum range of relevant topics.
- Provide data that are as specific as possible.
- Foster interaction that explores the participants' feelings in some depth.
- Take into account the personal context that participants use in generating their responses to the topic.

These criteria are named by the authors as *range, specificity, depth, and personal context*, successively.

13.4 Best Practices

In this section, we will cover issues pertaining to the following: *choosing the focus group for studying specific research topics, its sample design and setting, group processes when carrying out a focus group session, the role of the moderator, the data and its analysis, and finally, the research report*. But let us start with an **overview** of the steps of the general focus group methodology process:

- **At the preparatory stage:**
  - ○ Specify the research objective;
  - ○ Develop questions/Moderator outline.
- **Focus group execution:**
  - ○ Conduct the focus groups
    - ▪ Introduction;
    - ▪ Questions/Discussion;
    - ▪ Closure.

- **Analysis and report:**
  - ○ Analysis;
  - ○ Transcribe, coding, report.

Based on this overview, we will discuss the aforementioned issues in what follows.

13.4.1 *Choosing the focus group for studying specific research topics*

Choose focus groups over other research approaches when:

- Fundamental image and brand research are sought for;
- Policy product, concept, strategy development is at issue;
- An extensive inventory is asked for;
- When the research objective revolves around existing experiences/opinions with respect to some issue or phenomenon.

13.4.2 *Sample design and setting*

Earlier, we indicated that generally a focus group session is held with 8–12 participants. Kitzinger (1995, p. 301), on the other hand, argues that the ideal group size is between four and eight people. A general guideline here is that the group should be large enough to allow group dynamic forces to come into being while the maximum size of the group should be such that every individual participant has the opportunity to participate in the discussion frequently.

Also, the population of which the participants are part of must be defined, including its "unit of analysis" (e.g., individuals, households, companies, company teams, etc.). Most of the time the definition involves a number of characteristics an individual unit of the population must share. Next, the researcher has to answer the question whether the population is homogenous with respect to the research questions to be studied, or the process as specified in the conceptual model. If not, subgroups have to be defined that are homogenous as such. This may, for example, result in three or four subgroups. Now, for each of the subgroups of the sample design 8–12 (or less) participants have to be selected who participate in a focus group session. Of course, within each of the subgroups of the sample design multiple groups of participants may be selected and subjected to a focus group session.

A general issue concerns the degree of homogeneity/heterogeneity of the participants of a focus group session. When participants are extremely homogeneous with respect to the topics to be discussed during the session, they will just confirm each other's position, and no new insights are expected to arise. By contrast, when participants are extremely heterogeneous (different), they will have trouble understanding each other (f.i., using different words and languages as a result of different levels of education). The same is true when it comes to a lack of shared values, or perceived differences with respect to knowledge and experience. As a consequence, during the session individual participants will cling together, unwilling or unable to discuss matters with "other" participants who are not like them. The sensible researcher anticipates these malfunctioning processes and chooses a group composition which occupies a middle position with respect to the homogeneity/heterogeneity dimension of the participants involved.

Ordinarily, participants who do not know each other are chosen at the start of the session. This is an advantage, as no prior biases exist in this case. However, sometimes all participants are, or must be, employed at the same company, or institute. As a consequence, preconceptions with respect to other participants may exist. This situation is aggravated when hierarchical relationships exist between the participants of the session. Participants may want to impress their bosses, who also participate in the session. Also, low-ranked participants are aware that all they say may be remembered by their superiors long after the session. The moderator should device a strategy in advance to counteract the biases to be expected in this case.

A final word about the *environment* of the session in action. Obviously, the moderator creates a comfortable setting, offering refreshments, pleasant light, air condition, and a comfortable table and chairs. Normally, the layout of the participants is in the form of a circle, or a bar shoe. Thus, all participants can see each other, including the moderator. Sometimes, a table is chosen which has an oval shape. The reason is that it is believed that acute angles of the table may prohibit feelings of safety and relaxation among the participants.

13.4.3 *Group processes when carrying out a focus group session*

According to Gordon and Langmaid (1988), during any focus group session, specific group processes unfold stepwise and in a pre-defined order. This is called the theory of group processes.

Gordon and Langmaid (1988) described five consecutive stages of this group process:

1. *Forming*: The process of forming the group; the proposal round is being used to start the process of group creation. Also, the "rules of the game" (norms of the group) are introduced.
2. *Storming*: In this step, group members are in the process of arranging power and control. The rules of the game have been tried by the member, as well as the method of communication.
3. *Norming*: Mutual agreement and acceptance among the group members takes place. The felt agreements on visions create a bond between members, there is a feeling of relaxation, the members feel ready for the task.
4. *Performing*: An orientation on the task has been established, the members are prepared to cooperate, constructive positioning can be felt, while there is an acceptance of various visions, there is a general sense of "let's go for it".
5. *Mourning*: Upon completion of the group task there is a sense of "breaking off" the group. Participants are getting restless and they communicate non-verbal signals of that kind. The moderator concludes the discussion and checks for any remaining issues. Finally, she/he offers opportunity of the last word.

It is believed that these consecutive steps should be taken in order to produce the best outcomes of the group discussion. When a group fails to move to the next step problems may be expected, and the moderator should intervene to get things going again. Some failures in the group process have been documented, and labelled, because they form a distinct pattern. Below three of these failure patterns are presented and described, along with the corrective steps to be taken by the moderator.

The dependent group
Participants submit themselves to the "leader" (moderator); there is an attitude of helplessness: "we know nothing, we are useless". There are no initiatives (silence) other than upon specific instruction. A continuous, subtle undermining of the moderator's authority may be observed. Participants try to maintain this situation, as this is comfortable in that situation. A total deadlock is reached. Communication occurs only between individual participants and moderator. In order to force a break through the moderator shows and manifests dependencies to the group.

The 'fight-flight' group
The group feels threatened in its existence: *fight reactions* become manifest. A dominant respondent fights on behalf of the group. There is competitive behaviour among the group members. Some may be boasting, showing 'Status displaying' behaviour. Finally, diversionary tactics may be employed.

The group feels threatened in its existence: *flight reactions* become manifest. Group members take up a previously prepared position. They react only to this as work that is carried out "for free", suggesting distance between an individual and the group. In order to force a break through: the moderator confronts the group with this process and asks for comments.

The 'paired' group
Alliances are being formed between a few group members. Other group members are hoping these will produce new ideas and initiatives. Specific relations between group members are being formed, using the tools of presenting coffee and tea. Joint interests are pursued. The formation of a relation between a single group member and the moderator may be observed.

In order to force a break through the moderator displays the processes and asks for comments. The general action of the moderator in all of these cases is to 'relive' the steps of the process with the participants in order to lift the blockades. The conclusion of the group session is accompanied by participants getting restless. The group now must be transformed back to individuals. The technique to accomplish this is using ritual formulations and moderator behaviour. When all goes well the participants are satisfied, as they feel that the job has been done. In other words: the circle is closed: Group members are now individual persons again.

The *Practical closure* is initiated by the moderator say things like: 'We're going to finish the discussion', have any issues not been dealt with?', and 'Does anyone wish to make any closing statements?'

The *Psychological closure* is enforced by saying things like: 'We've come to the end of our discussion', 'It was a pleasant discussion, that will prove very useful', 'Thank you for your participation, you will shortly receive your reward', and 'Have a safe trip home!'.

As now has become obvious from our discussion of group processes during a focus group session the moderator plays a pivotal role in guiding and steering these group processes, while keeping focused at the questions to be asked and addressed. In Section 13.4.4, the role of the moderator is further explained and highlighted.

13.4.4 *The role of the moderator*

The skills of a moderator may be summarised as follows:

- Understand the research objectives and have knowledge about the topic.
- Be flexible without losing the focus of the objectives.
- Be trustful and sensitive while creating a comfortable atmosphere and while encouraging the participants to keep talking.
- Observe and listen while being prepared for non-verbal behaviour.

- Guide participations if necessary while facilitating and stimulating interactions between participants, always link their reactions during the discussion.
- Keep control over the conversations while stimulating some participants to raise their contributions to the group discussion and gracefully reducing the contributions of dominant participants.

In the following, we will draw on Kitzinger (1995), who has made important remarks about the tasks to be carried out by the moderator during a focus group session. Thus, Kitzinger (1995, p. 301) poses that the facilitator should explain that the aim of focus groups is to encourage people to talk to each other rather than to address themselves to the researcher. The researcher may take a back seat at first, allowing for a type of "structured eavesdropping". Later on in the session, however, the researcher can adopt a more interventionist style: urging debate to continue beyond the stage it might otherwise have ended and encouraging the group to discuss the inconsistencies both between participants and within their own thinking. Disagreements within groups can be used to encourage participants to elucidate their point of view and to clarify why they think as they do.

Kitzinger (1995, p. 301): continues by saying: "The facilitator may also use a range of group exercises. A common exercise consists of presenting the group with a series of statements on large cards. The group members are asked collectively to sort these cards into different piles depending on, for example, their degree of agreement or disagreement with that point of view or the importance they assign to that particular aspect of service."

Finally, the same author elucidates how interaction between participants can be used to achieve seven main aims (Kitzinger, 1995, p. 302):

1. To highlight the respondents' attitudes, priorities, language, and framework of understanding.
2. To encourage research participants to generate and explore their own questions and develop their own analysis of common experiences.

3. To encourage a variety of communication from participants-tapping into a wide range and form of understanding.
4. To help to identify group norms and cultural values.
5. To provide insight into the operation of group social processes in the articulation of knowledge (for example, through the examination of what information is censured or muted within the group).
6. To encourage open conversation about embarrassing subjects and to permit the expression of criticism.
7. Generally, to facilitate the expression of ideas and experiences that might be left underdeveloped in an interview and to illuminate the research participants' perspectives through the debate within the group.

In closing, we let Krueger (1994, pp. 104–105) finish. According to this author, the following two moderator roles are especially worth mentioning:

1. **The Seeker of Wisdom:** The moderator plays the role of a person who is trying to obtain understanding, insight, and wisdom; by asking the "right" questions he will achieve this; this is the moderator role most often chosen.
2. **The Enlightened Novice:** The moderator is highly engaged; however, he gives the impression of lacking certain (specialist) knowledge. Participants need to explain elements of the topics and the answers given (for instance focus groups in the domain of medicine and prescriptions, with doctors as participants). The need for explanations during the conversation provides the participants with a touch of authority, which enhances their motivation.

This concludes our overview of the role of the moderator. In Section 13.4.5, we will discuss both data and data analysis.

13.4.5 *Data and analysis*

As a result from the focus group sessions, textual data have become available in the form of tape recordings, transcriptions (a two-hour session may yield up to 40–50 pages), and field notes which may include all kinds of observations relevant to answering the research questions.

The data analysis is driven by the underlying research questions. The analysis is qualitative in that it is interpretive, while constrained by context, and topics are analysed as linked to group guidelines which, in turn, are based on the research questions that have to be answered.

A number of steps can be taken now. The first step may be described mechanical, involving both organising and subdividing of the data. Next, interpretations are made by developing subdivisions (code mapping), search for patterns within subdivisions, and eventually drawing meaningful conclusions. It should be noted that software programmes like, e.g., *Atlas.ti*, may be fruitfully utilised in the process of data analysis. In conclusion, the reliability of the analysis process should be established. To that end, a repeated review of data can be carried out. The independency of the analysis process may be established by having two experienced analysts carrying out the analysis separately while subsequently making comparisons between the two analysis outcomes. If differences show up the researcher discusses these with the two analysts in concert.

As contrasted to deductive qualitative analyses, inductive analysis approaches start from principles and heuristics. For instance, Krueger (1994, p. 157), while describing transcript-based analysis, provides instructions such as:

- Read transcripts and field notes one category at a time.
- Look for emerging themes (by question and then overall).
- Develop coding categories and code the data.
- Sort the data into coded categories.
- Construct topologies or diagram the analysis.

In addition, or as a consequence, Krueger (1994, p. 139), says: "Analysis takes special skills. Good analysts are like good athletes. They are born with certain skills or aptitudes that give them an advantage over others, but if those skills are not refined, disciplined, and honed their talents will not reach full potential. Some analysis attributes are inherited, whereas others can be acquired in the formative years."

These characteristics, as stated above, may make it more difficult to judge the quality of the analysis and the relevance of the recommendations.

We end this paragraph with a quote from Kitzinger (1995, p. 301), who praises the virtues of the focus group methodology in the context of the analysis of its data: "Differences between individual one-off interviews have to be analysed by the researchers through armchair theorising; differences between members of focus groups should be explored in situ with the help of the research participants."

13.4.6 *The research report*

Reporting the outcomes of a focus group study is not really different from reporting the results of an in-depth interview study. The research report takes the form of a text report with citations to illustrate the experience world of the respondents and to highlight their ideas, images, standpoints and attitudes, values and norms, and behaviours. As always, citations are never research outcomes as such in the sense the something can be proved by solely providing citations. However, careful use of citations may provide considerable assistance to the reader of the report while attempting to enter the inner world of the participants of the study.

Chapter 14

Interviews

14.1 Introduction

This chapter will discuss in-depth interviewing as a way to collect qualitative data from individual interviewees. During the interview, the interviewer has an eyeball-to-eyeball contact with the respondent. As a consequence, both verbal and non-verbal responses may be registered and interpreted by the interviewer. Furthermore, the interviewer has the unique opportunity to ask questions of clarification, and continuation questions in an interactive and personal context. Frequently, why-questions are asked in order to acquire a deeper level of understanding regarding the peculiar way the respondent answers the questions. As a result, in-depth knowledge and deep insights are acquired at the individual level regarding the issues under study.

14.2 Definition and Use

Boyce and Neale (2006) provide a succinct definition of interviewing: "In-depth interviewing is a qualitative research technique that involves conducting intensive individual interviews with a small number of respondents to explore their perspectives on a particular idea, program, or situation." Thus, the objective of interviews of this kind is to reveal the views of people, unbiased by evaluative responses on the researcher's part. Both in-depth interviews and expert interviews belong to this category of interviews. Questions must be carefully constructed (Fodd, 1993). Structured open-ended questions (Fontana and Frey, 2003) are more desirable than non-structured ones that run the risk of turning into conversations; structured interviews are more valid and reliable than non-structured interviews, as they are usually based on a preconceived approach (or even a conceptual model) to a phenomenon to be studied.

The context of an in-depth interview may be thought of as a conversation between one respondent and an interviewer; duration: 20–60 minutes. Generally, in-depth interviews, as a method of data collection, may be chosen in cases where insight is required into more individual processes of experience, backgrounds, motives leading to opinions, attitudes or actions with respect to a product or service. "Depth" refers to acquiring real insights into individually determined factors leading to attitudes and behaviour.

In-depth interviews are chosen and used as the preferred method of data collection in the following instances:

- When interpersonal contact is important.
- When you need more in-depth data.
- When you need to have some follow-up.
- When complex questions or behaviours need to be explored.
- When you suspect other methods aren't getting the whole picture.

We will now continue with an expose about the formulation of questions, and types of interviews. This section will end with a short summary of interview outcomes.

14.2.1 *Questions*

Interviews require open-ended questions to ask to the respondent, as they allow room for explanations; questions should be carefully worded, avoiding yes/no responses that lack detail. In addition, it is wise to design questions to reduce the possibility of responses reflecting *social desirability* (Arnold and Feldman, 1981; Arnold *et al.*, 1985; Crowne, 1960; Golembiewski and Munzenrider, 1975; Thomas and Kilmann, 1975; Zerbe and Paulhus, 1987). As a strategy to circumvent this problem, often (Freudian) *projective techniques* are used. For example, the interviewer could ask the following question: "Suppose somebody who has the same background, age, and education as you have would enter a small supermarket which is deserted at that moment. Would this person grasp the opportunity to take with him some of the products without paying?" The basic idea now would be that the respondent projects his own behavioural inclination to steal on this fictitious person. In that way he will find it easier to answer the question truthfully because this is not about himself (but it is).

Also, *past behaviour questions* (e.g., What did you do when demand for your product exceeded your ability to supply?) can complement *situational questions* (e.g., If a supplier were too slow, what would you do?) as discussed by Taylor and Small (2002). Most often, questions should point at contexts that are part of the actual, idiosyncratic experiences of the interviewees.

14.2.2 *Types of interviews*

The in-depth interview has a number of basic forms:

- The Structured Interview
  - Essentially a face-to-face survey format with some open-ended questions.
- The Semi-Structured Interview
  - Questions and prompts are designed ahead of time, but pace and question ordering are flexible, depending on the discussion and respondent.
  - Interviewee is encouraged to expand on answers and express new information that the interviewee thinks is important.
- Free-flowing, open-ended conversations
  - Informal in nature, the interviewer simply wants to allow the interviewee to expound.

- Observational Interviews
  - The context and surrounding are as important as the conversation.
  - i.e., Following a respondent through an average day.
- Focus Groups (see Chapter 13)
  - Multiple respondents are interviewed at the same time.
  - The researcher is especially interested in the group interaction.

Some *types of research* are particularly suitable for in-depth interviews. They include the following:

- Broad, explorative policy research
  - Studying complex assessment processes among citizens, or finding niches in the policy environment. Thus, a deeper understanding of psychological processes with (segments of) citizens may be acquired, also involving personal issues. In addition, longitudinal studies may be carried out in order to better understand development processes among citizens.
- New policy development
  - When a fundamentally new policy needs to be developed when only a few citizens/experts are available. Also, when policy reactions from individual family members are important, or when a SWOT-analysis of a formulated policy is needed for policy modifications.
- "Creative development"
  - May be fruitfully studied using in-depth interviews at later stages in the development process or for creative interpretation of policy principles. Finally, the evaluation of immediate emotional reactions of citizens on proposed, tangible policy interpretations.
- Communication research
  - Can be carried out using in-depth interviews. For instance, a campaign may be tested whether it is entertaining/humoristic, whether the message comes across, or how and whether communication tools are effective or not.

- Diagnostic research/tactical research
  - Lends itself to the single interview approach, for example finding out why a campaign is ineffective, or why a product steadily loses market share over time.

14.2.3 *Types of interview outcomes*

Finally, we will elaborate on the various outcome elements of the in-depth interview. The type of outcome of in-depth interviews consists of deep insights into personal processes, backgrounds, motivations, and experiences of a series of individuals. Additionally, insight into the reasons for a certain opinion/perception/attitude/behaviour of an individual is acquired, including the influence of external factors and the influence of own values/norms thereon. A full and deep understanding of the processes under study may for instance explain choices, decisions and preferences/user behaviour, may suggest a viable method of communication and information, or may materialise a real way of understanding satisfaction (what is satisfaction, and what makes a person satisfied?)

Section 14.3 will elucidate a number of advantages and disadvantages as associated with the in-depth interview.

14.3 Advantages and Disadvantages

The in-depth interview may be advantageously employed when:

- Choice and decision behaviour have to be penetrated.
- Communication (pre-test) is at issue.
- Product concepts are to be tested.
- Insight in the dimensions of satisfaction as a target concept is sought for.
- Information search behaviour has to be clarified.
- Values/norms have strong a strong influence in the process to be studied.
- Perception as a concept is highly individually determined within a specific research context.

Specific **advantages** include the following:

- You get rich, detailed material.
- You get the chance to go beyond the surface.
- Interviewing yields new insights.
- Participants describe what is important to them rather than being restricted to survey questions.
- Provides high reliability — clarification of responses to increase the likelihood of useful information.
- You can customise questions for the individual.
- Data analysis can lead to qualitative assessments.

Distinctive **disadvantages** are:

- Time consuming.
- Responses are variable.
- Interviewing effectively takes practice and experience.
- Large amounts of information to reduce and analyse.
- Less easily generalised.
- Dependent on researcher's personal attributes and skills.

Section 14.4 will provide a detailed overview of the ways the in-depth interview may be brought into action.

14.4 Best Practices

In this section, the in-depth interviewing process is discussed by focusing successively on each of the steps to be taken in the context of the research process. The discussion will provide ample details where possible.

Let us begin with an **overview of the interview process**. The following steps in the semi-structured process may be distinguished:

(1) Define the problem.
(2) State your purpose.
(3) Develop research questions.
(4) Select a sample.
(5) Perform the interview.

(6) Transcribe your data.

(7) Analyse your data.

(8) Report your findings.

In the following, we will expand a number of these steps, and we will provide suggestions for best practices when carrying out in-depth interviews as a way of collecting data for a study.

- **Defining the Problem — Goals**
  - ○ Remember, interviews are best used to solve a specific type of research problem:
    - ▪ Gathering generalisable information from a sample of respondents.
    - ▪ Discovering a particular piece of information.
    - ▪ Obtaining an important document or dataset.
    - ▪ Informing or guiding work that uses of other sources of data.
    - ▪ Sitting back and learning from an acknowledged expert.
    - ▪ Add colour for a quantitative study.
  - ○ Your research puzzle should dictate how you use the interview and the type of questions you ask.
  - ○ A good reason to use interviews is the need to flesh-out information that cannot be found by other ways (archival research, available datasets).
  - ○ A prime reason to using interviews is a need to answer the how/what questions.
- **Statement of Purpose**
  - ○ This should be a clearly written, concise statement that you can show to respondents and institutional sponsors.
  - ○ What information do you plan to obtain from the process?
  - ○ How long will it take?
  - ○ How will the information be used?
  - ○ Confidentiality requirements.
- **Selecting a Sample — What you need out the interview will determine who you sample.**
  Therefore, the following questions need to be addressed:
  - ○ Are you looking for generalizable patterns?
    - ▪ You will need to use some of the sampling procedures next week

- In the case of a small-n, you should use a "most similar" matching technique.
- If you are looking for detailed information from experts nested inside larger units (mayors in cities; CEOs in companies; principals in schools), you should match at the second level.
- Semi-structured interviews will always involve less respondents than a survey. Nevertheless, the rules of selection and non-response bias still apply, even though there is a small-n.
- Qualitative research can be fruitful, but it is not a synonym for sloppy.
  - o Do you need deep information from the few acknowledged experts in the area?
    - Talk to as many as time and budget allow. Sampling is not as important.
  - o Are you tracking down a particular case or journalistic-style story?
    - Treat the process like an investigative journalist. Talk to key players, learn more, and add new respondents to your list (snowball sampling).
    - Remember, that respondents in this type of interview settings have agendas. Try to cover all sides of the story. Do not let narratives from particular respondents drive your analysis.

14.4.1 *Sampling methods*

With regards to interviewees, these can be identified and selected using various sampling methods. Among these is snowball sampling, the focus of Goodman (1961). Where a universe is small, conducting a census may be a better investment than selecting a random sample that is too limited for statistical manipulation to give meaningful results (Dana, 1995). Based on the characteristics of the phenomenon under study, selection variables may be employed, resulting in subgroups of interviewees. It is expected that these subgroups will respond to certain characteristics in decidedly different ways.

Semi-Structured Questions
- Your survey form should have a mix of some closed and open-ended questions.
- Weight more heavily towards open-ended, as this is really the goal of the approach.
- Allow your respondents to elaborate but reign them in when necessary by:
  - Having a pre-programmed list of *wrangling* phrases (i.e., Could we return to…?; That is fascinating, but I want to make sure I understand … better).
  - Building conversational *bridges* between subjects directly into the survey script. ("Your answer leads me to wonder….; We have discussed how policy is made, now let's step back to the motivations of policy makers).
- Many of the question rules of survey design continue to apply the following:
  - Avoid double-barrelled questions.
  - Define complex terms carefully.
  - Don't editorialise.
  - Don't trap respondents into particular answers.

Additional Questions Types in Interviews
- Grand Tour Questions
  - "Could you describe a typical day in your office?"
  - Walk me through the stages of the business registration process.
  - Take me through the legal drafting process in your country.
- Asking for examples — These examples help elucidate complex points and add colour. They also help break a respondent out of "a message track".
- Prompts/Probes/Follow-ups
  - Can be built into checklist and spontaneous.
  - Can be oral or physical (the blank look, arched eye brows).
- The intentionally incorrect statement
  - State a law or fact incorrectly and gauge the respondent's reaction.

- Innocuous, but enlightening questions
  - o Sometimes it helps to avoid asking a sensitive question, when you can get the same information with a seemingly innocuous question.
  - o i.e., Gauging dual subordination in Vietnam — how many times do you meet with Party Secretary?
  - o What did you do this morning? Rather than, "Did you eat breakfast?"

More tips for good interviews

- Do your homework. The more you know, the better you can write questions, direct the interview, and probe.
- Sometimes it may be necessary to establish that you have some expertise on the subject to keep your interview from resorting to a canned speech.
- Don't be afraid to ask for documents, datasets, other interviews
  - o This often is of the utmost importance.
- End with an open question to elicit anything not covered
  - o Is there a question you expected me to ask that I didn't?

Observation

- Record your observations of the context of the interview.
- What is the setting like?
- Watch how respondent behaves with colleagues, family, etc.
  - o But remember the effects of observation: "Of course the introduction of the observer must not be misunderstood to imply that some kind of subjective features are to be brought into the description of nature. The observer has, rather, only the function of registering decisions, i.e., processes in space and time, and *it does not matter whether the observer is an apparatus or a human being*; but the registration, i.e., the transition from the "possible" to the "actual," is absolutely necessary here and cannot be omitted from the interpretation of quantum theory" (Heisenberg, 1958, p. 137). That is, in the process of observing an experimental setting, we may accidentally alter the environment around us. In other words, what we observe is not necessarily reality, but reality exposed to our method of questioning.

Post-Interview
- Put thoughts and questions into a reflexive journal.
- Transcribe tapes.
- Take out identifying information.
- Code transcription.
- If you have questions concerning clarification, contact the interviewee.
- Erase tapes as specified in consent form.
- Secure transcripts.

Triangulate after the Interview
- After the interview, find ways to verify the information given to you, i.e., engage in triangulation.
- If a respondent said they were at a meeting, do archival research to see if you can get a list of attendees.
- If a respondent mentions a particular law or decree, get a copy for yourself.
- If a respondent mentions a particular location, visit and verify the description (i.e., IRA attacks).

Initial Coding
- Coding text of the transcript means to break the text down into small, meaningful units by assigning labels to the unit.
- Use the smallest unit possible.
- Look for data pertinent to answering the research questions.
- Units may have multiple codes associated with them.
- Also look for new ideas or concepts to explore.
- Initially, don't worry about making relationships between the codes.

Developing Themes: "The best set of quotations is no substitute for thinking and formulating themes"
- After initial coding you should start to see repeating themes. Repeating ideas lead to Themes which lead to conclusions.
- Sort the coded units according to these themes.
- Assess the topics by asking "Does everything in this topic belong here? Can some of the topics be combined? Can some topics be

deleted because they don't relate to the research questions or because they don't have much data in them?"
- Develop a conceptual schema, or dimensions, for the data.
- The schema can have major and minor themes within it.

Coding Methods
- Traditional is by reproducing unit on an index card and grouping cards into categories and themes
- Qualitative software has taken the place of traditional methods
- Same concept except faster, more convenient and with greater analysis power
- NVivo and Atlas.ti prove to be the most popular coding and analysis software programs.

Reporting
- After the themes are developed start a narrative that explains the properties and dimensions of the categories and the circumstances under which they are connected.
- Findings, conclusions, recommendations, future research — provide a context for understanding the conditions under which the results were obtained.
- Remember to present information in a way that is verifiable and falsifiable.
- Report findings as they relate to each research question.
- What is the contribution of this study to knowledge and practice? What improvements can be made?

Boyce and Neale (2006, p. 8) warn against the use of *quantitative* descriptors in *qualitative* research reports such as based on interviews: "In presenting results of in-depth interviews, you need to use care in presenting the data and use qualitative descriptors rather than try to 'quantify' the information. You might consider using qualifiers such as 'the prevalent feeling was that...,' or 'several participants strongly felt that...,' or even 'most participants agreed that...' Numbers and percentages sometimes convey the impression that results can be projected to a population, and this is not within the capabilities of this qualitative research procedure."

The same authors (p. 9) also explain the correct use of *quotes* while reporting research outcomes. They say: "Providing quotes from respondents throughout the report adds credibility to the information." More specifically, quotes provide illustrations of the points made in the report. However, and this is important, they cannot be used as empirical outcomes as such.

Finally, Boyce and Neale (2006, p. 8) provide a *structure* for presenting the outcomes of an in-depth interview study. They explain: "In-depth interviews are flexible in that they can be presented in a number of ways — there is no specific format to follow. However, like all evaluation results, justification and methodology of the study should be provided, as well as any supporting information (i.e. copies of instruments and guides used in the study). In-depth interview data may stand alone or be included in a larger evaluation report. If presented as a **stand-alone report**, the following **outline** is suggested:

1. **Introduction and Justification**
2. **Methodology**
   a. How was the process carried out? (Describe the process of selecting the interviewees and conducting the interviews.)
   b. What assumptions are there (if any)?
   c. Are there any limitations with this method?
   d. What instruments were used to collect data? (You may want to include some or all in the appendix.)
   e. What sample(s) is/are being used?
   f. Over which period of time was this data collected?
3. **Results**
   a. What are the key findings?
   b. What were the strengths and limitations of the information?
   c. Where and how are the results similar and dissimilar to other findings (if other studies have been done)?
4. **Conclusion and Recommendations**
5. **Appendices** (including the interview guide(s))"

In closing, we will discuss both *general interviewing skills*, and the skill to *acquire depth* during the interview process. These skills are essential when it comes to conducting an in-depth interview. It is fair to say that these skills are the major determinants of the quality, and hence the usefulness of the outcomes of the in-depth interviews.

Interviewing skills

Interview technique determines credibility; the researcher must control his/her reactions. It is desirable for the researcher to be flexible in his or her approach to interviewees; the setting should be non-threatening to participants. As well, it is important to avoid influencing interviewees during interviews. Boyce and Neale (2006) provide directives for conducting in-depth interviews. Asking open-ended questions and probing are among the prime skills of a moderator.

The art of asking questions comes to the fore when conducting in-depth interviews. The interviewer may choose a (semi-)structured interview format. In that case, interview themes and questions are available in the checklist in a fixed order at the time of the interview. However, even here the interviewer may choose to tackle specific aspects, discuss aspects at a later stage, or neglect aspects. In that sense, the structure of the interview is still flexible. All questions are asked in an open-ended manner in order to obtain both rational and emotional responses regarding attitude and behaviour. This also leaves some room for using an interview format in accordance with the interviewer (style) and respondent (idiom). Also, the interviewer is supposed to keep on asking questions in accordance with the circumstances of the interview, and the answers received from the respondent. Finally, the questions to be asked may become more elaborated over time to some extent as the number of interviews that have been carried out advances, because of learning effects based on increasing knowledge and understanding of the interviewer. *Fixed elements* of the interview structure include the "psychological contract" between interviewer and respondent (during the interview the interviewer will ask questions and the respondent will address these questions) and the checklist, as derived from the objective/questions of the research, and the conceptual model. Next to a set of listed questions the checklist indicates the moment to show stimulus materials, and when to use projective techniques.

All in all, extensive interviewing skills are required, as the communication/confrontation is much more direct, a defensive attitude of respondent has to be conquered, the respondent's body language is (relatively) more important, and the use of projective techniques more important.

"Depth" of the interview

Finally, the "depth" of the interview is in part determined by the interviewer's interviewing skills. Depth refers to getting a deep understanding of why a person has certain views, opinions or evaluations, and why he displays certain behaviours. In terms of the conceptual model, a movement is made from the right-hand part of the model, containing the target behaviour to be studied, towards the left-hand part of the conceptual model, containing the explanatory concepts and the person-bound, or company-bound, characteristics.

As the skill of applying depth to the interview represents a core indicator of the quality (usefulness, relevance, degree of detail, full answers) of the outcomes of the interviews, this topic merits some attention. Applying depth may be accomplished by the following:

- **The use of projective techniques:** Using techniques such as word association, finish sentences, cartoons with (empty) speech balloons, personification, or mapping (subjective clustering). Projective techniques are used for breaking through cognitive barriers, finding new lines of approach, drawing on alternative communication channels, or for promoting lateral processes. Projective techniques may also be used for the sake of variety and when you get the feeling that the respondent fails to get to the point.
- **Phrasing the question with a positive and a negative component:** This is important in view of the "friendliness bias" that otherwise

may occur, i.e., the fact that respondents tend to be fair and friendly and thus tend to agree with you, no matter whether you ask the question positively-framed or negatively-framed. For that reason, the interviewer should always inquire after the positive as well as the negative pole. Also, answers like "the same", "both", "somewhere in the middle" should never be accepted. Ideally, the respondent should always be persuaded, or even seduced, to make choices. You don't need similarities; it's the differences you're after, no matter how small.

- **Phrasing and timing of the questions:** To this end, a set of instruments, a toolkit as it were, may be utilised. For instance, silences could be introduced during the interview. They should be used consciously, as they put pressure on the respondent. Also, after an initial response the interviewer could summarise the answer, as this will induce the respondent to provide the remaining components of the full answer. A variation is summarising overly simple as this will cause the respondent to "correct" (and elaborate) the summary. Another way to do this is to repeat the last sentence or phrase, then a silence is introduced, and the interviewer looks at the respondent questioningly. Finally, responses from the interviewer such as, pondering, quasi-consenting, a slow yes, yes, yes, reaction to the answer may result in better answers as well. Generally speaking, reacting assertively and using varying ways of keeping on asking "why?" is of prime importance.

- **Body language:** This is of significance in two ways: on the one hand, it is advised to continually observe the body language of the respondent during the interview. A respondent may show fatigue, loss of interest or focus, anxiety, etc. The interviewer should take action when necessary. On the other hand, the interviewer should continuously monitor his own body language as observed by the respondent. He should show interest through his attitude, as perceived by the respondent. The interviewer should change his pose regularly, as it livens up the conversation and loosens tension. It also helps to keep the respondent's attention.

- **The use of probing techniques:** The usefulness of the final answers upon completion of the interview can be evaluated on the following points: validity, completeness, relevance, and clarity. Probing techniques foster these qualities. Among the probing techniques to be employed by the interviewer are the following:

o Repeat or clarify the question if needed, using comparable words or expressions; formulate clearly using only words and expressions the respondent can understand.
o Do not run the risk of directing the answer by using examples.
o Repeat or summarise the answer using paraphrasing or repeat literally.
o Explicitly keep on asking untargeted questions, explicitly keep on asking targeted questions; silently keep on asking.
o Engage in both listening behaviour and non-verbal listening behaviour.
o Engage in post-conversation in case the interview didn't provide all the necessary information during the interview.

It will be obvious by now that successfully interviewing respondents in research requires considerable skills from the interviewer. These skills make the difference between a professional in-depth interview (this is why it is called in-depth) and a loose and shallow conversation by the layman.

14.5 Sample Study

In order to demonstrate how a study may employ interviewing as a major vehicle to collect data an overview of the study performed out by Dana *et al.* (2019) is provided, and the excellent interview process characteristics of this study are highlighted.

14.5.1 *Issue and relevance*

This study focuses on the entrepreneurial attitudes and activity of two matched groups comprising Memons and Non-Memons in Karachi, Pakistan, while identifying the social mechanisms that support the dynamics of intergenerational entrepreneurship support.

In particular, it attempts to unveil the interdependences among family, community, and ethnic capital, as contextual expressions of social capital that are manifest at different levels of the ethnic social system.

The authors indicate that this study provides a threefold contribution to the theory and practice of ethnic minority entrepreneurship from a social capital perspective: first, it clarifies the role and interdependence of family, community, and ethnic capital in facilitating self-employment in ethnic communities; second, it provides an overview of the social structures and mechanisms that contribute to the intergenerational transmission and support of an entrepreneurial mindset; and finally, it furthers an understanding of Memon community organisation and functioning.

14.5.2 *Research goal*

The purpose of this study is to describe the social and cultural profile of the Memons' ethnic minority; second, to compare the entrepreneurial attitudes and activity of Memon community members with non-Memons; and third, to identify the social mechanisms that support the dynamics of intergenerational entrepreneurship transmission and support in the Memons community, resulting in a comprehensive model integrating the concepts of ethnic, community, and family capital.

14.5.3 *Research design*

To achieve the research objectives, the authors collected and analysed both secondary and primary data. The entire process of data collection included three main stages, deployed during a two-year period:

In the first stage, secondary data was accessed about the Memon community in Pakistan, regarding their history, culture, and lifestyle.

In the second stage, primary data were collected through participant observation and semi-structured interviews with 20 Memons, and 20 non-Memons families, regarding their culture, lifestyle, and business orientation.

In the third stage of the data collection, the local author administered a 16-item questionnaire to each of the 40 main respondents — i.e., the male head of each family, to collect data regarding social capital and its influence on entrepreneurial activities within the community. As a complementary step, these questionnaires were then complemented by face-to-face interviews that averaged 37 minutes in length.

14.5.4 *Sample design*

The sample design for the semi-structured interviews was developed as follows: A sample of Memon and non-Memon families was built using the respondent-driven snowball method, a method which may be applied in the case of hard-to-reach populations. Respondents were selected from high-status neighbourhoods and evaluated by two independent real estate professionals. The matched neighbourhoods were used as controls of selected families' wealth.

In this way, a sample was created with an equal number of Memons and non-Memons men, matched in terms of wealth and age.

14.5.5 *Data collection*

A combination of qualitative and quantitative data collection was carried out. Qualitative data were obtained by carrying out semi-structured, in-depth interviews while using a checklist with open-ended questions as related to the social mechanisms that support the dynamics of intergenerational entrepreneurship support.

14.5.6 *Data analysis*

The interviews were transcribed, while the survey data was compiled in a SPSS database. Data analysis followed a three-stage iterative process of progressive, deeper investigation, going from general to more specific issues: first, the qualitative data collected during the general interview were analysed and interpreted, using an ethnographic method, in order to better understand the general social and cultural profile of the Memon community in Karachi; second, the survey data were analysed in terms of frequency, adopting a comparative approach between Memon and non-Memon respondents; and third, the final interviews were analysed in order to complete the overall image regarding the contribution of family, community and ethnic capital — as situated manifestations of social capital, to the dynamics of entrepreneurial initiatives within the two investigated groups.

The final analysis applied triangulation of secondary and primary data, to increase the reliability and robustness of the proposed model, which is based on a complex, multilayered integration of various sources of data and levels of interpretation. In this latter context, a distinction was made between micro level — the behaviours, perceptions, and opinions of various respondents; meso level — analysed and interpreted within the collective framework of community values, structures and mechanisms; and macro level — considered within the general, multiethnic context of the Pakistan society. The reliability of findings was realised using respondent selection and checking, follow-up, triangulation, peer reviews, and multistage, recurrent procedure of data collection.

14.5.7 *Report*

A text report that raises the issue to be studied, presents the relevant literature, and formulates research goals. Next, the research design is proposed, focusing on both the sample design and the principle method of data collection through the use of interviews. Then, the outcomes of the various forms of data analysis are presented and discussed. Findings indicate a complex range of community structures and mechanisms that reproduce the traditionally validated model of an entrepreneurially oriented ethnic enclave, based on ethnic group solidarity, reciprocity, trust, and social responsibility.

Finally, a figure is proposed, representing both the concepts, and the connections between these concepts. This is the comprehensive model integrating the concepts of ethnic, community, and family capital.

14.5.8 *Excellent interview process characteristics of the study*

For an interview-based study to be excellent a number of conditions have to be met. These include the following: The research problem has to be clear and relevant. The research design must be functional for the research purpose. Data collection must be to the point and exhaustive. Here, data analysis must be carried out in a multilevel approach. That is, interdependence among family, community, and ethnic capital, as contextual expressions of social capital that are manifest at different levels of the ethnic social system. All of this is the case in this study.

This study focused on the specific social structure and functioning of the Memons' community in Karachi, Pakistan. In view of the complexities of culture and society in this area — characterised by current extortion risks and security concerns — special measures were taken to obtain valid and reliable interview data as set forth in the following. The bias related to data collection, analysis, and interpretation was minimised by applying follow-up and triangulation procedures: each family was visited three times, and all adult family members were involved in the discussion. After each wave of data collection, the interviewer used various testimonies to identify both convergent and divergent opinions. All divergences were further investigated, addressing additional questions and requiring further details and explanations, and requiring objective proofs for factual elements (such as, for example, the level of education of the family head). Then, the information provided by various members of each family was triangulated to achieve a coherent narrative structured around the main research themes.

In the light of the foregoing it is easy to appreciate the care with which interviewing, as a major method of data collection, has been utilised in this study. Starting with a well-thought out sample design, taking care of avoiding possible biases, and ending up with procedures to apply forms of triangulation, this study sets an excellent standard for the purposeful and effective use of interviewing as a vehicle to collect meaningful and reliable empirical data.

Chapter 15

Elicitation Techniques in Qualitative Research

15.1 The Use and Operation of Elicitation Techniques

A checklist is basically filled with questions regarding the topics to be studied. These are open-ended questions, aimed at unravelling the perceptions of the respondent with regard to these topics. By asking these questions, the interviewer aims to reach the cognitive, affective, and conative (behavioural inclinations) worlds of the respondent. In order to do so, however, only verbal utterances from the interviewer are used as stimuli to the respondent. Consequently, answers from the respondent may produce preponderantly rationalised and superficial answers. As a matter of fact, additional ways of evoking responses do exist. They are generally called "elicitation techniques". These are techniques for verbal or non-verbal promotion. They are used at an individual in order to evoke ill-considered and non-rationalised, but genuine responses (verbal behaviour and actual behaviour) that provide a (deeper) insight into the primary perceptions of that individual (see for instance, Mariampolski, 2001). More specifically, they comprise techniques to be used during the in-depth interview, or with a focus group, and they are aimed at facilitating deeper, broader, and more complete responses to the issues raised. This chapter introduces these techniques while providing a framework for making reasoned choices regarding the appropriate selection of a particular elicitation technique. It is

249

largely inspired by Stalpers (2007), but with several adaptations. This chapter has the following set-up: It will start with an introduction regarding the use and operation of elicitation techniques. Next, existing divisions of elicitation techniques will be discussed. The main part of the chapter introduces a comprehensive classification structure. This structure is called "Information Driven Elicitative Action" (IDEA). It is a taxonomy of elicitation techniques based on three psychological dimensions including: affective elicitation techniques, cognitive elicitation techniques, and conative elicitation techniques. The text concludes with a few final remarks about the usefulness of the IDEA taxonomy.

When preparing a new research project, the researcher starts with making an inventory of the topics to be covered during the interviews. As a next step, the researcher analyses each of these topics in order to decide which *type of information* is required. In this context, information might possess the basic characteristic of cognitive information or affective information. Also, information might be behaviour-related. Based on these characteristics the researcher may decide to make use of an elicitation technique that fits the type of information required.

The basic choice to use, or refrain from using, elicitation techniques is based on two considerations: On the one hand, it is obvious that using an elicitation technique will yield richer information, which will generally enhance the quality of the study to a great extent; On the other hand, carrying out a single elicitation technique will take time and may cost money. While time is a scarce commodity during the interview, costs may be incurred by the application of these techniques. Hence, the question is: Is the issue to be dealt with during the interview so important or essential that spending five or ten minutes, or even more time on using such a technique is justified? This is up to the researcher who makes a rational decision about this.

Apart from considerations about the quality of the data, another consideration may come into play. Using elicitation techniques may elevate the general motivation level of the respondent(s), as it introduces variation in the interview process for them. For instance, starting an interview session with a short association task may have a lively and focusing effect on the respondent that may last during the entire interview.

The operation of elicitation techniques is often based on psychological mechanisms which produce expressions of respondents that are both observable and interpretable. Thus, these expressions allow the researcher an entrance into the experiences of respondents. In particular, two elicitation techniques are used frequently in qualitative research: (i) association techniques; and (ii) projective techniques.

Association techniques focus on the associative world of the respondents. From a psychological perspective, many — often diverse — associations are connected in a frequently complex way. That is, in the individual's experience world, often quite different experiences and evaluation elements are present in a complex cohesion. Associations, such as those expressed by the individual, will provide insight into the patterns of these related experiences and perceptions to the researcher. By collecting and analysing these associations, the researcher may acquire a deeper understanding of respondents' true experiences. Association tasks are administered in such a way that there is no opportunity for the respondent to reflect on his associations prior to voicing them to the interviewer. That is, he is instructed to utter all associations quickly and without prior thinking. If he does engage in thinking, the so-called "diplomat effect" may take precedence. This means that the respondent makes a pre-selection of what he will tell based on what he thinks is appropriate to the interview setting. In this way, it is a cognitive underpainting. Obviously, the interviewer wishes to hear it all, as for instance social undesirable associations may contain important clues and insights.

Projective techniques refer to the psychological mechanism of projection as developed by Freud (1911). Freud explains that individuals project their negative character traits on others, so the threat of punishment imposed on these negative properties will be reduced. The basic idea is that individuals attempt to avoid possible negative consequences of being honest about their undesirable behaviour.

Instead, they will project this behaviour on (comparable) others. In a research setting, this technique may for instance be used to study social undesirable behaviour such as the act of stealing in a supermarket or engaging in tax evasion. While a direct question will result in biased denials, using a projection technique may result in reporting that "others" (like themselves) show this misbehaviour. If one accepts Freud's interpretation actually the respondent projects his own behaviour on a virtual other and thus reports about his own behaviour. Summarising the above, individuals can disclose their deeper thoughts and feelings with regard to stimuli (individuals or objects) much easier when they can project them onto another individual or object, or on another situation. This is especially important in topics where social desirability plays a role.

15.2 Existing Divisions of Elicitation Techniques

Both association techniques and projective techniques have been discussed above. For some researchers these two techniques are the only techniques they have come across. For that reason, a first, but limited division of elicitation techniques is expressed under the general label of Elicitation techniques: *associative and projective techniques.*

A second way of dividing elicitation techniques is a division based on *type.* Gordon and Langmaid (1988) make a distinction between projective and enabling techniques. While the projective techniques are the same as discussed earlier, the enabling techniques represent all other techniques that facilitate respondents when trying to express their perceptions and drives. Obviously, this rather crude division makes it difficult for a researcher to decide on a specific elicitation technique for his research.

A third way of dividing elicitation techniques is to use as a starting point the way these techniques are actually *being used in qualitative research settings.* In this way, the techniques are divided into those used in focus groups, individual interviews, and observational settings. Clearly, this is an eclectic and non-theoretical division. It cannot be used to decide on a specific elaboration technique in relation to type of information (type of research question).

Ideally, the specific research questions raised in a study point to the elicitation techniques that are relevant and eligible to choose from. This in turn would make it possible for the researcher to make a reasoned choice. For the divisions discussed above, this is not possible. Therefore, we are in need of a division of elicitation techniques which allows us to make well-reasoned choices. An example of such a division is called "Information Driven Elicitative Action", and this will be introduced next.

15.3 Information Driven Elicitative Action

From the field of psychology, three dimensions of meaning may be distinguished: (i) Thinking — cognitive; (ii) Feeling — affective; and (iii) Doing (behaviour) — conative. While IDEA connects directly to the individual perception of the respondent it claims to allow for a reasoned choice of technique on the basis of the specific research questions. The research questions point to the type of information that is sought after in the study including both affective information, cognitive information, and conative information. Consequently, in the following we will introduce the categories of Affective elicitation techniques, Cognitive elicitation techniques, and Conative elicitation techniques, in that order. For each of these techniques, a few prototypical examples will be elaborated. In these examples, *products, services,* and *societal issues* may be mentioned. From the perspective of using elicitation techniques, they are interchangeable as these elements as such do not represent criteria for the choice of an elicitation technique.

15.4 IDEA: Affective Elicitation Techniques

Affective elicitation techniques are appropriate tools to obtain insights into the feelings of an individual with respect to a product, a service or a societal issue. These affective techniques can be further classified on the basis of **two dimensions**: The first dimension is the degree of elaboration by the individual, i.e., the "depth" of the exploration of the feelings by the individual. That is, the individual

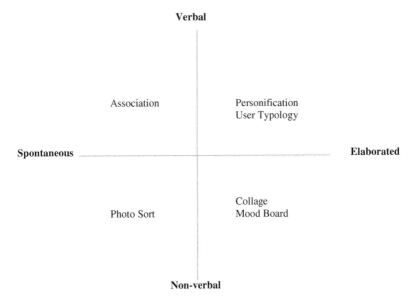

Verbal

Association   Personification
                      User Typology

Spontaneous _____ Elaborated

                      Collage
Photo Sort   Mood Board

Non-verbal

Figure 15.1:   Categorisation of *Affective* Elicitation Techniques.

can be moved to explore his emotional life in depth to a greater or
lesser extent. The two extremes of this dimension are "spontaneous"
and "elaborated". The second dimension relates to the way in which
the individual is asked to express his feelings. The extremes of this
dimension are "solely verbal" and "solely non-verbal". Hybrids of
verbal and non-verbal expression lie in between.

Figure 15.1 displays various prototypical *affective* elicitation techniques in four quadrants.

15.4.1 *Prototypical affective techniques*

In *associative* techniques, the respondents are asked to provide primary responses to a specific stimulus. That stimulus can be a word
or a phrase, or also a photo, a piece of music, etc. Associative techniques have multiple variants. *Free association*, for example, means
that a respondent is completely free in the way he associates. In the
case of *Aided association*, there is less freedom: for example, a
respondent may be asked to indicate which words or pictures from
a given set will fit to a particular service. *Sentence completion* is a

well-known, other, associative technique: the researcher provides the respondent with a portion of a sentence, and this must be further supplemented by the respondent.

Personification is a technique in which a respondent is asked to propose a brand as a person, and then to describe this person. This description can vary from quite concrete characteristics such as gender or appearance, to more abstract attributes such as hobbies and leisure.

In the *User typology*, the respondent describes the typical user of a product, or the typical proponent or opponent regarding an issue. In the latter case, these two typical individuals may be contrasted by the respondent.

With *Collage*, or *Mood board* techniques the reactions of respondents to a complex stimulus are being examined. In the first case — collage — respondents should (the technique is applied more frequently in groups than to individuals) express their feelings towards a societal issue through a collage which they create themselves. This collage is then discussed and explained by the creators. With a mood board, the researcher has at his disposal a collage or a set of different collages designed to evoke a certain mood or feeling. These collages are being offered to the respondents and they are elaborated with one another.

The *Photo sort* technique entails that stimuli are being offered to respondents in the form of photographs. Respondents must then indicate which of the photos fit best (least well) to a given service, and the choices made by the respondent can then be jointly evaluated. However, often photos are used of which the associative meanings have already been established in earlier (quantitative) research using other respondents. In this case, the Photo sort is called a validated instrument.

15.5 IDEA: Cognitive Elicitation Techniques

Cognitive techniques are deployed when the researcher wishes to obtain insights in the cognitive domain of the mental world of the individual, that is to say, in thinking, reasoning, organising, etc.

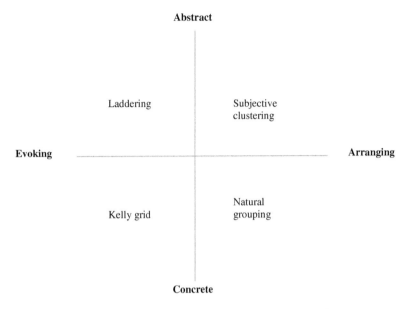

Figure 15.2:   Categorisation of *Cognitive* Elicitation Techniques.

Again, several techniques are available, and these can also be classified on the basis of two dimensions:

1.   The first dimension may be the type of task which must be car-
     ried out by the respondent, to be interpreted as a sliding
     dichotomy, with "evoking" and "arranging" as the extremes of
     the dichotomy.
2.   The second dimension can be termed as "common denomina-
     tor", with as extremes "concrete" and "abstract". This concerns
     the extent to which the dimensionality and significance of a
     brand is being elaborated with the respondent.

A number of distinctive cognitive techniques are included in
Figure 15.2 positioned *vis-à-vis* these two dimensions.

15.5.1 *Prototypical cognitive techniques*

Laddering is used to gain insight into the structure of meanings a
brand has for the individual, and in the manner in which they are

linked. Typically, one starts with fairly superficial attributes of the brand, but by asking further questions the researcher attempts to penetrate into deeper layers of meaning.

Subjective clustering is used to understand the dimensions that are used by respondents to assess and compare products. Respondents are being offered a variety of product attributes and they must divide them into different groups (categorise).

Natural grouping seeks the same as subjective clustering, but an essential difference is that in natural grouping concrete stimuli are presented to the respondent. For example, different brands within one product category. The respondent must divide the stimuli into two groups and explain in what way the two groups differ. This procedure may be repeated for each of the groups until no further division is possible.

The *Kelly grid* is used to discover what specific attributes are used for the assessment and comparison of brands. In the standard version, various sets of three brands are offered to the respondent repeatedly. The respondent is required to indicate in what way two of them match and at the same time differ as compared to the third brand. Often, the Kelly grid is executed prior to Laddering.

15.6 IDEA: Conative Elicitation Techniques

Conative techniques are applied when insight is desired in the behavioural inclinations of an individual in relation to a particular service. The techniques that promote this again may be arranged by two dimensions:

1.   The first dimension indicates the perspective, or the subject, as a continuum with the extremes of the "researcher" and the "respondent". At one extreme it is the researcher who perceives a situation and reports about it; at the other end, it is the respondent who carries out this task. Hybrid forms in which both researcher and respondent are active lie in between.
2.   The second dimension refers to the degree of interference in the situation, with as extremes "observation" (the existing

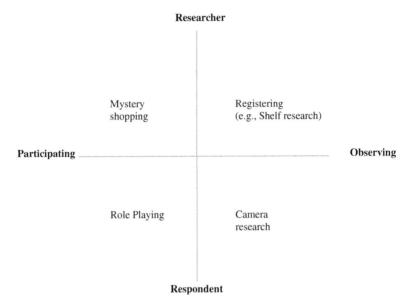

Figure 15.3:   Categorisation of *Conative* Elicitation Techniques.

situation remains unchanged) and "participation" (the situation is affected by the subject).

Figure 15.3 displays various prototypical *conative* elicitation techniques in four quadrants.

15.6.1 *Prototypical conative techniques*

Mystery shopping means that the researcher will acknowledge the role of the consumer and will enter realistic situations with respect to a specific service in the same way a consumer would experience such a situation, while taking an active role. The investigator assesses the service according to pre-defined criteria.

Registering (such as Shelf research) occurs when a researcher observes the behaviour of a consumer in a realistic setting (cf. shopping behaviour).

Camera research is an example of a technique where a respondent is asked to capture his own acts (for example, making daily errands) in this case with a camera. This recording is then evaluated.

Role-play is used to gain insight into the behaviour of respondents in specific situations by having them mimic these situations first, to be followed by an evaluation of this behaviour. In view of its requirements, the technique is specifically suitable for group settings. The individual variant is used with two roles, one for the researcher and one for the respondent.

15.7 Conclusion

The IDEA taxonomy clearly, and logically, connects two elements: the characteristics of information as required by the researcher for the study and the ensuing deliberate choice of one or more elicitation techniques.

The author (Stalpers, 2007) ends his publication by presenting his view on IDEA (quotes translated):

> "IDEA represents an attempt to arrange and categorise elicitation techniques in such a way that there is a functional link between the characteristics of the information to be acquired (see the problem analysis and especially the research questions) on the one hand, and the targeted choice of elicitation techniques on the other hand."
>
> "As such, the proposed taxonomy can be viewed as a further contribution to the *scientific substantiation* of *applied qualitative research*."

Chapter 16

Observation and Participant Observation

16.1 Introduction

Observation and participant observation are methods of data collection, mostly used in qualitative studies. Participant observation refers to the process of being part of a group or an organisation for a certain period of time while making systematic observations of, for instance, their ideas, values, convictions, perceptions, preferences, judgments, and behaviour.

As Mintzberg (1979, p. 583) says in a comparison between quantitative methods and observation approaches: "Too many of the results have been significant only in the statistical sense of the word. In our work, we have always found that simpler, more direct methodologies have yielded more useful results. Like sitting down in a manager's office and *watching* what he does. Or tracing the flow of decisions in an organization." It is his conviction that some forms of knowledge and insights can only be gained from a process of extended observation, and the creative interpretation of these observations. In this chapter, we will review the definitional characteristics of observation, and the various steps to be taken when carrying out observational processes as part of a qualitative study.

Webb *et al.* (1966) identified observational studies in which the investigator acts as a passive recorder who avoids provoking or interrupting responses. Cochran (1983) focused on the planning and analysis of observational studies. The observer systematically seeks out and organises data rather than focusing on achieving one, situationally-defined goal. It is required to keep detailed records of what occurs, including those things taken for granted in other contexts. Observations are closely monitored for evidence of bias, and the researcher detaches himself/herself from the situation to review notes from a neutral perspective.

Rather than simply observe, researcher(s) during the process of participant observation actively participate(s) in the firm/society being studied. This was the focus of Friedrichs and Luedtke (1975) and Spradley (1980). Whyte (1991) used the term "participatory action research". Examples of research conducted using participant observation include Brednikova and Pachenkov (2002), and Dana and Light (2011).

16.1.1 *Mere observation versus participant observation*

Mere observation should be distinguished from *participant* observation. Webb *et al.* (2000, p. 102) indicate that current examples of a mere observational process would involve "the rug on the floor, the drapes on the window, the white telephone, the second secretary and the corner office as signs of the employee's success with the firm". The difference between observation and participant observation, however, is that in the case of participant observation the researcher(s) actively participate(s) in the firm/society being studied.

Mintzberg (1979, p. 585) notes in this context: "we have always tried to go into organizations with a well-defined focus to collect specific kinds of data systematically. In one study we wanted to know who contacts the manager, how, for how long, and why; in the second we were interested in the sequence of steps used in making certain key decisions; in the third, we are after chronologies of decision in various strategic areas. Those are the 'hard' data of our research, and they have been crucial in all of our studies." The author goes on and proposes (p. 587) that *systematic* data are to be supported by anecdotal data. "For while systematic data create the foundation for our theories, it is the *anecdotal data that enable us to do the building.* Theory building seems to require rich description, the richness that comes from anecdote. We uncover all kinds of relationships in our "hard" data, but it is only through the use of this "soft" data that we are able to "explain" them, and explanation is, or course, the purpose of research."

Bryman *et al.* (2015, p. 444) make a comparison between the concepts of participant observation and ethnography and indicate that these are rather entangled. "The common definitional element is that the participant observer/ethnographer immerses himself or herself in a group for an extended period of time, observing behaviour, listening to what is said in conversations both between others, and with the field worker, and asking questions." The denotational value of the term "participant observation" is such that in this case the data collection aspect of the process — observation — tends to be called up.

16.1.2 *Participant observation*

Participant observation is a research approach aimed at (Denzin, 1989, p. 157) recording "the ongoing experiences of those observed, through their symbolic world." The observer may be either known to those observed, or not. An attempt is made to observe (p. 157) "the evolution and unfolding of social action through time and across situations" while taking the perspective of those observed as a starting point. More specifically, people may be interviewed by asking open-ended questions, documents from the past are analysed, census data are collected, informants may be employed, and direct observations of on-going events are made.

The researcher tries to keep an open mind when it comes to outcome expectations and hypotheses throughout the research process. He attempts to *understand the experiences* of those observed by interpreting the meanings of their social actions.

Participant observation involves being together with the observed individual (or group) who behaves in his (their) natural setting. This might, for instance, mean that the researcher starts to work as a dock worker, while living and being housed in the part of the city where they all work. Also, he would engage in their social lives and spend leisure time together. By learning more of the symbolic world those observed live in he also learns about their culture, norms and values, habits, thoughts, and behaviours.

The researcher may decide to create a suitable (but false) identity, or he may decide to present his own identity. In either case the idea is that the observer is accepted by the individual or the group, and that he gets permission to ask questions from time to time.

Observers may experience what is called (p. 164) a "cultural shock", as they may enter an entirely new world. Generally speaking, researcher may move through a four-phased process: the honeymoon phase (no problems), the crisis phase, the recovery stage, and a state of adjustment.

While paying attention both to principles, strategies, procedures, methods and techniques of participant observations researcher Jorgensen (1989, pp. 13–14) defines this research methodology in terms of seven basic features:

1. An interest in human meaning and interaction as viewed from the perspective from the people involved in the situation or setting under research.
2. Location in the here and now.
3. A form of theory or theorising stressing interpretation and understanding of human existence.
4. A logic and process of inquiry that is flexible and amenable to constant redefinition of the problem.
5. An in-depth, qualitative case study approach and design.
6. The performance of a participant role while maintaining a relationship with those individuals who are to be observed.
7. Data collection through the use of direct observation as one of the ways to collect these data.

Spradley (1980, pp. 53–58) takes another angle, that is, the angle of role definition. He portrays the differences between an *ordinary participant* in a social situation on the one hand, and the *participant observer* in the same situation on the other hand. It turns out that the participant observer takes a number of roles as follows:

- **Dual purpose:** Engaging in activities which are appropriate to the situation combined with making observations of the "activities, people, and physical aspects of the situation".
- **Explicit awareness:** Instead of blocking out all kinds of information as an ordinary participant (wisely) does, the participant observer tries to "increase his awareness, to raise the level of attention, and to tune in things usually turned out".
- **Wide-angle lens:** "Taking in a much broader spectrum of information".
- **The insider/outsider experience:** On the one hand, being a full participant in a social situation, and on the other hand being a "detached observer".
- **Introspection:** Using the process of introspection, or reflection, to gain an understanding of the dynamics of the events of the social situation.
- **Record keeping:** Keeping a "detailed record of both objective observations and subjective feelings."

Finally, participant observation may also be defined through the steps to take when carrying out a full research project. Thus, when carrying out a participant observation study a number of steps are taken, Jorgensen (1989, p. 176):

- A problem analysis is carried out.
- A field setting is selected.
- Initial field contacts are made.
- Key concepts are defined, specific research methods are selected.
- Data are collected, if necessary theoretical notions are adapted.
- General categories are developed for the data analysis to carry out.
- Analysis of the data takes place.
- The writing of the research report is taking place; if necessary, additional data are collected.

16.2 Advantages and Disadvantages

Let us start with some broad statements about the general advantages of the participant observation approach. Mintzberg (1979, p. 588), while making a plea for qualitative observations, says: "We can [also] question whether the human brain prefers to think in terms of continuous and bivariate relationships, or searches for another kind of order, characterized by clusters or configurations, ideal or pure types."... (p. 588): "But to generate those configurations, I have more faith in typologies than taxonomies. In other words, while I believe we need empirical data to generate our categories — systematic data reinforced by a good deal of anecdote — I do not expect them to come from mechanical data reduction techniques. It is pattern recognition we are after, in the form of those creative leaps, and I believe that human, not electronic, brains are most capable of achieving those leaps."

In more concrete terms, Bryman *et al.* (2015, p. 453) observe both advantages and disadvantages when it comes to the "covert role in ethnography", that is, the role of being engaged in participant observation. We will present these in the words of the authors.

Advantages include:

- There is no problem of access because the researcher does not have to seek permission to gain entry to a social setting or organisation.
- Reactivity is not a problem because participants do not know the person conducting the study is a researcher. Therefore, they are less likely to adjust their behaviour because of the researcher's presence.

Disadvantages include:

- The problem of taking notes. When people do not realise you are conducting research it may be difficult, or even impossible, to take notes and relying solely on memory may be risky.
- The problem of not being able to use other methods. It is not really possible to carry out interviews. In addition, steering spontaneous conversations in order to collect specific data for fear of detection.

- **Anxiety:** The researcher experiences stress or anxiety when he imagines that his cover may be blown at any moment. When this should happen, a consequence could be that the research project abruptly and unavoidably comes to a halt.
- **Ethical problems:** The subjects are deceived as to the real objectives of the researcher and the subjects do not have the opportunity to wilfully consent to their role in the research design. Finally, privacy issues may play a role for the subjects.

Finally, Patton (1980, pp. 124–126) puts forward six strengths of observational methods in general. When applied to the process of participant observation the following can be said:

- Being in direct contact with those involved makes it possible to assess the context within which the observations are to be made.
- The observer is able to directly observe a phenomenon as such which allows him to utilise an "inductive, discovery-oriented approach".
- An observer may observe particulars of a phenomenon that otherwise would not have been recognised.
- Aspects of the phenomenon which are sensitive to the interviewee's may be observed directly instead of asking questions; as a consequence, no such questions need to be asked, and resulting biases may be avoided.
- The observer adds his own observations to the — often — selective perceptions of the subjects. And even if the observations of the observer are selective to a point, the availability of multiple sources of information may improve the general comprehensiveness of the body of data.
- The observer may benefit from first-hand experience by being able to use and access personal knowledge and direct experiences as related to the phenomenon under study.

Also, the *validity* of the participant observation approach must be addressed as it may influence its advantage/disadvantage balance. Denzin (1989, pp. 171–175) proposes that "issues regarding the **validity** of such a study may require attention". The author makes the following remarks:

External validity, focusing on the generalisation of the study's outcomes, may be degraded by the fact that the respondents have (a set of) unique characteristics. Furthermore, the population may not be stable over time, or may not be stable in terms of location and geography.

Internal validity may be threatened by a number of factors or circumstances such as:

- Historical factors, which may include prior events, intervening events, the larger historical scene, the inner history (a shared history of for instance a group).
- Subject maturation (relationships between the observer and the ones observed will result in biased outcomes).
- Subject bias (not all of the characteristics of the subjects observed are uncovered).
- Subject mortality (those subjects who leave the research setting).
- Reactive effects of the observer (observers produce unwanted effects on subjects).
- Changes in the observer (they have to be recorded).
- Peculiar aspects of situations (they must be comparable and documented).

Having discussed both advantages and disadvantages of the participant observation approach we will now turn to its best practices.

16.3 Best Practices

The structure of this section is as follows. First, we will discuss the role of the observer in the process of (participant) observation, followed by data collection practices and field notes. Finally, the data analysis will be sketched.

16.3.1 *The role of the observer*

Patton (1980, pp. 137–138) describes various different approaches to the observation process. These approaches are defined by a specific combination of five "primary dimensions". The researcher must make choices regarding each of these five dimensions and combine them in order to arrive at a detailed and functional observation approach. The aforementioned dimensions, as focused on the observation process, include the following:

- **Role of the observer:** Full participant observation versus onlooker observation as an outsider.
- **Portrayal of the observatory role to others:** Overt observations (it is known that observations are being made and by whom) versus covert observations (no knowledge about observations being made).
- **Portrayal of the purpose of the observations:** Ranging from full explanation, partial explanation, no explanation, and false explanation.
- **Duration of the observations:** Single observation with limited duration versus long-term, multiple observations.
- **Focus of the observations:** Narrow focus (only specific features of a phenomenon are observed) versus broad focus (all of the features of a phenomenon are observed in a holistic way).

Bruyn (1966, pp. 14–15), provides a more interpersonal, experiential perspective when he argues that the role of the participant observer requires both detachment and personal involvement. "Sympathetic identification" "includes empathic communication in the life of the observed through identification and role-taking. In this type of involvement, the observer is both detached and effectively participating."

Turning to the level of general methods, Webb *et al.* (2000, pp. 113–114) make a distinction between three types of observational methods:

1. Observational methods to be applied when the observer "plays an unobserved, passive, and non-intrusive role in the research situation."
2. Observational methods to be applied when the "observer plays an active role in structuring the situation, but in which he is still

unobserved by the actors." In this case, for instance, recording devices may be brought into the situation which are being used to make the observations. Web *et al.* (2000, p. 143) call this type of observation "*contrived observation*".

3. The visible "research-observer approach and the participant-observation method"; however, they may create comparatively high risks of reactivity (of the subject to be observed), in contrast to the first two types of observational methods. An example: when the people in a specific street at some point become aware that they are being observed they are likely to change their mental focus and their behavior, introducing in this way bias with respect to the observations as carried out by the observers.

16.3.2 *Data collection*

When it comes to data collection methods, the following observation may be made. The observer systematically seeks out and organises data rather than focusing on achieving one situationally defined goal. It is required to keep detailed records of what occurs, including those things taken for granted in other contexts.

Turning to *types of data,* Jorgensen (1989, pp. 22–23) lists a number of ways to collect these data. First and foremost, direct observation is in order. Next to this, documents, and other forms of communication may be utilised. Also, informants may be employed as sources of information. Finally, conversations, formal and informal interviews, and even questionnaires may serve as useful vehicles to collect relevant data. Also, the use of only one researcher, or conversely, a team of researchers may be chosen for the data collection. In all cases, data need to be recorded whenever possible.

Multiple observer roles may be chosen from. Gans (1968), as cited in Bryman *et al.* (2015, p. 458), observes that researchers generally do not take up a particular role as a participant observer; rather they assume various different roles *during the process of collecting data* as part of the study they aim to carry out. In this context, Gans distinguishes between three participant observer roles:

1. **Total participant:** The researcher is completely involved in a certain situation, only afterwards he writes his notes.
2. **Researcher-participant:** The researcher participates in the situation. However, he is only partially involved, thus being able to fully function as a researcher in the situation.
3. **Total researcher:** The researcher makes observations while not being involved in the situation. Consequently, he is able to fully focus on the observations as a researcher.

With respect to research and *data collection* in organisational settings, the researcher (p. 459) again may play various different roles, such as "consultant", "apprentice", of "confidant", even within one research project. The role taken may imply joining, to some degree, in activities of the subjects to observe.

Finally, Symon and Cassell (2013, p. 246) discuss *participant selection*. The authors state that two principles must be adhered to:

1. **Representativeness:** Some breadth and variation among interviewees belonging to a certain defined category provides a better coverage of this category of interviewees intended.
2. **Quality in the interview responses:** Not only selecting key informants who are able to express themselves at an excellent level in terms of intellectual, verbal, emotional, and moral responses.

In summary, a certain balance must be found in seeking both a breadth of representation and depth with respect to the choice of interviewees.

16.3.3 *Field notes*

In general terms, one could say that observations are closely monitored for evidence of bias, and the researcher detaches himself/herself from the situation to *review notes* from a neutral perspective. Let us zoom in on the production and use of *field notes*.

The process of data collection, first and foremost, implies taking field notes as based on their observations. Bryman *et al.* (2015, pp. 461–462) describe field notes as "fairly detailed summaries of events and behaviour and the researcher's initial reflections on them." And also, "the notes need to specify key dimensions of whatever is observed or heard."

The authors go on to present a number of general principles that guide the structure and content of field notes. These principles include the following:

- Notes have to be written down as quickly as possible after observing or hearing something of interest to the study.
- Full field notes should be created the same day as the observations were made; details to be included are "location, who was involved, what prompted the exchange, date and time of the day, etc."
- Using a digital recorder to make initial notes implies making lengthy transcriptions of these recordings.
- Notes must be written in such a way that its content remains comprehensible even after an extended period of time.
- Notes should be made in abundance, with rich detail.

Obviously, the task of making observations and taking notes while being immersed in the research scene may be a daunting task, requiring much perseverance.

Finally, Bryman *et al.* (2015, pp. 462–463) present a *classification*, or *types* of *field notes*. They distinguish between three types of notes: *mental notes*, to be made when it is not feasible to take notes using paper and pencil; *jotted notes*, very brief notes (short phrases, quotes, key words) jotted on a piece of paper; these notes have to be written out at a later point in time when the researcher has some privacy to dot this; and *full field notes*, i.e., fully fledged and elaborated notes that serve as the data to be analysed at a later time. Such kinds of notes typically would include "information about events, people, conversations". Full field notes should be elaborated as soon as possible, and preferably before the end of the day they were taken. These notes may also contain ideas about interpretation and recordings of impressions and feelings.

According to the authors (pp. 463–464), the process of data collection may come to a close because of a number of reasons. For instance, an agreed time period has come to an end, or deadlines are reached. Also, all of the money available for research may have been spent. Or a point of saturation was reached in the sense that the researcher is of the opinion that all has been observed that matters for the study and the data available at that point warrant answering all of the research questions that were raised at the start of the study.

16.3.4 *Data analysis*

We will end with a brief note on data analysis approaches. These approaches will be sketched in general terms, suggesting only basic steps.

Jorgenson (1989, pp. 107–115) describes the process of analysing the data and theorising on its outcomes in terms of principles and procedures. The coding process starts with coding and labelling field notes. Next, the analysis process focuses on spotting (p. 115) "essential features, patterns, relationships, processes and sequences, comparing and contrasting, as well as formulating types and classes"... (p. 116), "theory and theorizing take a variety of forms, including analytic induction, sensitizing concepts, grounded theory, existential theory, and hermeneutic theory." Thus, it is clear that the researcher may choose from multiple analysis approaches for the analysis of participant observation data. The choice should be based on the research paradigm and the type of knowledge and insights required by the researcher.

16.4 Sample Study

In order to demonstrate how a study employing participant observation techniques may be carried out an overview of Dana's (2008) study is provided, and the excellent participant observation characteristics of this study are highlighted.

16.4.1 *Issue and relevance*

The Sámi people live in the indigenous nation of Sápmi (formerly known as Lapland), covering Norway, among other places. Until the middle of the twentieth century, a self-employed Sámi reindeer herder in Norway could subsist on 250 reindeers. These were owned individually but cared for collectively by means of flexible entrepreneurial networks.

Reindeer herders, interviewed for this study, have been adapting successfully to technological, regulatory, and other changes. Yet, they are concerned that, if herding is reduced to an element of the food industry, the essence and efficiency of their community-based, symbiotic entrepreneurship will be undermined. While reindeer herders are attracted or pulled towards traditional community entrepreneurship, many are forced or pushed into secondary money-driven enterprises, less close to their tradition.

16.4.2 Research goal

The purpose of this study is to add to the understanding of the traditional culture and value system of the Sámi people, including the striking form of their entrepreneurships, in the light of current technological changes and the march of the present-day global market system and economic system that act as a force for them to change their culture and their way of living, and their traditional entrepreneurial system.

16.4.3 Research design

A classic participant observation study based on the immersion of the researcher in the community of the Sámi people for an extended period in order to develop "inside" knowledge and understanding.

16.4.4 Sample design

The population to be studied was the Sámi people community in Norway; the sample consisted of a number of Sámi families and individuals.

16.4.5 Data collection

Data were collected using participant observation and interviews as the primary tools.

16.4.6 *Data analysis*

Data were analysed through a process of meaning making as based on the notes of the interviews and the field notes made. Direct on-site observations were supplied by several sources of data. Triangulation was used to cross-validate across these.

16.4.7 *Report*

A text report describing and explaining the observations and interview outcomes, thus offering meaning as to the experience world of the subjects involved, their thoughts, feelings, and their behaviours. Outcomes were related to the relevant academic literature in order to offer more insights to the reader and to contribute and to fill knowledge gaps of the scientific community.

16.4.8 *Excellent participant observation characteristics of the study*

For a participant observation study to be excellent a number of conditions have to be met. These include the following: The research problem has to be clear and relevant. The research design must be functional for the research purpose. Data collection must be to the point and exhaustive. Data analysis must involve the culture of the members of the community while providing novel and deep insights into the social and entrepreneurial world of the community. That is, above all, interpreting meaning processes as these provide an explanation of the mental processes and the behaviours of community members. All of these are the case in this study.

This is a classical participant observation study. The research objective was clearly formulated, as based on the extensive literature. The following characteristics of the study point to its excellence:

- The researcher was able to live with the Sámi people for a prolonged time in order to make observations and do the work in the field as a coworker of the Sámi reindeer herders, and as a truly participant observer.

- The research team became accepted into the community, while individuals became increasingly open. Triangulation was used for verification purposes.
- The researcher focused on the cultural history of the Sámi people, and the way this shaped their remarkable entrepreneurial structure. Next, he was able to fathom the ways new, Western techniques and the Western economic system influenced, and threatened, their culture and their entrepreneurial system, and how they responded to these threats.
- The analysis elaborates on these characteristics and evolutions, being a mix of description and meaning-making. Systematically, all aspects of the Sámi people's life, their culture and habits, their basic values and normative beliefs, and the traditional entrepreneurial structure that defines their way of herding reindeer are presented and described and explained. Moreover, the analysis chooses as an angle the external threats they face, as described earlier.
- The report is written in such a way that the reader easily picks up life, life conditions, cultural values, and entrepreneurial behaviour of the Sámi people. Thus, clear insights are offered into the enchanting world of this community.

Chapter 17

Conclusion

Looking back on the concept of methodology, and the specific qualitative methodologies as discussed, two observations may be made:

1. The choice of a specific methodology should be based on the type of knowledge and insight you would like to acquire, and the context of the study.
2. For each type of methodology specific starting points and ensuing methodological characteristics must be observed. Generally, when a (fully) matured theory is the starting point, it will prescribe a way to "see the world", a coherent way to collect the data, and a consistent way to analyse the data.

If, and only if these requirements are met manuscripts unveiling methodological rigour may be anticipated.

17.1 10 Steps to Increase Rigour

1. Clearly identify a useful research objective, a research framework, and a realistic and worthy research objective, question. Verschuren and Doorewaard (2010) assist the scholar in doing this. Be focused and avoid data overload. The task of analysing data will be facilitated if the study is based on a conceptual framework.

277

2. Read the research that has already been done and search whether there is a void in the literature.
3. Establish a strategic research protocol, i.e., a map of your research, with a time line; include (i) what you will be doing; (ii) how; and (iii) why this is important. Decide how to analyse your data before collecting it.
4. Be flexible with regards to data collection methods. As stated by Sandelowski, "Qualitative descriptive designs typically are an eclectic but reasonable combination of sampling, and data collection, analysis, and re-presentation techniques" (2000, p. 334). Let the unexpected happen if it can be beneficial. Piore (1979) explained how he adopted the interview method of data collection.
5. To maintain validity during interviews, be a good listener; interviewees should be allowed to provide the majority of the research input.
6. Record accurately all impressions including those that do not seem very important at the time (Eisenhardt, 1989, p. 539); incorrect grammar, typos, and/or inconsistencies jeopardise the validity of an otherwise good study.
7. It is the researcher's task to properly interpret the responses of the research subject(s). Analysis should be on going as data is collected; unlike the case of quantitative research, the distinction between data collection and analysis is less sharp for qualitative studies. Overlap data collection with analysis including field notes. Denzin and Lincoln (2011) discussed the qualitative researcher as a *bricoleur*. As discussed by Denzin (1970), triangulation, i.e., the gathering of data on the same theme from a variety of sources, can be very useful; triangulation may increase accuracy and enhance dependability. Denzin (1978) identified several types of triangulation: (i) the convergence of multiple data sources; (ii) methodological triangulation which involves the convergence of data from multiple data collection sources; and (iii) investigator triangulation in which multiple researchers are involved in an investigation. Triangulation reduces the risk that the research outcomes are partly dependent on characteristics of the research process. Thus, potential biases of this kind may be reduced, or eliminated.

8. Analysis is central to the production of meaningful and valid research; data must be turned into useful information. Content analysis is among the many tools available for this.

9. Seek feedback from interviewees as well as colleagues.

10. In your submission, present evidence from your data (including observations and quotations) to support interpretations. Avoid using percentages if numbers are small. Avoid describing what is in a table in the text; explore implications instead. Do not over-generalise and never claim things that are not there. Include primary data in your manuscript submission; this allows reviewers to see the basis on which the researcher's conclusions were made. It is better to include too much detail than too little. Also, admit limitations in data collection as this demonstrates reflexivity of researcher(s) and contributes to the research validity.

We end with a quote from Eisenhardt *et al.* (2016). In their article (p. 1113) they elaborate on the ways inductive methods may tackle the so-called "grand challenges", that is problems such as urban poverty, insect-borne disease, and global hunger. The authors state (p. 1121): "Our broader aim is to further the agenda of grand challenges by clarifying inductive methods — that is, how to avoid false rigor or what we term 'rigor mortis' and instead how to embrace 'rigor' (and quality) in inductive research by generating strong theory that is well grounded in rich data and achieves insight."

References

Adair, J. G. (1984). The Hawthorne Effect: A Reconsideration of the Methodological Artifact. *Journal of Applied Psychology* **69** (2), pp. 334–345.

Ahrens, T. and Chapman, C. S. (2006). Doing Qualitative Research in Management Accounting: Positioning Data to Contribute to Theory. *Accounting, Organizations and Society* **31**, pp. 819–841.

Ahuvia, A. (2001). Traditional, Interpretive and Reception Based Content Analysis: Improving the Ability of Content Analysis to Address Issues of Pragmatic and Theoretical Concern. *Social Indicators Research* **54** (2), pp. 139–172; Liu, K., Clarke, R. J., Andersen, P. B. and Stamper, R. K. (2001). *Technology Studies in Organisational Semiotics*. Norwell: Kluwer.

Andersen, T. H., Boeriis, M., Maagero, E. and Tonnessen, E. S. (2015). *Social Semiotics Key Figures, New Directions*. London: Routledge.

Arnold, H. J. and Feldman, D. C. (1981). Social Desirability Response Bias in Self-Report Choice Situations. *Academy of Management Journal* **24**, pp. 377–385.

Arnold, H. J., Feldman, D. C. and Purbhoo, M. (1985). The Role of Social Desirability Response Bias in Turnover Research. *Academy of Management Journal* **28**, pp. 955–966.

Avenier, M.-J. and Thomas, C. (2015). Finding One's Way Around Various Methodological Guidelines for Doing Rigorous Case Studies: A Comparison of Four Epistemological Frameworks. *Systèmes d'Information et Management* **20** (1), pp. 61–98.

Baker, S. M., Holland, J. and Kaufman-Scarborough, C. (2007). How Consumers with Disabilities Perceive "Welcome" in Retail Servicescapes: A Critical Incident Study. *Journal of Services Marketing* **21** (3), pp. 160–173.

Barkhuizen, G. (2013). Introduction: Narrative Research in Applied Linguistics. In: *Narrative Research in Applied Linguistics*. G. Barkhuizen (Ed.). Cambridge University Press.

Barling, J., Weber, T. and Kelloway, E. K. (1996). Effects of Transformational Leadership Training on Attitudinal and Financial Outcomes: A Field Experiment. *Journal of Applied Psychology* **81** (6), pp. 827–832.

Beach, R., Muhlemann, A. P., Price, D. H. R., Paterson, A. and Sharp, J. A. (2001). The Role of Quantitative Methods in Production Management Research. *International Journal of Production Economics* **74**, pp. 201–212.

Bengtsson, M. (2016). How to Plan and Perform a Qualitative Study using Content Analysis. *NursingPlus Open* **2**, pp. 8–14.

Berg, B. L. (1995). *Qualitative Research Methods for the Social Sciences*. Pearson Education.

Berg, B. L. (2001). *Qualitative Research Methods for the Social Sciences*. Boston: Allyn and Bacon.

Bertrand, M. and Mullainathan, S. (2004). Are Emily and Greg More Employable than Lakisha and Jamal? A Field Experiment on Labour Market Discrimination. *American Economic Review* **94** (4), pp. 991–1013.

Beverland, M. and Lindgreen, A. (2010). What Makes a Good Case Study? A Positivist Review of Qualitative Case Research Published in Industrial Marketing Management, 1971–2006. *Industrial Marketing Management* **39**, pp. 56–63.

Bitner, M. J., Booms, B. H. and Tetreault, M. S. (1990). The Service Encounter: Diagnosing Favorable and Unfavorable Incidents. *Journal of Marketing Research* **54**, pp. 71–84.

Blumer, H. (1969). *Symbolic Interactionism: Perspective and Method*. Englewood Cliffs, New Jersey: Prentice-Hall.

Bohnet, I. (2016). *What Works: Gender Equality by Design*. Cambridge, MA: Belknap Press of Harvard University Press.

Bolman, L. and Deal, T. E. (2008). *Reframing organizations Artistry, Choice, and Leadership*, 4th edn. San Francisco: Jossey-Bass.

Bolognini, M. (2001). *Democrazia elettronica (Electronic Democracy)*. Rome: Carocci.

Bowen, G. A. (2003). Social Funds as a Strategy for Poverty Reduction in Jamaica: An exploratory study. Dissertation Abstracts International. University Microfilms AAT 3130417, Doctoral dissertation, Florida International University, A65/04, 1557.

Bowen, G. A. (2009). Document Analysis as a Qualitative Research Method. *Qualitative Research Journal* **9** (2), pp. 27–40.

Boyce, C. and Neale, P. (2006). *Conducting In-depth Interviews: A Guide for Designing and Conducting In-Depth Interviews for Evaluation Input.* Watertown, Massachusetts: Pathfinder International.

Braun, V. and Clarke, V. (2006). Using Thematic Analysis in Psychology. *Qualitative Research in Psychology* **3** (2), pp. 77–101. ISSN 1478-0887.

Brednikova, O. E. and Pachenkov, O. V. (2002). Migrants: 'Caucasians' in St. Petersburg. *Anthropology & Archeology of Eurasia* **41** (2), pp. 43–89.

Bristor, J. M., Lee, R. G. and Hunt, M. R. (1995). Race and Ideology: African-American Images in Television Advertising. *Journal of Public Policy and Marketing* **14** (1), pp. 48–62.

Bruce, C. (2007). Questions Arising about Emergence, Data Collection, and Its Interaction with Analysis in a Grounded Theory Study. *International Journal of Qualitative Methods* **6** (1), pp. 51–68.

Bruner, E. M. (1997). Ethnography as Narrative. In: *Memory, Identity, Community: The Idea of Narrative in the Human Sciences.* L. P. Hinchman and S.K. Hinchman (Eds.). New York: State University of New York Press, Albany.

Bruyn, S. T. (1966). The Human Perspective in Sociology: The Methodology of Participant Observation. Englewood Cliffs, New Jersey: Prentice-Hall.

Bryan, J. H. and Test, M. A. (1966). A Lady in Distress: The Flat Tire Experiment, Princeton, New Jersey: Educational Testing Service.

Bryman, A. and Bell, E. (2015). *Business Research Methods* (Fourth edn.). Oxford: Oxford University Press.

Busch, C., De Maret, P. S., Flynn, T., Kellum, R., Le, S., Meyers, B., Saunders, M., White, R. and Palmquist, M. (1994–2012). Content Analysis. Writing@ CSU. Colorado State University. Available at https://writing.colostate.edu/guides/guide.cfm?guideid=61.

Cameron, W. B. (1963). *Informal Sociology: A Casual Introduction to Sociological Thinking.* New York: Random House.

Chell, E. and Pittaway, L. (1998). A Study of Entrepreneurship in the Restaurant and Café Industry: Exploratory Work Using the Critical Incident Technique as a Methodology. *International Journal of Hospitality Management* **17** (1), pp. 23–32.

Chomsky, N. (1957). Syntactic Structures, The Hague/Paris: Mouton, ISBN 978-3-11-021832-9

Cochran, W. G. (1983). *Planning and Analysis of Observational Studies.* New York: Wiley.

Conger, J. A. (1998). Qualitative Research as the Cornerstone Methodology for Understanding Leadership. *Leadership Quarterly* **9** (1), pp. 107–121.

Cope, J. and Watts, G. (2000). Learning by Doing — An Exploration of Experience, Critical Incidents and Reflection in Entrepreneurial Learning. *International Journal of Entrepreneurial Behaviour & Research* **6** (3), pp.104–124.

Creswell, J. W. (2007). *Qualitative Inquiry and Research Design. Choosing Among Five Approaches,* Second edn. London: Sage.

Creswell, J. W. (2009). *Research Design: Qualitative, Quantitative, and Mixed Methods Approaches.* Los Angeles: Sage.

Creswell, J. W. (2014). *Educational Research: Planning, Conducting and Evaluating Quantitative and Qualitative Research,* 4th edn. Pearson Education.

Crowne, D. P. (1960). A New Scale of Social Desirability Independent of Psychopathology. *Journal of Consulting Psychology* **24** (4), pp. 349–354.

Curry, A. and Copeman, D. (2005). Reference Service to International Students: A Field Stimulation Research Study. *The Journal of Academic Librarianship* **31** (5), pp. 409–420.

Czarniawska, B. (2004). *Narratives in Social Science Research.* London: Sage Publications.

Czinkota, M. R. and Ronkainen, I. A. (1997). International Business and Trade in the Next Decade: Report from a Delphi Study. *Journal of International Business Studies* **28** (4), pp. 827–844.

Czinkota, M. R. and Ronkainen, I. A. (2005). A Forecast of Globalization, International Business and Trade: Report from a Delphi Study. *Journal of World Business* **40**, pp. 111–123.

Daft, R. L. (1983). Learning the Craft of Organizational Research. *Academy of Management Review* **8** (4), pp. 539–546.

Dalkey, N. and Helmer, O. (1962). An Experimental Application of the Delphi Method to the Use of Experts. Memorandum RM-727/1 — abridged.

Dana, L.-P. (1990). Saint Martin/Sint Maarten: A Case Study of the Effects of Culture on Economic Development. *Journal of Small Business Management* **28** (4), pp. 91–98.

Dana, L.-P. (1995). Entrepreneurship in a Remote Sub-Arctic Community: Nome, Alaska. *Entrepreneurship: Theory and Practice* **20** (1), pp. 55–72. Reprinted in N. Krueger (Ed.) *Entrepreneurship: Critical Perspectives on Business and Management,* Volume IV. London: Routledge, 2002, pp. 255–275.

Dana, L.-P. (2007). A Humility-Based Enterprising Community: The Amish People in Lancaster County. *Journal of Enterprising Communities: People and Places in the Global Economy* **1** (2), pp. 142–154.

Dana, L.-P. (2008). Community-Based Entrepreneurship in Norway. *Entrepreneurship and Innovation* **9** (2), pp. 77–92.

Dana, L.-P. (2011). Entrepreneurship in Bolivia: An Ethnographic Enquiry. *International Journal of Business and emerging markets* **3** (1), pp. 75–88.

Dana, L.-P. and Anderson, R. B. (2007). Taos Pueblo: An Indigenous Community Holding on to Promethean Values. *Journal of Enterprising Communities: People and Places in the Global Economy* **1** (4), pp. 321–336.

Dana, L.-P. and Dana, T. E. (2005). Expanding the Scope of Methodologies Used in Entrepreneurship Research. *International Journal of Entrepreneurship and Small Business* **2** (1), pp. 79–88.

Dana, L.-P. and Dana, T. E. (2008). Ethnicity and Entrepreneurship in Morocco: A Photo-Ethnographic Study. *International Journal of Business and Globalisation* **2** (3), pp. 209–226.

Dana, L.-P. and Galbraith, C. S. (2006). Poverty, Developing Entrepreneurship and Aid Economics in Mozambique: A Review of Empirical Research. In: *Developmental Entrepreneurship: Adversity, Risk, and Isolation*, C. S. Galbraith and C. H. Stiles (Eds.). Oxford: Elsevier, pp. 187–201.

Dana, L.-P., Gurau, C., Light, I. and Muhammad, N. (2019). Family, Community, and Ethnic Capital as Entrepreneurial Resources: Toward an Integrated Model. *Journal of Small Business Management.* DOI: https://doi.org/10.1111/jsbm.12507.

Dana, L.-P. and Light, I. H. (2011). Two Forms of Community Entrepreneurship among Reindeer Herding Entrepreneurs in Finland. *Entrepreneurship & Regional Development* **23** (5–6), pp. 331–352.

Dana, L.-P., Manitok, P. and Anderson, R. B. (2010). The Aivilingmiut People of Repulse Bay (Naujaat), Canada. *Journal of Enterprising Communities: People and Places in the Global Economy* **4** (2), pp. 162–178.

Dana, L.-P. and Wright, R. W. (2009). International Entrepreneurship: Research Priorities for the Future. *International Journal of Globalisation and Small Business* **3** (1), pp. 90–134.

De Loe, R. C. (1995). Exploring Complex Policy Questions Using the Policy Delphi: A Multi-round, Interactive Survey Method. *Applied Geography* **15** (1), pp. 53–68.

Deakins, D. and Freel, M. (1998). Entrepreneurial Learning and the Growth Process in SMEs. *The Learning Organization* **5** (3), pp. 144–155.

Delbecq, A. L., van de Ven, A. H. and Gustafson, D. H. (1975). *Group Techniques for Program Planning*. Glenview, Illinois: Scott Forseman.

Denzin, N. K. (1970). *The Research Act in Sociology: A Theoretical Introduction to Sociological Methods*. Chicago: Aldine.

Denzin, N. K (1978). *The Research Act: A Theoretical Introduction to Sociological Methods*. New York: McGraw-Hill.

Denzin, N. K. (1989). *The Research Act: A Theoretical Introduction to Sociological Methods*, 3rd edn. Englewood Cliffs, NY: Prentice Hall.

Denzin, N. K. and Lincoln, Y. S. (2011). The Discipline and Practice of Qualitative Research. In: Norman K. Denzin, and Yvonna S. Lincoln (Eds.), *The SAGE Handbook of Qualitative Research*, 4th edn. Thousand Oaks, California: Sage Publications, pp. 1–19.

Downey, H. K., and Ireland, R. D. (1979). Quantitative Versus Qualitative: Environmental Assessment in Organizational Studies. *Administrative Science Quarterly* **24** (4), pp. 630–637.

Duffield, C. (1993). The Delphi Technique: A Comparison of Results Obtained Using Two Expert Panels. *International Journal of Nursing Studies* **30** (3), pp. 227–237.

Duriau, V. J., Reger, R. K. and Pfarrer, M. D. (2007). A Content Analysis of the Content Analysis Literature in Organization Studies: Research Themes, Data Sources, and Methodological Refinements. *Organizational Research Methods* **10**, pp. 5–33.

Edvardsson, B. (1992). Service Breakdowns: A Study of Critical Incidents in an Airline. *International Journal of Service Industry Management* **3** (4), pp. 17–29.

Eisenhardt, K. M. (1989). Building Theories from Case Study Research. *The Academy of Management Review* **14** (4), pp. 532–550.

Eisenhardt, K. M. and Graebner, M. E. (2007). Theory Building from Cases: Opportunities and Challenges. *Academy of Management Journal* **50** (1), pp. 25–32.

Eisenhardt, K. M., Graebner, M. E. and Sonenshein, S. (2016). From the Editors. Grand Challenges and Inductive Methods: Rigor without Rigor Mortis. *Academy of Management Journal* **59** (4), pp. 1113–1123.

Elliott, J. (2005). *Using Narrative in Social Research: Qualitative and Quantitative Approaches*. London: Sage Publications.

Erlingsson, C. and Brysiewicz, P. (2017). A Hands-On Guide to Doing Content Analysis. *African Journal of Emergency Medicine* **7** (3), pp. 93–99. Available at: http://creativecommons.org/licenses/by-nc-nd/4.0

Etherington, K. (2009). Narrative Approaches to Case Studies. [Online]. Last accessed 30 July 2019 at http://www.keele.ac.uk/

Fairclough, N. (2003). *Analysing Discourse: Textual Analysis for Social Research.* New York: Routledge.

Feldman, M. S. (1995). *Strategies for Interpreting Qualitative Data.* Qualitative Research Methods, Vol. 33. Sage Publications.

Figueroa, S. K. (2008). The Grounded Theory and the Analysis of Audio-Visual Texts. *International Journal of Social Research Methodology* **11**, pp. 1–12.

Fisher, W. R. (1997). Narration, Reason, and Community. In: *Memory, Identity, Community: The Idea of Narrative in the Human Sciences,* L. P. Hinchman and S. K. Hinchman (Eds.). New York: State University of New York Press, Albany.

FitzGerald, K. N., Seale, S., Kerins, C. A. and McElvaney, R. (2008). The Critical Incident Technique: A Useful Tool for Conducting Qualitative Research. *Journal of Dental Education* **72** (3), pp. 299–304.

Flanagan, J. C. (1954). The Critical Incident Technique. *Psychological Bulletin* **51** (4), pp. 327–358.

Fletcher, A. J. and Marchildon, G. P. (2014). Using the Delphi Method for Qualitative, Participatory Action Research in Health Leadership. *International Journal of Qualitative Methods* **13**, pp. 1–18. Available at: http://creativecommons.org/licenses/by-nc-sa/4.0/.

Flick, U. (2006). *An Introduction to Qualitative Research.* London: Sage Publications.

Flick, U. (2014). *The Sage Handbook of Qualitative Data Analysis.* London: Sage.

Fodd, W. (1993). *Constructing Questions for Interviews and Questionnaires: Theory and Practice in Social Research.* Cambridge: Cambridge University Press.

Fontana, A. and Frey, J. H. (2003). The Interview: From Structured Questions to Negotiated Text. In: *Collecting and Interpreting Qualitative Materials,* 2nd edn., N. K. Denzin and Y. S. Lincoln (Eds.), pp. 61–106. Thousand Oaks, California: Sage.

Fox-Wolfgramm, S. J. (1997). Towards Developing a Methodology for Doing Qualitative Research: The Dynamic-Comparative Case Study Method. *Scandinavian Journal of Management* **13** (4), pp. 439–455.

Fraser, H. (2004). Doing Narrative Research: Analysing Personal Stories Line by Line. *Qualitative Social Work* **3** (2), pp. 179–201.

Freud, S. (1911). Psycho-Analytical Notes on an Autobiographical Account of a Case of Paranoia. In: *The Standard Edition of the Complete Psychological Works of Sigmund Freud,* Volume XII, J. Strachey (Ed.). London: The Hogarth Press.

Friedrichs, J. and Luedtke, H. (1975). *Participant Observation: Theory and Practice.* Lexington, Massachusetts: Lexington Books.

Gabbott, M. and Hogg, G. (1996). The Glory of Stories: Using Critical Incidents to Understand Service Evaluation in the Primary Healthcare Context. *Journal of Marketing Management* **12** (6), pp. 493–503.

Gans, H. J. (1968). The Participant-Observer as Human Being: Observations on the Personal Aspects of Fieldwork. In: *Institutions and the Person: Papers Presented to Everett C. Hughes*, H. S. Becker (Ed.). Chicago: Aldine.

Geertz, C. (1973). *The Interpretation of Cultures: Selected Essays.* New York: Basic Books.

Gibbert, M. and Ruigrok, W. (2010). The 'What' and 'How' of Case Study Rigor: Three Strategies Based on Published Work. *Organizational Research Methods* **13** (4), pp. 710–737.

Giske, T. and Artinian, B. (2007). A Personal Experience of Working with Classical Grounded Theory: From Beginner to Experienced Grounded Theorist. *International Journal of Qualitative Methods* **6** (4), pp. 67–80.

Glaser, B. G. (1968). *Theoretical Sensitivity.* San Francisco: The Sociology Press.

Glaser, B. G. (2002). Conceptualization: On Theory and Theorizing Using Grounded Theory. *International Journal of Qualitative Methods* **1** (2), pp. 23–38.

Glaser, B. G. and Strauss, A. L. (1967). *The Discovery of Grounded Theory: Strategies for Qualitative Research.* New Brunswick, N.J. and London: Transaction Publishers.

Gnatzy, T., Warth, J., von der Gracht, H. and Darkow, I.-L. (2011). Validating an Innovative Real-Time Delphi Approach — A Methodological Comparison between Real-Time and Conventional Delphi Studies. *Technological Forecasting & Social Change* **78**, pp. 1681–1694.

Goldin, C. and Rouse, C. (2000). Orchestrating Impartiality: The Impact of "Blind" Auditions on Female Musicians. *American Economic Review* **90** (4), pp. 715–741.

Golembiewski, R. T. and Munzenrider, R. F. (1975). Social Desirability as an Intervening Variable in Interpreting OD Effects. *Journal of Applied Behavioral Science* **11**, pp. 317–332.

Goodman, C. M. (1987). The Delphi Technique: A Critique. *Journal of Advanced Nursing* **12**, pp. 729–734.

Goodman, L. A. (1961). Snowball Sampling. *The Annals of Mathematical Statistics* **32** (1), pp. 148–170.

Goodsell, C. T. (1976). Cross-Cultural Comparison of Behaviour of Postal Clerks Towards Clients. *Administrative Science Quarterly* **21**, pp. 140–150.

Gordon, W. and Langmaid, R. (1988). *Qualitative Market Research: A Practitioner's Buyer's Guide.* Aldershot: Gower.

Green, K. C., Armstrong, J. S. and Graefe, A. (2007). Methods to Elicit Forecasts from Groups: Delphi and Prediction Markets Compared. MPRA Paper No. 4663. Monash University Business and Economic Forecasting Unit. Available at: http://mpra.ub.uni-muenchen.de/4663/.

Gremler, D. D. (2004). The Critical Incident Technique in Service Research. *Journal of Service Research* **7** (1), pp. 65–89.

Grisham, T. (2009). The Delphi Technique: A Method for Testing Complex and Multifaceted Topics. *International Journal of Managing Projects in Business* **2** (1), pp. 112–130.

Groenland, E. A. G. (2014). The Problem Analysis for Empirical Studies. *International Journal of Business and Globalisation* **12** (3), pp. 249–263.

Groenland, E. A. G. (2018a). A review strategy for carrying out an academic literature analysis as part of the problem analysis for an empirical study. *International Journal of Business and Globalisation,* **20** (4), pp. 497–508.

Groenland, E. A. G. (2018b). Employing the matrix method as a tool for the analysis of qualitative research data in the business domain. *International Journal of Business and Globalisation,* **21** (1), pp. 119–134.

Gubrium, J. and Holstein, J. (1997). *The New Language of Qualitative Method.* New York: Oxford University Press.

Hammersley, M. and Atkinson, P. (1983) *Ethnography: Principles in Practice.* London and New York: Tavistock.

Hauser, O. P., Linos, E. and Rogers, T. (2017). Innovation with Field Experiments: Studying Organizational Behaviours in Actual Organizations. *Research in Organizational Behaviour* **37**, pp. 185–198.

Health and Safety Laboratory for the Health and Safety Executive (2009). Buxton, Derbyshire: HSE Books.

Heisenberg, W. (1958). *Physics & Philosophy: The Revolution in Modern Science.* London: George Allen & Unwin.

Helmer, O. (1967). *Analysis of the Future: The Delphi Method.* DTIC Document. Retrieved from http://oai.dtic.mil/oai/oai?verb=getRecord&metadataPrefix=html&identifier=AD064964 0.

Hodder, I. (1994). The Interpretation of Documents and Material Culture. In: N. K. Denzin and Y. S. Lincoln (Eds.), *Handbook of Qualitative Research.* Thousand Oaks, California: Sage Publications.

Hoepfl, M. C. (1997). Choosing Qualitative Research: A Primer for Technology Education Researchers. *Journal of Technology Education* **9** (1), pp. 47–63.

Hoon, C. (2013). Meta-Synthesis of Qualitative Case Studies: An Approach to Theory Building. *Organizational Research Methods* **16** (4), pp. 522–556.

Hsieh, H.-F. and Shannon, S. E. (2005). Three Approaches to Qualitative Content Analysis. *Qualitative Health Research* **15** (9), pp. 1277–1288. Available at: http://qhr.sagepub.com/content/15/9/1277.short?rss=1&ssource=mfc.

Hsu, C.-C. and Sandford, B. A. (2007). The Delphi Technique: Making Sense of Consensus. *Practical Assessment, Research & Evaluation* **12** (10), pp. 1531–7714.

Hughes, H., Williamson, K. and Lloyd, A. (2007). Critical Incident Technique. In: L. Suzanne, (Ed.), *Exploring Methods in Information Literacy Research*, Topics in Australasian Library and Information Studies. Number 28. Centre for Information Studies, Charles Stuart University, Wagga Wagga, N.S.W., pp. 49–66.

Hyvarinen, M. (2007). Analyzing Narratives and Story-Telling. In: P. Alasuutari, L. Bickman and J. Brannen (Eds.), *The Sage Handbook of Social Research Methods*. London: Sage Publications.

Insch, G. S. and Moore, J. E. (1997). Content Analysis in Leadership Research: Examples, Procedures, and Suggestions for Future Use. *Leadership Quarterly* **8** (1), pp. 1–25.

Jacob, E. (1998). Clarifying Qualitative Research: A Focus on Traditions. *Educational Researcher* **27** (1), pp. 16–24.

Jick, T. D. (1979). Mixing Qualitative and Quantitative Methods: Triangulation in Action. *Administrative Science Quarterly* **24** (4), pp. 602–611.

Jones, R. (1996). *Research Methods in the Social and Behavioral Sciences*. Sunderland, Maine: Sinauer Associates.

Jorgensen, D. L. (1989). *Participant Observation: A Methodology for Human Studies*. London, England: Sage Publications.

Kai-Chieh, H., Mingying, L., Chia-Yu, T. and William, J. (2013). Applying Critical Incidents Technique to Explore the Categories of Service Failure and Service Recovery for Taiwanese International Airlines. *Journal of the Eastern Asia Society for Transportation Studies* **10**, pp. 2255–2273.

Kassarjian, H. H. (1977). Content Analysis in Consumer Research. *Journal of Consumer Research* **4**, pp. 8–18.

Kaulio, M. (2003). Initial Conditions or Process of Development? Critical Incidents in Early Stages of New Ventures. *R&D Management* **33** (2), pp. 65–175.

Kerlinger, F. N. (1986). *Foundations of Behavioral Research*, 3rd edn. Fort Worth: Harcourt Brace College Publishers.

Kim, J.-H. (2016). *Understanding Narrative Inquiry: The Crafting and Analysis of Stories as Research*. London: Sage Publications.

Kitzinger, J. (1995). Qualitative Research: Introducing Focus Groups. *British Medical Journal* **311**, pp. 299–302.

Kozinets, R. V. (1998). On Netnography: Initial Reflections on Consumer Research Investigations of Cyberculture. In: J. Alba and W. Hutchinson (Eds.), *Advances in Consumer Research*, Vol. 25, pp. 366–371. Provo, UT: Association for Consumer Research.

Krefting, L. (1991). Rigor in Qualitative Research: The Assessment of Trustworthiness. *The American Journal of Occupational Therapy* **45** (3), pp. 214–222.

Krippendorff, K. (1980). *Content Analysis: An Introduction to Its Methodology*. Newbury Park: Sage.

Krippendorff, K. (2004). *Content Analysis. An Introduction to Its Methodology*, 4th edn. Sage.

Krippendorff, K. (2013). *Content Analysis*, 3rd edn. Thousand Oaks, CA: Sage Publications.

Krueger, R. A. (1994). *Focus Groups: A Practical Guide for Applied Research*, 2nd edn. London: Sage.

Krueger, R. A. and Casey, M. A. (2015). *Focus Groups: A Practical Guide for Applied Research*, 5th edn. Thousand Oaks, CA: Sage.

Kuhn, T. & Koschel, K.-V. (2018). *Gruppen-diskussionen. Ein Praxis-Handbuch*. Second edn. Wiesbaden: Springer Fachmedien.

Lamnek, S. (2005). *Gruppendiskussion. Theorie und Praxis*. Second edn. Weinheim and Basel: Beltz Verlag.

LaPierre, R. T. (1934). Attitudes vs. Actions. *Social Forces* **13**, pp. 230–237.

Lincoln, Y. S. (2002). On the Nature of Qualitative Evidence. A paper for the Annual Meeting of the Association for the Study of Higher Education, November 21–24, Sacramento, California.

Linstone, H. A. and Turoff, M. (1975). Introduction. In: H. A. Linstone and M. Turoff (Eds.)., *The Delphi Method: Techniques and Applications*. London: Addison-Wesley.

Linstone, H. A (1975). Eight Basic Pitfalls: A checklist. In: H. A. Linstone and M. Turoff (Eds.), *The Delphi Method: Techniques and Applications*. London: Addison-Wesley Publishing Company.

Linstone, H. A. and Turoff, M. (2002). (Eds.) *The Delphi Method: Techniques and Applications*. Available at: https://web.njit.edu/~turoff/pubs/delphibook/delphibook.pdf.

Liu, K. (2000). *Semiotics in Information Systems Engineering*. Cambridge University Press.

Löffler, S. and Baier, D. (2013). Using Critical Incidents to Validate the Direct Measurement of Attribute Importance and Performance When Analyzing Services. *Journal of Service Science and Management* **6**, pp. 1–11.

Maanen van, J. (1979). The Fact of Fiction in Organizational Ethnography. *Administrative Science Quarterly* **24** (4), pp. 539–550.

Machungwa, P. D. and Schmitt, N. (1983). Work Motivation in a Developing Country. *Journal of Applied Psychology* **68** (1), pp. 31–42.

Man, T. W. Y. (2006). Exploring the Behavioural Patterns of Entrepreneurial Learning: A Competency Approach. *Education + Training* **48** (5), pp. 309–321.

Manetti, G. (2010). Ancient Semiotics. In: P. Cobley (Ed.), *The Routledge Companion to Semiotics*. New York: Routledge.

Manning, P. K. and Cullum-Swan, B. (1994). Narrative, Content and Semiotic Analysis. In: N. K. Denzin and Y. S. Lincoln (Eds.), *Handbook of Qualitative Research*. Sage.

Manning, P. and Smith, G. (2010). Symbolic Interactionism. In: A. Elliott (Ed.), *The Routledge Companion to Social Theory*, pp. 37–55. New York: Routledge.

Mariampolski, H. (2001). *Qualitative Market Research: A Comprehensive Guide*. Thousand Oaks: Sage.

Märtsin, M. (2018). Beyond Verbal Narratives: Using Timeline Images in the Semiotic Cultural Study of Meaning Making. *Integrative Psychological and Behavioral Science* **52**, pp. 116–128.

Maxwell, J. A. (1992). Understanding and Validity in Qualitative Research. *Harvard Educational Review* **62**, pp. 279–300. (in Flick) Five types of validity for qualitative research.

May M., and Andersen P.B. (2001). Instrument semiotics. In: Liu K, Clarke RJ, Andersen PB, Stamper RK (eds.) *Information, Organisation and Technology: Studies in Organisational Semiotics*. Boston: Kluwer, pp 271–298.

Mayring, P. (1983). *Qualitative Inhaltsanalyse: Grundlagen und Techniken*. Weinheim: Deutscher Studien Verlag.

Mayring, P. (2014). *Qualitative Content Analysis: Theoretical Foundation, Basic Procedures and Software Solution*. Klagenfurt. Available at: http://nbn-resolving.de/urn:nbn:de:0168-ssoar-395173.

McClintock, C. C., Brannon, D. and Maynard-Moody, S. (1979). Applying the Logic of Sample Surveys to Qualitative Case Studies: The Case Cluster Method. *Administrative Science Quarterly* **24** (4), pp. 612–629.

Mead, G. H. (1934). *Mind: Self and Society.* Chicago, Illinois: University of Chicago Press.

Mead, G. H. (1938). *The Philosophy of the Act.* Chicago, Illinois: University of Chicago Press.

Mead, M. (1959). *An Anthropologist at Work: Writings of Ruth Benedict.* New York: Houghton Mifflin.

Merton, R. K., Fiske. M. and Kendall, P. L. (1990). *The Focused Interview* (2nd edn.). New York: Free Press.

Miles, M. B., Huberman, A. M. and Saldana, J. (2014). *Qualitative Data Analysis: A Methods Sourcebook,* 3rd edn. Los Angeles: Sage.

Miles, M. B. (1979). Qualitative Data as an Attractive Nuisance: The Problem of Analysis. *Administrative Science Quarterly* **24** (4), pp. 590–601.

Miller, R. B. and Flanagan, J. C. (1950). The Performance Record: An Objective Merit-rating Procedure for Industry. *American Psychologist* **5**, pp. 331–332.

Mingers, J. and Brocklesby, J. (1997). Multimethodology: Towards a Framework for Mixing Methodologies. *Omega, International Journal of Management Science* **25** (5), pp. 489–509.

Mintzberg, H. (1979). An Emerging Strategy of Direct Research. *Administrative Science Quarterly* **24** (4), pp. 582–589.

Mintzberg, H. and Waters, J. A. (1982). Tracking Strategy in an Entrepreneurial Firm. *The Academy of Management Journal* **25** (3), pp. 465–499.

Mitchell, M. and Egudo, M. (2003). A Review of Narrative Methodology. DSTO Systems Sciences Laboratory, PO Box 1500, Edinburgh South Australia 5111 Australia.

Morgan, D. L. (1988). *Focus Groups as Qualitative Research.* Newbury Park: Sage.

Morgan, D. L. (1997). *Focus Groups as Qualitative Research.* London: Sage.

Morgan, G. (Ed.) (1983). *Beyond Method: Strategies for Social Research.* Newbury Park: Sage.

Nake, F. (2002). Data, Information, and Knowledge: A Semiotic View of Phenomena of Organization. In: *Organizational Semiotics Evolving a Science of Information Systems,* K. Liu, R. J. Clarke, P. B. Andersen and R. K. Stamper (Eds.). London: Kluwer; Network of Signs, Toronto: University of Toronto Press.

Neuendorf, K. (2002). *The Content Analysis Guidebook.* Thousand Oaks, California: Sage.

O'Leary, Z. (2014). *The Essential Guide to Doing Your Research Project* (2nd edn.). London: Sage Publications.

Ogilvie, M. and Mizerski, K. (2011). Using Semiotics in Consumer Research to Understand Everyday Phenomena. *International Journal of Market Research* **53** (5), pp. 651–668.

Okoli, C. and Pawlowski, S. D. (2004). The Delphi Method as a Research Tool: An Example, Design Considerations and Applications. *Information & Management* **42**, pp. 15–29.

Oswald, L. R. (2015). The Structural Semiotics Paradigm for Marketing Research: Theory, Methodology, and Case Analysis. *Semiotica* **205**, pp. 115–148.

Patterson, M. E. and Williams, D. R. (2002). *Collecting and Analyzing Qualitative Data: Hermeneutic Principles, Methods, and Case Examples.* Sagamore Publishing.

Patton, M. Q. (1980). *Qualitative Evaluation Methods.* London: Sage Publications.

Patton, M. Q. (1982). Qualitative Methods and Approaches: What Are They? In: *Qualitative Methods for Institutional Research,* E. P. Kuhns and S. V. Martorana (Eds.), pp. 3–16. San Francisco: Jossey-Bass.

Patton, M. Q. (1990). *Qualitative Evaluation and Research Methods* (2nd edn.). Newbury Park, CA: Sage.

Patton, M. Q. (2002). *Qualitative Research & Evaluation Methods* (Third edn.). London: Sage Publications.

Pentland, B. T. (1999). Building Process Theory with Narrative: From Description to Explanation. *Academy of Management Review* **24** (4), pp. 711–724.

Petrilli, S. and Ponzio, A. (2005). *Semiotics Unbounded: Interpretive Routes Through the Open.* Network of Signs, Toronto: University of Toronto Press.

Petty, N. J., Thomson, O. P. and Stew, G. (2012). Ready for a Paradigm Shift? Part 2: Introducing Qualitative Research Methodologies and Methods. *Manual Therapy* **17** (5), pp. 378–384.

Pinson, C. (1992). Semiotics of Marketing. INSEAD working paper Nr. 92/22/MKT.

Piore, M. J. (1979). Qualitative Techniques in Economics. *Administrative Sciences Quarterly* **24** (4), pp. 560–569.

Polkinghorne, D. E. (2007). Validity Issues in Narrative Research. *Qualitative Inquiry.* **13** (4), 471–486.

Powell, C. (2003). The Delphi Technique: Myths and Realities. *Journal of Advanced Nursing* **41**(4), 376–382

Ramadani, V., Bexheti, A., Dana, L.-P. and V. Ratten (2019). Informal Ethnic Entrepreneurship: An Overview. In: *Informal Ethnic Entrepreneurship. Future Research Paradigms for Creating Innovative Business Activity,* V. Ramadani, L.-P. Dana, V. Ratten and A. Bexheti (Eds.). Springer Nature Switzerland.

Rapley, T. (2007). *Doing Conversation, Discourse and Document Analysis*. The Sage qualitative research kit, U. Flick (Ed.). London: Sage.

Rastier, F. (2018). Computer-Assisted Interpretation of Semiotic Corpora. In: *Quantitative Semiotic Analysis*, D. Compagno (Ed.). Lecture notes in Morphogenesis Series, A. Sarti (Ed.). Springer.

Riessman, C. K. (2008). *Narrative Methods for the Human Sciences*. CA: SAGE.

Rist, R. C. (1977). On the Relations among Educational Research Paradigms: From Disdain to Détente. *Anthropology and Education* **8** (2), pp. 42–49.

Robson, C. (1993). *Real World Research: A Resource for Social Scientists and Practitioners-researchers*. Oxford: Blackwell.

Romano, C. A. (1989). Research Strategies for Small Business: A Case Study Approach. *International Small Business Journal* **7** (4), pp. 35–43.

Romer, D., Bontemps, M., Flynn, M., McGuire, T. and Gruder, C. L. (1977). The Effects of Status Similarity and Expectation of Reciprocation upon Altruistic Behaviour. *Personality and Social Psychology Bulletin* **3** (1), pp. 103–106.

Roth, S. and Dana, L.-P (2016). 'What is Your Self-Made Expat Story?' Netnography of Entrepreneurial Re-Users of a Popular Semantic. *International Journal of Entrepreneurship and Small Business* **28** (4), pp. 492–503.

Rotondi, A. and Gustafson, D. (1996). "Theoretical, methodological and practical issues arising out of the Delphi method." In: *Gazing into the Oracle: The Delphi Method and Its Application to Social Policy and Public Health*, M. Adler and E. Ziglio (Eds.). London: Jessica Kingsley Publishers.

Rowe, G. and Wright, G. (1999). The Delphi Technique as a Forecasting Tool: Issues and Analysis. *International Journal of Forecasting* **15**, pp. 353–375.

Rowe, G. and Wright, G. (2001). Expert Opinions in Forecasting: The Role of the Delphi Technique. In: *Principles of Forecasting. International Series in Operations Research & Management Science*, Vol. 30, J. S. Armstrong (Eds.). Boston, MA: Springer.

Ruspini, E. (2002). *Introduction to Longitudinal Research*. London: Routledge.

Sackman, H. (1974). *Delphi Assessment: Expert Opinion, Forecasting, and Group Process*. Santa Monica: Rand Corporation.

Salancik, G. R. (1979). Field Stimulations for Organizational Behavior Research. *Administrative Science Quarterly* **24** (4), pp. 638–649

Sanday, P. R. (1979). The Ethnographic Paradigm(s). *Administrative Science Quarterly* **24** (4), pp. 527–538.

Sandelowski, M. (2000). Focus on Research Methods: What Ever Happened to Qualitative Description? *Research in Nursing & Health* **23**, pp. 334–340.

Schmid, H. (1981). Qualitative Research and Occupational Therapy: The Foundation. *The American Journal of Occupational Therapy* **35** (2), pp. 105–106.

Schreier, M. (2014). Qualitative Content Analysis. In: *The Sage handbook of qualitative of qualitative data analysis*, U. Flick (Ed.). London: Sage.

Schwartz, R. D. and Skolnick, J. H. (1962). Two Studies of Legal Stigma. *Social problems* **10** (2), pp. 133–142.

Sharkin, B. S. and Birky, I. (1992). Incidental Encounters between Therapists and Their Clients. *Professional Psychology: Research and Practice* **23** (4), pp. 326–328.

Sieber, S. (1973). The Integration of Field Work and Survey Methods. *American Journal of Sociology* **78**, pp. 1335–1359.

Silverman, D. (2005). *Doing Qualitative Research*, 2nd edn. London: Sage.

Simao, L. M., Guimaraes, D. S., de Freitas, D. F. C. L., Bastos, S. and Sanchez Rios, H. (2016). Researcher-Participant Relationships in Different Settings: Theoretical and Methodological Issues within the Framework of Semiotic-Cultural Constructivism. In: *Particulars and Universals in Clinical and Developmental Psychology (Critical reflections)*. M. Watzlawik, A. Kriebel and J. Valsiner Charlotte (Eds.). North Carolina: Information Age Publishing.

Smith, J. K. (1983). Quantitative versus Qualitative Research: An Attempt to Clarify the Issue. *Educational Researcher* **12** (3), pp. 6–13.

Snodgrass, R., Gervais, R. L., Corbett, E. and Wilde, E. (2009). The usefulness of Critical Incident Technique (CIT) in eliciting plant competencies. A Pilot Study.

Spinelli, S. (2018). Semiotics and Sensory Sciences: Meaning between Texts and Numbers. In: *Quantitative Semiotic Analysis*, D. Compagno (Ed.). Lecture notes in Morphogenesis. Springer.

Spradley, J. P. (1980). *Participant Observation*. New York: Holt, Rinehart and Winston.

Stalpers J. (2007). Elicitatietechnieken in kwalitatief onderzoek [Elicitation techniques in qualitative research]. *Kwalon* **34**, **12** (10), pp. 32–39.

Stamper, R. K. (2001). Organisational Semiotics: Informatics without the computer? In: *Information, Organisation and Technology Studies in Organisational Semiotics*. K. Liu, R. J. Clarke, P. B. Andersen and R. K. Stamper (Eds.). Norwell: Kluwer.

Sullivan, R. (2000). Entrepreneurial Learning and Mentoring. *International Journal of Entrepreneurial Behaviour & Research* **6** (3), pp.160–175.

Suneetha, S. D. and Vidhyadhara, A. R. (2016). A Conceptual Study of Mystery Shopping as an Ancillary Method for Customer Surveys. *Global Journal of Management and Business Research: EMarketing* **16** (2), 11–17.

Symon, G. and Cassell, C. (2013). *Qualitative Organizational Research: Core Methods and Current Challenges.* London: Sage.

Talib, R., Hanif, M. K., Ayesha, S. and Fatima, F. (2016). Text Mining: Techniques, Applications and Issues. *International Journal of Advanced Computer Science and Applications* **7** (11), 414–418.

Tavory, I. and Timmermans, S. (2013). A Pragmatist Approach to Causality in Ethnography. *American Journal of Sociology* **119** (3), pp. 682–714.

Taylor, C. R. and Stern, B. B. (1997). 'Asian-Americans' Television Advertising and the 'Model Minority' Stereotype. *Journal of Advertising* **26** (2), pp. 47–60.

Taylor, P. J. and Small, B. (2002). Asking Applicants What They *Would* Do versus What They *Did Do*: A Meta-analytic Comparison of Situational and Past Behaviour Employment Interview Questions. *Journal of Occupational and Organizational Psychology* **75**, pp. 277–294.

Thia, H. and Ross, D. (2011). Using Content Analysis to Inquire into the Influence of Public Opinion on the Success of Public Private Partnerships. *International Journal on GSTF Business Review* **1** (1), pp. 237–242.

Thomas, K. W. and Kilmann, R. H. (1975). The Social Desirability Variable in Organizational Research: An Alternative Explanation for Reported Findings. *The Academy of Management Journal* **18** (4), pp. 741–752.

Tjosvold, D. and Weicker, D. W. (1993). Cooperative and Competitive Networking by Entrepreneurs: A Critical Incident Study. *Journal of Small Business Management* **31** (1), pp. 11–21.

Törrönen, J. (2002). Semiotic Theory on Qualitative Interviewing Using Stimulus Texts. *Qualitative Research* **2** (3), pp. 343–362.

Tsang, E. W. K. (2013). Case Study Methodology: Causal Explanation, Contextualization, and Theorizing. *Journal of International Management* **19** (2), pp. 195–202.

Tsotra, D., Janson. M. and Cecez-Kecmanovic, D. (2004). Marketing on the Internet: A Semiotic Analysis. Proceedings of the Tenth Americas Conference on Information Systems, New York, August 2004, pp. 4210–4220.

Twelker, P. A. (2007). The Critical Incident Technique: A Manual for Its Planning and Implementation. Available at: www.tiu.edu/ psychology/ Twelker/critical_incident_technique.htm.

Usability Body of Knowledge (http://usabilitybok.org) Source URL (retrieved on 2016-07-21 08:31): http://usabilitybok.org/critical-incident-technique.

Verschuren, P. and Doorewaard, H. (2010). *Designing a Research Project.* The Hague: Eleven International.

Veryard, R. (1985). What Are Methodologies Good For? *Policy* **27** (6), pp. 8–12.

Vitouladiti, O. (2014). Content Analysis as a Research Tool for Marketing, Management and Development Strategies in Tourism. *Procedia Economics and Finance* **9** (2014), pp. 278–287.

von Bertalanffy, K. L. (1968). *General System Theory.* New York: George Braziller.

Wagstaff, C., Fletcher, D. and Hanton, S. (2012). Positive Organizational Psychology in Sport: An Ethnography of Organizational Functioning in a National Sport Organization. *Journal of Applied Sports Psychology* **24**, pp. 26–47.

Webb, E. J. and Salancik, J. R. (1970). Supplementing the Self-Report in Attitude Research. *Attitude Measurement,* pp. 317–327.

Webb, E. J., Campbell, D. T., Schwartz, R. D. and Sechrest, L. (1966). *Unobtrusive Measures: Nonreactive Research in the Social Sciences.* Chicago: Rand McNally; revised 2000, London: Sage.

Whyte, W. F. (1991). *Participatory Action Research.* Newbury Park: Sage.

Woolsey, L. K. (1986). The Critical Incident Technique: An Innovative Qualitative Method of Research. *Canadian Journal of Counselling/Revue Canadienne de Counseling* **20**, 242–254.

Woudenberg, F. (1991). An Evaluation of Delphi. *Technological Forecasting and Social Change* **40**, pp. 131–150.

Yin, R. K. (1981). The Case Study Crisis: Some Answers. *Administrative Science Quarterly* **26** (1), pp. 58–65.

Yin, R. K. (1984). *Case Study Research: Design and Methods.* London: Sage.

Yin, R. K. (2003). *Case Study Research: Design and Methods,* 3rd edn. Thousand Oaks, CA.

Yin, R. K. (2009). *Case Study Research. Design and Methods,* 4th edn. London: Sage.

Zainol, A. and Lockwood, A. (2014). Understanding Service Experience: A Critical Incident Technique Approach. *Academic Research International* **5** (4), 189–203.

Zerbe, W. J. and Paulhus, D. L. (1987). Socially Desirable Responding in Organizational Behavior: A Recognition. *Academy of Management Review* **12** (2), pp. 250–264.

Ziglio, E. (1995). The Delphi Method and Its Contribution to Decision-Making. In: *Gazing into the Oracle: The Delphi Method and Its Application to Social Policy and Public Health,* M. Adler and E. Ziglio (Eds.), pp. 3–33. Bristol, PA: Jessica Kingsley Publishers.

CPSIA information can be obtained
at www.ICGtesting.com
Printed in the USA
JSHW010730171119
2461JS00003B/2